D0516544

VIOLENCE AND SECURITY ON CAMPUS

VIOLENCE AND SECURITY ON CAMPUS

FROM PRESCHOOL THROUGH COLLEGE

~

James Alan Fox and Harvey Burstein

 PRAEGER

AN IMPRINT OF ABC-CLIO, LLC
Santa Barbara, California • Denver, Colorado • Oxford, England

Library of Congress Cataloging-in-Publication Data

Fox, James Alan.
    Violence and security on campus :   from preschool through college   /   James Alan Fox
and Harvey Burstein.
        p. cm.
    Includes bibliographical references and index.
    ISBN 978-0-313-36268-2 (hard copy : alk. paper)—ISBN 978-0-313-36269-9 (ebook)
1. School violence. 2. Campus violence. 3. Students—Violence against. I. Burstein, Harvey. II. Title.
    LB3013.3.F69 2010
    371.7'82—dc22   2009053026

ISBN: 978-0-313-36268-2
EISBN: 978-0-313-36269-9

14   13   12   11   10   1   2   3   4   5

This book is also available on the World Wide Web as an eBook.
Visit www.abc-clio.com for details.

Praeger
An Imprint of ABC-CLIO, LLC

ABC-CLIO, LLC
130 Cremona Drive, P.O. Box 1911
Santa Barbara, California 93116-1911

This book is printed on acid-free paper ∞

Manufactured in the United States of America

In memory of the far too many innocent lives senselessly lost as the result of campus violence.

CONTENTS

List of Tables and Figures

TABLES

FIGURES

PREFACE

For millions of Americans, the notion of terrorism invokes frightful images of hijacked airliners crashing into the twin towers of New York's World Trade Center and suicide bombers wreaking devastation on countless innocents for political leverage. However, years before the identities of Osama bin Laden and al Qaeda became widely recognized, another form of terror—based not on religious fundamentalism but on adolescent rage—had surfaced in once-obscure places like Moses Lake, Washington; Pearl, Mississippi; and Jonesboro, Arkansas. And the word "Columbine," once reflecting the colorful beauty of the Colorado state flower, became linked to the horror of children being gunned down in the halls of their school. Adding to the irony, the diary of one of the young shooters from Columbine High described a fantasy about following up the massacre by flying an airplane into the skyline of New York; of course, the journal entry was made years before the Twin Towers collapsed.

It may seem a stretch to characterize school shootings as a form of terrorism. Yet, the issues of international terror and schoolyard terror are remarkably similar. Prompted by a string of school massacres in the late 1990s, school administrators were eager to profile dangerous students, just as airport security officials strived to identify violent extremists among those who boarded commercial airplanes. While the U.S. Congress voted to permit airline pilots to carry weapons in the cockpit to guard against a possible in-air take-over, state legislators around the country debated the wisdom of arming school teachers. Moreover, the fine balance between privacy and security that troubles many Americans with regard to the ongoing "War on Terror" has been a thorny matter as well at educational institutions of all levels, from elementary schools to colleges.

As widespread fear and apprehension over the safety of students pushed school security onto the national agenda, the body of research and scholarship on the topic of school violence and its prevention grew dramatically. Although at one time the theme would have seemed far too narrow, in 2002 the *Journal of School Violence*, an inter-disciplinary quarterly on theory, research, and practice focused only on violence and disorder in schools, released its inaugural issue. In addition, over 80 percent of the peer-reviewed journal publications uncovered from searching for "school violence" in the *Social Science Abstracts* dating back to the mid-1970s were published between 2000 and 2008. The growth in interest and concern has also been reflected outside of the academic literature. A cottage industry has developed for school security hardware, technology, guidebooks, and consulting.

In collaborating on this book, we sought to blend our divergent yet complementary perspectives. One of us has brought to the partnership an extensive background in social science research, scholarship, and consulting related to youth and school violence, including participation on several national advisory panels devoted to the issue. The other of us has expertise honed from decades of executive employment in federal law enforcement and corporate/campus security, consulting with companies and organizations worldwide, and teaching and writing in the area of security management and law. Our objective was to approach the complex topic of school violence, safety, and security by integrating criminological theory and research with security policy and practice.

In the first part of the book, we attempt to distinguish hard facts from hyped fictions. We detail the nature, patterns, and trends of school violence; assess some of the common myths and misconceptions about violence, bullying, and other school safety perils; discuss an array of factors associated—or at least believed to be associated—with violent offending at school; and critically address the nexus between school crime and media coverage.

In the next portion of the book, we review and discuss for each level of schooling (preschool through college) the specific security concerns and best practices for protecting students and staff, as well as buildings and other school property. Importantly, the concern—sometimes bordering on obsession—over the problem of school violence has, at times, caused school administrators and security officials to overlook other issues that relate to protecting school assets. In addition, dealing effectively with the wide range of school security risks includes many routine but no less significant management issues. We emphasize, therefore, the importance of school personnel matters—recruitment, training, supervision, retention, and termination—all of which impact on school security. Finally, several appendices provide background and reference material, including a detailed list of major episodes of school violence, best-practice approaches for bullying prevention and security technology, and key prescriptive documents arising from legislative and judicial acts.

Finally, we are grateful to several individuals for their support, encouragement, and assistance. Above all, Jenna Savage provided skillful suggestions in terms of both substance and style. Several Northeastern University graduate students—Sarah Rustan, David Hutchinson, Amanda Reich, and Aviva Rich-Shea—helped us in assembling sources of data and research. Also providing valuable direction and insight were: Beth Cooney, Director of University Administration Human Resources at Harvard University; Professor Dewey G. Cornell of the University of Virginia; Peter Langman, Clinical Director of KidsPeace; Dianne Layden, former professor at University of Redlands; Professor Jack Levin of Northeastern University; Jon Oliver, President of the Lesson One Company; Dan O'Neill of Applied Risk Management, Inc.; Katherine N. Pendergast, Vice President of Human Resources Management at Northeastern University; Professor Kenna Quinet of Indiana University–Purdue University, Indianapolis; and Amanda Warman, Director of Public Safety at Keene State College. Finally, we appreciate the confidence of the editorial staff at ABC-CLIO Publishers for the opportunity to contribute this text.

James Alan Fox
Harvey Burstein

1

VIOLENCE IN PRIMARY AND SECONDARY SCHOOLS

Previous to the events of September 11, 2001, when two hijacked commercial jets were deliberately crashed into the twin towers of New York's World Trade Center and America was drawn into a "war on terror," the nation had already been engaged in a very different kind of war against a very different form of terrorism. For the five years leading up to that contemporary date of infamy, the country had been shocked by murderous rampages perpetrated by mere youngsters. Schools everywhere, in big cities and the rural hinterlands, were reacting—and sometimes overreacting—to the potential for open warfare in the halls and classrooms of learning.

As listed in Table 1.1, between February 1996 and March 2001, eight multiple-victim school shootings perpetrated by middle or high school students in America claimed over three dozen lives, including a pair of gunmen who committed suicide as police arrived (see also Appendix A). Although the table lists only those episodes that took place in the United States, similar events occurred in distant lands—from Scotland to Yemen, from Germany to Argentina. Within the United States, specifically, the fear provoked by school shootings was so intense and the media coverage so widespread that the word "epidemic" was often used to characterize the crisis of school violence, at least until the events of September 11th drew our attention elsewhere.

SCHOOL-RELATED HOMICIDES

In March 2001, following yet another multiple-victim shooting—this time at Santana High School, just outside of San Diego, California—the venerable Dan Rather, one of the nation's best-known and well-respected TV journalists, had declared school shootings to be an epidemic.[1] While calling the spate of school shootings an "epidemic" may have been more hyperbole than reality, there is little

Table 1.1
Five years of multiple-victim school shootings

Date	School, Location	Shooter(s), Age(s)	Victim Count
Feb 2, 1996	Frontier Junior High School, Moses Lake, WA	Barry Loukaitis, 14	1 teacher and 2 students killed; 1 wounded
Feb 19, 1997	Bethel Reg. High School, Bethel, AL	Evan Ramsey, 16	1 teacher and 1 student killed; 2 wounded
Oct 1, 1997	Pearl High School, Pearl, MS	Luke Woodham, 16	2 students killed; 7 wounded; mother fatally stabbed
Dec 1, 1997	Health High School, West Paducah, KY	Michael Carneal, 14	3 students killed; 5 wounded
Mar 24, 1998	Westside Middle School, Jonesboro, AR	Mitchell Johnson, 13 and Andrew Golden, 11	1 teacher and 4 students killed; 10 wounded
May 21, 1998	Thurston High School, Springfield, OR	Kipland Kinkel, 15	2 students killed; 25 wounded; mother and father fatally shot
Apr 20, 1999	Columbine High School, Littleton, CO	Eric Harris, 18 and Dylan Klebold, 17	1 teacher and 12 students killed; 23 wounded (plus 2 suicides)
Mar 5, 2001	Santana High School, Santee, CA	Charles Andrew Williams, 15	2 students killed; 13 wounded

Note: Columbine High School is actually situated in an unincorporated area of Jefferson County, just outside of Littleton, CO, and has a Littleton postal address.

question that the level of fear and anxiety over school safety was spreading wide and fast. With impressions heavily impacted by tragedies at Columbine High School and elsewhere, there was pervasive concern among school officials and parents of school-age children that school violence was definitely on the rise.

Notwithstanding the unmitigated horror and outrage associated with the succession of high-profile schoolyard massacres over the five-year time span from Moses Lake to Santee, schools were, in reality, not only safe relative to other settings in which children typically spend their time, but growing safer —and not necessarily because of steps that were being taken to fortify them.

Unfortunately, no "official" (i.e., "known to the police") national data series for school crime exists. However, there are available several sources of data pertaining to school violence, based either on student/staff surveys or news media reports, all of which vary with regard to their coverage, completeness, and accuracy.[2] Arguably the most accurate data available come from incident reports of school-associated violent deaths maintained by the National School Safety Center (NSSC) in Westlake, California—a private organization launched in 1984 initially through federal funding directed by President Ronald Reagan. The data accuracy stems from the fact that school homicides, given their severity, are presumably always reported in some media outlet somewhere.

Table 1.2 displays annual counts for several measures of school-related homicides (perpetrated by students or nonstudents), extracted from the NSSC documents. In addition to these measures, the rate of homicide victimization per million students is calculated based on annual public and private school enrollment figures. Notwithstanding the news saturation during the five-year span in which several school mass shootings occurred, the number of incidents and the number of victims—both overall and students only—were appreciably larger in the early 1990s, when concerns about school violence were not as center-stage in public discourse. As one measure of attention, *The New York Times,* widely considered the newspaper of record, published 268 articles with the key phrase "school violence" between 1990 and 1994, compared to as many as 684 in the years 1995 to 1999.

Part of the reason for the disconnect between incidence and awareness involves the changing nature of the offenses. Many of the homicides near the beginning of the 1990s reflected gang activity, interpersonal disputes, and arguments—violence unrelated to school issues spilling onto school grounds. There was certainly no lack of awareness regarding the youth crime problem in the early 1990s or alarm associated with the notion of young "superpredators" terrorizing the streets of urban America, but this problem was not particularly related to schools. Although some of the urban violence was occurring at school, the source of the conflict was located elsewhere.

The widely publicized episodes of school violence that marked the late 1990s contrasted with the sharply declining homicide rate that America had been enjoying for most of the decade. However, the more significant change in the pattern of school-related lethal violence between the early and late 1990s was the emergence of mass shootings and multiple-victim homicides.

Statistical Trends

Among other things, the trend data contained in Table 1.2 highlight the distinction between incidence and victim count. In the early 1990s, a point in time when the school homicide count was at its peak, the victim and incident counts were nearly identical, that is, one victim per incident. By contrast, from the 1995/1996 through 2000/2001 school years, the homicide victim tally outpaced

Table 1.2
School-related homicide trends, 1992/93 – 2007/08

Academic Year	Incidents	Victims	Student Victims	Shooting Victims	Multiple Homicide Incidents	Multiple Homicide Victims	Student Victims per Million
1992/1993	45	47	38	37	2	4	0.78
1993/1994	45	46	32	35	1	2	0.65
1994/1995	17	17	15	12	0	0	0.30
1995/1996	26	30	22	23	3	7	0.43
1996/1997	23	25	17	14	2	4	0.33
1997/1998	27	35	28	27	5	13	0.54
1998/1999	11	24	23	18	2	15	0.44
1999/2000	20	22	14	11	2	4	0.26
2000/2001	17	18	8	14	1	2	0.15
2001/2002	4	4	2	2	0	0	0.04
2002/2003	13	13	11	7	0	0	0.20
2003/2004	32	36	21	25	4	8	0.38
2004/2005	19	24	14	17	2	7	0.25
2005/2006	5	5	4	5	0	0	0.07
2006/2007	12	16	13	12	1	5	0.23
2007/2008	2	2	2	2	0	0	0.04
Total	318	364	264	261	25	71	0.31

Source: Adapted from National School Safety Center, "School Associated Violent Deaths."

the number of incidents. Thus, whereas the homicide incidents in the early 1990s were almost exclusively single-victim episodes, the late 1990s witnessed a significant number of multiple-victim shootings.

Single-victim episodes, which were more abundant in the early 1990s, tend only to be noticed in the local area owing to the limited scope of news coverage and community distress. These homicides receive little, if any, attention from the press. By contrast, multiple-victim murders are reported nationally: the more victims, the more expansive the coverage. Thus, it wasn't until school shootings became worthy of the news spotlight coast to coast that the issue moved to the top of the national agenda.

The last column of Table 1.2 provides the level of risk (i.e., the victimization rate per million students) and shows how it has changed over the 15-year time span from 1993 to 2008. Notwithstanding the considerable fluctuation—which is to be expected of calculations based on small numbers of cases—the rate of homicide victimization during the school-violence panic of the late 1990s was half the comparable rate during the early part of the decade. Overall, a rate of 0.31 per million (or about 1 homicide for every 3 million students) is on par with or lower than that of a wide range of perils that children face on a daily basis but that do not inspire nearly as much attention and anxiety.

To place the risk of school homicide in some perspective, Table 1.3 compares the number of school-related homicide victims for the years 1999 to 2005 with cause-specific mortality figures drawn from coroner reports compiled by the National Center for Health Statistics (NCHS).[3] As the top portion of the table confirms, the number of children slain at or near school (a total of 89 victims over the seven-year time frame) is akin to that of other rare occurrences such as deaths from storm/lightning (105 cases) or animal bites (79 cases). Moreover, the risk of school homicide is substantially lower than that of accidental deaths due to careless handling of guns or of drowning in swimming pools. At the extreme, children are killed while on a bicycle 12 times more often than murdered while attending school. Yet, rather than ensuring that their children wear a helmet when bicycling around the neighborhood, many parents worry more deeply about the safety of their children when they are at school and demand tighter security measures to protect them. Government seems to be complicit in the relative neglect, as the majority of states do not require the use of helmets for children or adults.[4]

Another useful contrast is between the incidence of school-related homicides versus those that occur away from school—at home, at the mall, or in the neighborhood. As shown in the bottom panel of Table 1.3, less than 1 percent of all youth homicides during the years 1999 to 2005 occurred in the school setting. At the peak level by age group—10- to 14-year-olds—only about 1.4 percent of homicides were school-related. In addition, the number of children murdered by family members over the 1999 to 2005 time frame (1,285, based on FBI data) is 15 times larger than the number killed by classmates or others at school.

Of course, all of these comparisons hardly negate the seriousness of school-related homicides. Indeed, school shootings impact more than just the victims and assailants involved in the crime; they affect the entire student population, the local community, and sometimes even the nation as a whole. While a drowning or hunting accident may affect the lives of friends and family of the victim, a schoolyard killing sends shockwaves far and wide.

Some observers have suggested a strong gender component to school shootings (specifically, boys systematically targeting girls). For example, Katherine Newman of Princeton University, author of *Rampage: The Social Roots of School Shootings*, noted that "the predominant pattern in school shootings of the past three decades is that girls are the victims."[5] Based on an analysis of a dozen school shootings between 1997 and 2002, Jessie Klein of Lehman College suggested that "nearly all the boys who killed in these shootings specifically targeted girls who rejected them, or minimally implied that they acted due to a perceived rejection by a girl."[6]

There have indeed been several lethal assaults inspired at least partially by romantic conflict in which certain victims were chosen out of jealousy or spite. Mitchell Johnson, one of two boys responsible for the mass murder at the Westside Middle School in Jonesboro, Arkansas, reportedly told classmates that he was going to shoot all the girls who had rejected him. Notwithstanding this and other illustrations of school homicides by lovelorn boys, more generally, there is little evidence to support a particularly significant anti-female factor. Among the 364 victims of school-related homicides between 1992 and 2008, only 24 percent were female. Focusing just on the 265 student victims killed by classmates, 22 percent were female. Of the 181 student victims killed with a firearm, 24 percent were female. Only when narrowing the victim pool to students murdered in a

Table 1.3
Cause of death by age group, 1999–2005

Cause of death	Age Group			
	5–9	10–14	15–19	Total
Bicycle accident	283	480	337	1,100
Accidental fall	132	187	680	999
Pool drowning	349	234	223	806
Gun accident	17	66	131	214
Storm/Lightning	22	35	48	105
School homicide	**7**	**18**	**64**	**89**
Animal attack	42	23	14	79
Bus accident	7	21	18	46
Homicide	850	1,274	12,690	14,814
Percentage at school	0.8%	1.4%	0.5%	0.6%

Source: Based on National Center for Health Statistics Mortality data file (Underlying Cause of Death) and Federal Bureau of Investigation Supplementary Homicide Reports.

multiple-victim shooting by another student does the gender breakdown come close to even: Nearly half (23 out of 47) of these victims were female.

Whatever the victim-offender gender patterns, a factor underlying many school rampages may be associated more with gender identity than with gender itself. Of course, adolescence can be a difficult life stage for many boys and girls in terms of issues related to sex, sexual orientation, and gender. However, according to Kimmel and Mahler, these pressures and conflicts were implicated in a good number of school shootings. In a careful analysis of 28 random school shootings, they uncovered substantial evidence that certain shooters acted in retaliation for frequent teasing and insults that challenged their masculinity. In essence, for these beleaguered and much-maligned students, violence served as the ultimate vehicle for proving their power and manhood.[7]

NONLETHAL VIOLENCE

The tabulations and calculations thus far have focused on the risk of school-related homicide, though it is just the most extreme and visible tip of a much larger iceberg of violence, harassment, and intimidation in school settings. Measuring the level and rate of nonlethal violence with precision is compromised by the sometimes subjective and varying definition of what constitutes violence. For example, should a slap or a push, neither resulting in injury (other than psychological), be included?

With the notable exception of mandated reporting of campus crime data from colleges and universities, official police statistics on school violence are not routinely available. Although certain large school districts around the country collect and tabulate their own school-related crime data, the geographic coverage is not national in scope or representative.

Of course, violent crimes occurring at school are included in police data from the FBI's Uniform Crime Reporting program; however, aggregate crime counts do not distinguish crimes at school from those in the larger community within the particular police jurisdiction. On a very limited basis, some school crime data are available from the FBI's expanded program, the National Incident-Based Reporting System (NIBRS); however, these reports, coming from a select group of states and law enforcement agencies, are not nearly representative of the nation as a whole.

The school-related homicide data presented earlier, although not the product of any official police reporting process, are based primarily on news reports. Because of the low frequency yet newsworthiness of such serious crimes, incident counts extracted from various news archives are fairly reliable and complete.

The same certainly cannot be said for nonlethal offenses. For example, Alan Lampe has compiled a large database on acts of school violence and the associated count of victims killed and wounded in the United States and abroad based primarily on news reports, contemporary and archival.[8] The growth over time in case counts, from 39 in the 1970s, 84 in the 1980s, 386 in the 1990s and 1,383 for eight years of the 2000s—surely reflects increases in the extent and availability of news reporting much more than real change in the rate of school violence. As further evidence of the insurmountable measurement problems related to varying practices in news reporting, the average number of victims per incident in cases abroad is more than quadruple that of cases in the United States (see Table 1.4). It is doubtful that students in other countries have any greater propensity for claiming large victim counts. Most likely, either the American press is more apt to report episodes that are limited to nonfatal injuries or American press coverage of lesser crimes is just more widely accessible in newspaper archives. Either way, the validity of using news archives for tallying nonfatal cases and victims is extremely suspect. However, various surveys exist that provide a glimpse into the nature and trends in nonlethal violence in schools.

The most prominent source of data on nonlethal school violence comes from regular surveys of criminal victimization in the United States. With assistance of interviewers and other professional staff from the U.S. Bureau of the Census, the Bureau of Justice Statistics has for several decades sponsored the National Crime Victimization Survey (NCVS). On an annual basis, the NCVS collects survey responses from nationally representative samples of about 75,000 households comprising nearly 135,000 individuals ages 12 and over, concerning the occurrence, characteristics, and consequences of criminal victimization. Moreover, on a bi-annual rotation, the NCVS conducts supplementary interviews with over 10,000 school children, ages 12 to 18, concerning victimization, bullying, drug availability, and safety measures. The great detail of these victimization data permits a comparison of incidents occurring at school and those outside of school.

Although the samples are large and representative, the prevalence estimates and rates generated from the NCVS are subject to sampling error simply because they are based on random subsets of the population. In addition to the question of reliability due to sampling is the greater concern over what constitutes a serious violent crime. Furthermore, as mentioned previously, the definition of violence or bullying depends in part on the respondent's recall

Table 1.4
Historical counts of incidents of school violence in the U.S. and abroad, 1960–2007

Classification	United States	Abroad
Acts of school violence	1,281	373
Students and teachers killed	680	993
Students and teachers wounded	1,720	2,489
Victims per incident	1.9	9.3

Source: Adapted from http://www.columbineangels.com/School_Violence.htm.

and interpretation of events. Also, willingness to reveal and discuss an incident in an interview setting rests with the respondent.

With these cautions and caveats in mind, the NCVS provides the opportunity to track changes over time in the rate of nonlethal violence involving school-age children (12- to 18-year-olds) as victims. As shown in Figure 1.1, the rate of serious violence (rape, sexual assault, robbery, and aggravated assault) at school is consistently lower than that away from school. Moreover, although both rates have generally declined over the past two decades, the gap between that away from school and that at school has narrowed. Whereas in the early 1990s about one-quarter of victimization occurred in school or on school grounds, the share has grown to around one-third in more recent years. School children became safer, but not so much at school.

Importantly, the vast majority of serious crime victimizations involve aggravated assaults. To ensure that the overall trends do not just reflect the somewhat unclear distinction between simple assault (e.g., a slap or push) and aggravated assault (e.g., nonfatal attack with a knife or gun), the same comparison of school and nonschool rates for violent crime victimization, including simple assault, is displayed in Figure 1.2. The pattern of change over time remains the same after expanding the definition of violence to include less serious altercations. However, the gap between school and nonschool victimization rates that holds for serious violence virtually disappears when the more minor forms of violence are considered. Thus, whereas the school setting is far less dangerous than other locations in terms of homicide and other serious forms of violent crime, school provides no safe haven for many children and adolescents from the common forms of aggression—shoving, pushing, and bullying.

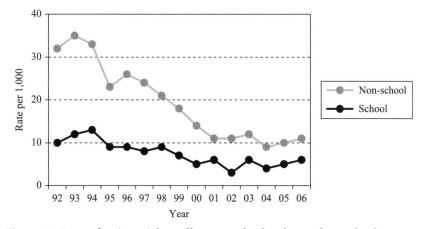

Figure 1.1 Rates of serious violent offenses at school and away from school

Note: Serious violent offenses include rape, sexual assault, robbery, and aggravated assault, but not homicide (given that the data come from victim surveys).

Source: Bureau of Justice Statistics, National Crime Victimization Survey, 1992–2006.

It is noteworthy that the overall trends in violent crime victimization (with and without the less serious assaults)—with a peak in the early 1990s, a decline thereafter until the early 2000s, and a modest rise in the most recent years—generally mimics overall youth violent crime trends for the nation as a whole. Still, the slight upsurge in school-related violence since the mid-2000s is worthy of some attention and perhaps a reinvestment in violence prevention efforts.

Although most of the attention and concern has focused on violence by and against students, the problem of student-on-teacher violence is far from trivial. As shown in Table 1.5, the percentage of teachers who report having been threatened with injury or physically assaulted by a student is highest in schools situated in a central city and lowest in small town schools, consistent with patterns of violence generally based on locale. More important, the prevalence of both threats and assaults declined over the decade time span from the 1993/1994 to 2003/2004 school years. This overall improvement in the prevalence of student-on-teacher violence parallels the reduction in violence among students.

The risk of victimization of teachers poses a special problem for schools in terms of faculty retention. Whereas most students have little choice in attending school, educators who fear for their safety can always decide to seek alternative placements or even to abandon the teaching profession altogether.

WEAPONS IN SCHOOLS

Whether or not they are ever used to scare or harm a classmate or teacher, the presence of weapons in school has been a long-standing concern. After all,

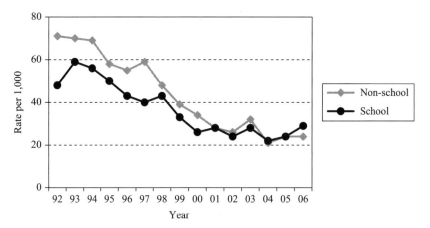

Figure 1.2 Rates of violent offenses at school and away from school
Note: Violent offenses include rape, sexual assault, robbery, and both simple and aggravated assault, but not homicide (given that the data come from victim surveys).
Source: Bureau of Justice Statistics, National Crime Victimization Survey, 1992–2006.

Table 1.5
Percentage of teachers reporting having been threatened or physically attacked

Locale	Threatened with injury			Physically attacked		
	1993–1994	1999–2000	2003–2004	1993–1994	1999–2000	2003–2004
Total	11.7%	8.8%	6.8%	4.1%	3.9%	3.4%
Central city	15.2%	11.4%	10.0%	5.5%	5.4%	4.8%
Urban fringe	10.7%	7.5%	5.8%	4.0%	3.4%	3.1%
Small town	9.8%	8.3%	4.6%	3.1%	3.0%	2.3%

Source: National Center for Education Statistics, Schools and Staffing Survey, various years.

deadly weapons (guns and knives, in particular) are used in the majority of serious acts of school violence. A quarter-century ago, a 1983 survey at four public high schools in Boston estimated that as many as 17 percent of the girls and 37 percent of the boys had brought a weapon to school at some point during the school year.[9] By the early 1990s, the problem of guns in particular was perceived to be worrisome enough that the U.S. Congress passed the 1990 Gun-Free Zone Act (GFZA), making it a federal offense for anyone to possess a firearm within 1,000 feet of a school, and later, the 1994 Gun-Free Schools Act (GFSA), mandating a one-year expulsion for any student who possesses a firearm at school or near school property (see Appendix B). In 1995, the law was broadened to include weapons other than guns.

As shown in Figure 1.3, from the 1996/1997 to 2003/2004 school years, just over 24,000 students were expelled by virtue of the GFSA prohibitions, a tiny fraction of the overall school enrollment of around 50 million annually. Compared with even the most conservative estimates of the prevalence of guns in schools, the risk of expulsion for gun possession has remained extremely small. In addition, the use of expulsion as a sanction for gun possession declined steadily over the eight years reported, from 4,787 in 1996/1997 down to 2,165 in 2003/2004. It is not clear, at least from these data, whether there was a reduction in gun carrying or, alternatively, lesser willingness by school officials to follow through with the mandates of the GFSA.

Some measure of the actual change in gun possession is available from the bi-annual surveys of high school students from the Centers for Disease Control and Prevention-sponsored Youth Risk Behavior Surveillance System (YRBSS). Developed in 1990, the YRBSS is designed to monitor patterns and trends in certain health-related issues among America's children and adolescents, such as smoking, drinking, drug use, obesity, exercise, and a variety of violence-related concerns. Although not restricted to firearms alone, these surveys solicit self-reports of weapon possession while at school.

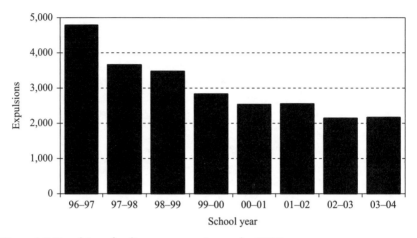

Figure 1.3 Expulsions for firearm possession under GFSA
Source: U.S. Department of Education, Report on the Implementation of the Gun-Free Schools Act in the States and Outlying Areas, School Year 2003–04, p. 12.

As shown in Figure 1.4, there has been a precipitous decline over the past two decades in the prevalence of weapons possession. The percentages of males and of females who admit to carrying a weapon have been halved between 1993 and 2007—from 17.9 percent to 9.0 percent for high school males and from 5.0 percent to 2.6 percent for their female counterparts. Given the potential for response bias that surrounds any type of survey effort, it is possible that students have become less willing to admit to a behavior that, if revealed, could potentially result in a severe penalty. In addition, it is not exactly realistic to consider

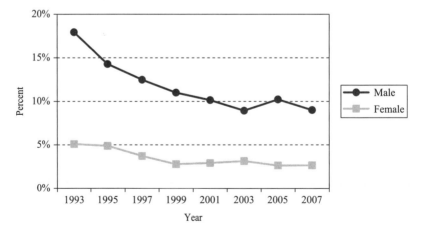

Figure 1.4 Percentage of high school students carrying a weapon at school
Source: Based on Centers for Disease Control, Youth Risk Behavior bi-annual surveys for 1993–2007.

the downward trend in reported weapons possession as any affirmation of the impact of the GFSA. The data series does not extend a sufficient number of years prior to the passage of GFSA to assess the implementation effects of the federal law. Moreover, it is not possible to determine the extent to which the downturn is in response to the threat of suspension or some other factors, such as the existence of metal detectors or random searches for contraband.[10]

Notwithstanding the methodological concerns related to the veracity of weapons possession self-reports, the YRBSS also includes questions related to school-based victimization from threats and injuries involving a gun or other weapon. Trends in victimization do not track those in self-reported weapons possession. As shown in Figure 1.5, there has been little if any change in the percentages of students reporting that they had been threatened with a weapon during the previous 12 months. Consistent with most other victimization data, males face weapons threats more often than females—a gender gap that has remained fairly constant over time.

The analyses of lethal and nonlethal school violence presented above indicate that, by virtually any measure, our nation's schools are safe—and for some children, possibly safer than any other place. Schools, even those in high-crime neighborhoods, provide children with a structured environment and adult monitoring—a level of supervision that may exceed that which they have at home.

THREATS, FEAR, AND PROTECTION

There are several reasons why students bring weapons onto school grounds. Some arm themselves for offensive purposes—to assault or intimidate the

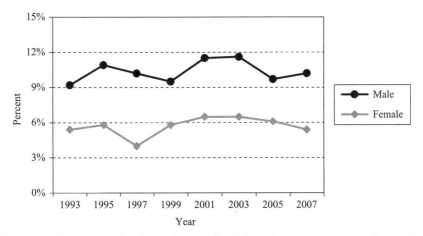

Figure 1.5 Percentage of students threatened or injured by a weapon in past 12 months
Source: Based on Centers for Disease Control, Youth Risk Behavior bi-annual surveys for 1993–2007.

more vulnerable. Others view weapons as a sign of status, even brandishing the gun or knife before their friends' eyes as a show of bravado. Finally, students sometimes choose to be armed for defensive purposes, particularly when feeling threatened or afraid at school.

Surveys of school-age populations often solicit reports of fear, avoidance, and weapons possession. However, these factors should be considered, not in isolation, but as parts of an integrated whole. The interactions among fear, avoidance, and weapons possession can be assessed using data from the YRBSS. The YRBSS data files for the years 1993 through 2007, each based on self-administered questionnaires, contain reasonably comparable items related to several school violence/safety matters and respondent attributes, including age, grade, gender, and race/ethnicity. The violence-related questions specifically concern the frequency of being threatened or injured with a weapon while at school (during the past year); skipping school because of feeling unsafe at school or on the way to or from school (during the past month); and carrying a gun, knife, or other weapon while on school property (during the past month).

The questionnaires solicited the number of occasions on which the respondents experienced or engaged in the above behaviors; however, these data were severely skewed. That is, most respondents reported none, and very few students reported more than once or twice. Moreover, the wording of the questions appears to have changed slightly over the years. For these reasons, it was best to dichotomize or reduce the variables into a yes/no form, rather than to keep them calibrated in terms of frequencies.

Table 1.6 shows the prevalence of the three school violence items (being threatened/injured, feeling unsafe, and carrying a weapon) by respondent age, sex, and race for all years combined. Not surprisingly, victimization decreased with age, as did school avoidance because of feeling unsafe. There was a slight and uneven tendency for increased prevalence of weapon possession among older students. With regard to gender, boys were twice as likely as girls to have been threatened or injured, slightly more likely to have felt unsafe, and about 3.5 times more apt to have had a weapon at school on some occasion. Finally, in comparison to white respondents, minority students (blacks and Hispanics, in particular) were somewhat more likely to have been threatened or injured, twice as likely to have felt unsafe, and slightly more likely to have carried a weapon on school property.

The fact that the questions were repeated in each of the bi-annual surveys from 1993 through 2007 (but not the first round in 1991) allows us to look for any trends that may have occurred over time. Of course, the respondents changed with each successive survey, introducing some small element of sampling error. Though desirable, it would not have been possible, of course, to survey the same panel of students because of their limited number of years in high school.

Figure 1.6 displays trends in the percentages of respondents who reported having been threatened, having felt unsafe, and having brought a weapon to school. Reports of threats and lack of safety have generally increased over the

Table 1.6
Percentage of students who were threatened, felt unsafe, and brought a weapon

	N	Percentage of respondents saying they		
		Were threatened	Felt unsafe	Brought a weapon
Age				
14 years old	11,962	9.5%	5.3%	6.6%
15 years old	28,217	9.6%	6.1%	7.5%
16 years old	30,165	7.8%	5.1%	8.2%
17 years old	28,410	6.7%	4.3%	7.8%
18 years old or older	16,374	6.7%	4.6%	7.8%
Sex				
Female	55,969	5.6%	5.3%	3.4%
Male	58,973	10.2%	4.9%	11.8%
Race				
White	73,155	7.0%	3.5%	7.2%
Nonwhite	40,967	9.6%	7.9%	8.5%
Overall	115,128	8.0%	5.1%	7.7%

Source: Centers for Disease Control, Youth Risk Behavior bi-annual surveys, 1993–2007.

time span, while gun possession has tailed off steadily. The latter, however, may have much to do with changing policies and security measures implemented in schools across the country, particularly after the string of school massacres in the late 1990s, rather than being a reflection of any reduction in perceived need for armed protection.

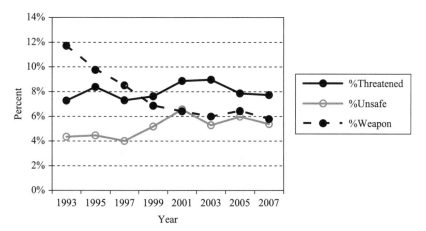

Figure 1.6 Students who were threatened, felt unsafe, and had a weapon in school
Source: Based on Centers for Disease Control, Youth Risk Behavior bi-annual surveys for 1993–2007.

Given the wealth of data, it is also possible to establish empirically a model of the interrelationships among the three behavioral variables (having been threatened, having felt unsafe, and having carried a weapon), and the influence of student demographics (grade level, sex, and race). Each of the arrows shown in Figure 1.7 suggests a causal linkage from one variable to another. Thus, being threatened impacts feeling unsafe, and both of these then influence the likelihood of carrying a weapon at school. Furthermore, all three of these behavioral variables are affected by a student's grade level, sex, and race.

Alongside each of the arrows (causal paths) in the figure is a quantity that reflects the extent to which the odds of a behavioral outcome (threatened, unsafe, or weapon) increases or decreases due to the influence of a particular causal factor. Quantities greater than 1.0 indicate increased odds, while those below 1.0 suggest reduced odds. A value of 1.0 means no impact (i.e., multiplying odds by 1.0 changes nothing).

All three background variables (grade, sex, and race) have substantial direct and indirect effects on the odds of having been threatened, having felt unsafe, and having carried a weapon. As would be expected, gender greatly impacts the likelihood of all three behavioral measures. Compared to females, males have twice the odds of having been threatened, lower odds of having felt unsafe, and well over three times the odds of having carried a weapon.

The effects of grade and race are not quite as pronounced, but are important nonetheless. Upper-grade students (11th or 12th grade) as compared to lower-grade high school students (9th and 10th grades) are considerably less likely to have been threatened or to have felt unsafe, yet slightly more apt to have carried a weapon. Here, the increased likelihood of weapon possession is a function of age, but not connected to threat, victimization, or fear. Finally, as compared to their white counterparts, nonwhite students are somewhat more likely to have been threatened, considerably more likely to feel unsafe, and only slightly more likely to carry a weapon.

The background variables create a context for the more interesting and important relationships among the three behavioral variables. Having been threatened magnifies by over eight times the odds of having felt unsafe, and quadruples the odds of having carried a weapon. Finally, feeling unsafe more than doubles the odds of weapon possession.

The technical complexities aside, it is clear that intimidation, fear, and weapon-carrying are strongly intertwined. Intervention strategies that reduce bullying, threats and fighting will significantly reduce levels of fear and likely will lower the perceived need for armed protection.

BULLYING

As the summer of 2005 drew to a close, just as the back-to-school shopping season was about to begin, Old Navy, a popular clothing retailer for teens, launched an online advertising campaign at *www.schooliscoming.com*.[11] Hardly

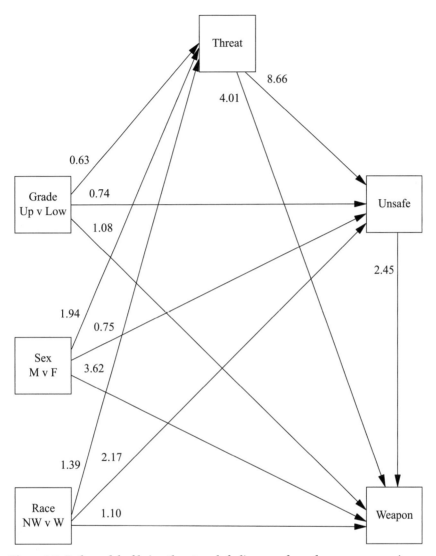

Figure 1.7 Path model of being threatened, feeling unsafe, and weapon possession
Source: Based on Centers for Disease Control, Youth Risk Behavior bi-annual surveys for 1993–2007.

a promotion for flip-flops or sleeveless tops, the Website contained such chilling features as a tool for scrawling your name in dripping blood, free "scream-tones" for your cell phone, and a create-your-own horror flick. There was even a short video, *From Desk 'til Dawn*, in which a pretty teenager, startled during a fireside embrace with her boyfriend, is chased screaming through the woods by a menacing school desk.

Old Navy may have been clever in exploiting kids' fascination with horror as a hook to sell jerseys and jeans; but the Web site was frighteningly accurate about how millions of children view the daily experience at school. Of course, children do not worry literally about wooden desks lurking in the corridors, but about menacing bullies in the halls.

Despite their relative safety, schools can still *feel* dangerous to children, particularly in the face of harassment and intimidation. In fact, most bullying in school does not involve actual violence or fighting, but rather the constant *threat* of violence, which can make school halls (and bathrooms) tremendously fear-provoking.

Bullying at school or in the schoolyard is hardly a new concern for students and their parents, or for teachers and administrators. Harassing behavior—from teasing to intimidation, from targeted vandalism and malicious pranks to shoving and fighting—has been a problem for decades, if not centuries, likely for as long as there have been schools. Previously dismissed as normal and relatively harmless child's play—"boys being boys," "girls being catty"—in recent years bullying has taken on an entirely different meaning, occasionally with devastating repercussions.

Chronic bullying has frequently been cited as an underlying precipitant for suicide and homicide. Eric Mohat, 17, of Mentor, Ohio, was harassed so mercilessly that when one of his tormenters said out loud in class, "Why don't you go home and shoot yourself; no one will miss you," he did just that. Claiming that their son was not the only victim of "bullicide," William and Janis Mohat filed suit in federal court alleging that bullying had been a significant factor in a cluster of suicides by Mentor High School students during 2007.[12]

Several high-profile cases of school homicide have involved a victim of long-term bullying seeking payback with a gun. In October 1997, for example, 16-year-old Luke Woodham of Pearl, Mississippi, took a rifle from home and used it to murder two female classmates (one of whom was his former girlfriend) and wound seven other students at his high school. He also killed his mother with a knife and baseball bat. In what apparently was meant to be a suicide note (were it not for the fact he lived), Woodham wrote, "I am not insane! I am angry. I kill because people like me are mistreated every day. I do this to show society—push us and we will push back. I have suffered all my life. No one ever truly loved me."

Woodham was not the only beleaguered student to have avenged repeated bullying with a counter-assault. Ann Marie C. Lenhardt of Canisius College assembled case profiles of 15 young assailants involved in 13 episodes of school homicide in the United States between 1996 and 2005. She found that 73 percent of the 15 perpetrators had apparently been the victims of bullying and persecution.[13] Of course, bullying itself is hardly sufficient to produce the level of rage seen in recent school rampages; it is usually harassment in combination with poor coping skills that produces this extreme response. Lenhardt's results show that 71 percent of attackers felt rejected and isolated by peers, 64 percent had poor coping skills, and 64 percent demonstrated an exaggerated need for attention and respect.

It is important to keep in mind that school shootings reflect only the most severe and visible responses to bullying, a long-standing and widespread problem in American schools. However, it was largely the high-profile slayings that encouraged school administrators to take a more serious look at the devastating effects of this insidious form of "child's play" on victims.

Bullying can take on many forms, extending well beyond overt acts of aggression. In their definition, one widely accepted in the literature, Nansel and colleagues have identified several elements that constitute bullying: aggressive behavior or intentional "harm doing" by one person or a group, which is carried out repeatedly and over time, and which is targeted toward someone less powerful.[14] Consistent with this definition, bullying can be verbal (such as insulting someone or making threats), psychological (such as rumor-spreading, purposeful embarrassment, or social ostracism), or physical (such as knocking down or hitting the person).

Bullying Prevalence and Trends

Given the broad and fairly limitless definition of bullying, it is rather difficult to estimate with precision the scope of the problem. Much depends on the data source and how, exactly, bullying is defined in the research.

The first attempts to measure the extent of school bullying were undertaken in Scandinavian countries, largely taking the lead from Dan Olweus's early-1970s work with school children in Norway. Following a series of suicides involving adolescent boys, the Norwegian Ministry of Education commissioned Olweus to conduct a large-scale survey of bullying and victimization, in which it was found that one of seven students were involved in bullying behavior, either as victims or perpetrators (and often both).[15]

Olweus's research opened many eyes around the globe regarding the prevalence of bullying. However, it was not until the late 1990s that the first systematic and large-scale studies of bullying prevalence were conducted in the United States. In 1998, the National Institute of Child Health and Human Development (NICHD) sponsored a nationally representative survey on bullying of 15,686 students in grades 6 through 10.[16] Overall, 30 percent of young people nationwide at the time of the survey were involved in moderate to frequent bullying during the previous couple of months, as perpetrators, victims, or both. Based on these survey data, it was estimated that as many as 3.2 million students nationwide were victims of bullying and 3.7 million were bullies. That there were more bullies than victims reflects the common pattern whereby several children gang up on one. Finally, these estimates included 1.2 million who both bullied others and were themselves victims of bullying.

According to the survey results, just over 17 percent of students had recently experienced some form of victimization, and nearly 10 percent had experienced it on a weekly basis. Levels of victimization were greater among younger children in middle or junior high school, consistent with the experience of many school officials regarding the social difficulties at this stage. For children in 6th and 7th grades, nearly half had recently been victimized, as opposed to only about 30 percent for 10th graders. Of course, some of this age differential can be the result of response bias, in that older students may be less inclined to admit to having been victimized, being especially concerned about not being seen as weak.

Victimization varied somewhat by race, with white children reporting greater victimization than blacks and Hispanics. Part of this difference may also reflect differential perceptions about what constitutes victimhood. Victimization also varied considerably by gender: Nearly half of the boys and slightly more than a third of the girls reported having been the target of bullying. Because the data relied on self-reports, the gender differential may have much to do with the types of bullying behavior common within the two groups. Physical bullying, which is far more common among boys, would be hard to define as anything other than bullying. However, it is the more subtle, psychological forms—such as malicious gossiping—that frequently impacts on girls. In a survey context, this type of victimization may not be perceived or self-defined by a respondent as actual bullying, as opposed to just meanness.

The survey also solicited self-reports of bullying and harassment perpetrated by respondents against other students. The patterns of offending were remarkably similar to those of victimization. In part, this may reflect the tendency for the victim-offender relationship to be same-gender, usually intra-racial and most often within the same grade level—consistent with general patterns of violence. Finally, the survey also examined differences in the nature of the harassment according to victim gender. Mean-spirited comments or actions associated with race or religion represented the least frequent form among both genders.

The NICHD survey results were roughly similar to those found from research in other countries and other studies done in the United States. For example, a study of roughly 1,000 young people in the 5th through 12th grades done for the Family Work Institute found that 12 percent of the students interviewed had been bullied five times or more in the prior month.[17]

However, a series of surveys from the U.S. Department of Justice paints a rather different picture of the extent of bullying. In bi-annual surveys from 1999 to 2003, as special school supplements to the regular National Crime Victimization Survey (NCVS), the levels of bullying victimization were considerably lower than other research had found. Specifically, the percentage of

12- to 18-year-old students who reported having been bullied during the previous six months was only 5.1 percent in 1999, 7.9 percent in 2001, and 7.2 percent in 2003.

Findings related to the prevalence of bullying victimization and offending, as well as correlates by age/grade, gender, and race, unfortunately do not produce clear-cut conclusions. Estimates of the extent of bullying have ranged from below 10 percent to well over one-third.[18] Moreover, although some studies suggest that bullying is more common among boys than girls, others have failed to identify any gender gap.

Unlike other forms of interpersonal conflict, there are no routine data collection protocols for measuring bullying and harassment. Attempts to estimate prevalence have come from disparate surveys of varying populations of students—varying in terms of geographic coverage, grade levels, and school type. Moreover, lack of uniformity in sampling designs, question wording, and data collection method has contributed to the empirical confusion.

In fact, for the 2005 School Supplement of the NCVS, the approach to measuring bullying was altered from earlier versions of the survey. Rather than just asking generally whether the respondent had been victimized in the previous six months, as had been done in the 1999 to 2003 surveys, the survey now asked a series of questions regarding specific behaviors, including various forms of aggression, harassment, and intimidation.[19] Because of this change in method, the prevalence of reported bullying victimization was as high as 28.1 percent, as compared to less than 8 percent from the earlier surveys. Responses to the various prompts ranged from as high as 18.7 percent for teasing and 14.7 percent for being the subject of rumors, down to 9.0 percent for physical forms of bullying (e.g., shoving, pushing, and tripping) and 4.6 percent for social exclusion. Clearly, estimates of the extent of bullying behavior depend on the severity of definition.

The NCVS School Supplement data for 2005 also showed wide variation by grade level. In terms of overall extent of bullying victimization, the figures ranged from 36.6 percent for 6th graders down to 19.9 percent for 12th graders. Other differences were not so dramatic, including a small gender gap (27.1 percent for boys and 29.2 percent for girls), modest differences among racial/ethnic groups (30.0 percent for whites, 28.5 percent for blacks, and 22.3 percent for Hispanics), and small location differences (from 29.0 percent for rural students down to 26.0 percent for those in urban areas).

One of the most reliable and extensive data sources for measuring prevalence, patterns, and trends in bullying—both in terms of victimization and offending—comes from the periodic national surveys of health-related behavior among children sponsored by the U.S. Department of Health and Human Services, as part of a multi-nation initiative coordinated by the World Health Organization. The most recent available data come from a 2001–2002 survey of a nationally representative sample of 14,817 school children in grades 6 through 10.[20] Table 1.7 displays overall prevalence figures for recent (within a

Table 1.7

Prevalence of bullying victimization and offending by school level and sex

Role in Bullying	Middle School		High School	
	Boy	Girl	Boy	Girl
Victim	35.2%	32.6%	30.6%	25.1%
Offender	41.9%	34.6%	42.1%	30.9%

Source: Analysis of 2001–02 Health Behavior in School-Aged Children Survey (HBSC).

couple of months) bullying victimization and offending, respectively, by combinations of school level and gender. Victimization is lower for high school students than for middle school students, and lower for girls than for boys, with the gender gap widening slightly from middle school to high school. In terms of offending levels, boys report bullying considerably more often than do girls, and while offending levels decrease for girls moving from middle school to high school, those for boys remain virtually unchanged.

Differences across the various subforms of bullying victimization are shown in Figure 1.8 by level of schooling and in Figure 1.9 by gender. Consistent with results from other studies, middle school students report higher levels of bullying victimization than do high school students for every type of behavior. In terms of comparative ratios, the difference between the two groups is greatest with regard to physical bullying (16.3 percent for middle school students versus 11.6 percent for their older counterparts). Interestingly, teasing about sexual matters is fairly common at both age levels, whereas teasing about race and religion is relatively taboo. In terms of gender differences, boys report victimization more often than do girls for all forms of bullying except sexual jokes, where girls slightly outnumber boys. The higher prevalence of sexual teasing reported by girls may derive from the greater awkwardness that girls experience associated with the physical changes of puberty, some of which are more visible in girls than boys. Alternatively, rather than an actual gender reversal in victimization, when it comes to sexual teasing, girls may be more likely than boys to define teasing as harassment.

The greater level of victimization among girls involving sexual teasing and ridicule speaks to the argument that sexual harassment should not be considered as a form of bullying at all. Presumably, the move toward blending sexual harassment into the general context of bullying—mixing it with such behaviors as name-calling and social ostracism—was accomplished under the assumption that the increased attention given to bullying prevention would carry over to gender-specific issues. Although well-meaning, this broad-based approach may have caused there to be less focus on sexual harassment, rather than more. As Chesney-Lind and Irwin point out, "the vague and overly inclusive definition of 'bullying' runs the risk of depriving girls of important civil rights in the areas of sexual harassment."[21]

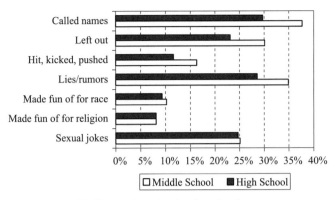

Figure 1.8 Prevalence of bullying victimization by school type
Source: Analysis of 2001−02 Health Behavior in School-Aged Children Survey (HBSC).

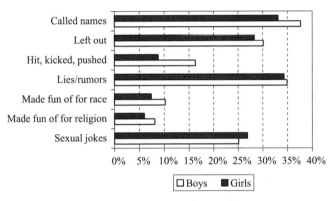

Figure 1.9 Prevalence of bullying victimization by gender
Source: Analysis of 2001−02 Health Behavior in School-Aged Children Survey (HBSC).

Cyberbullying

The victimization results according to bullying subtype shown in Figure 1.9 clearly suggest that verbal harassment—name-calling and spreading rumors— stands out as the most common form of harassment among both boys and girls and in both middle school and high school. In recent years, psychological rather than physical forms of harassment, which can be no less hurtful, have been glorified in movies like *Mean Girls* and television programs like the CW television network series *Gossip Girl.* The old adage "sticks and stones may break my bones, but names will never hurt me" could not have been farther from the truth. Making matters worse, the increased level and expanding types of Internet use have opened a new dimension for harassment. Although not occurring in the school setting, these venues for harassing behavior still involve an extension of the school experience and interactions with classmates.

What at one time may have been scribbled on the wall of a bathroom stall, only seen by relatively few people (and potentially not the victim), can now be broadcast widely through online blogs, chat rooms, and social networks like *Facebook* and *MySpace*. Compounding the problem is that the technical skills of children and adolescents—not to mention the enormous hours spent online—far exceed the limited skills of parents and other guardians to use the technology or comprehend the cryptic language of cyberspeak (e.g., "ih8u"), thereby interfering with their ability to detect or monitor this behavior.

On January 14, 2010, 15-year-old Phoebe Prince of South Hadley, Massachusetts committed suicide, apparently driven by repeated acts of cyberbullying. The teenager had recently emigrated from Ireland, and was not well-received at school, especially after she started dating a senior football player. As a cruel postscript to the tragedy, disparaging comments, reportedly from classmates, were posted, to a Facebook page created in the young girl's memory.

Paralleling the technology-driven changes in bullying context, several researchers have started to examine patterns of cyberbullying. Hinduja and Patchin, for example, conducted an exploratory investigation of the prevalence and correlates of cyberbullying, which they defined as "when someone repeatedly makes fun of another person online or repeatedly picks on another person through email or text message or when someone posts something online about another person that they don't like," through an online survey that yielded well over 6,000 responses.[22] Restricting their analysis to just the nearly 1,400 respondents who were under the age of 18, divided evenly by gender, they found that 32 percent of the boys and 36 percent of the girls indicated that they had been the victim of online bullying at some point in time. Cyberbullying occurred most often in chat rooms, followed by harassing or threatening text messages. Interestingly, victimization by cyberbullying was correlated with victimization by more traditional (offline) forms of harassment and intimidation.

Online surveys are subject to a host of methodological limitations and biases. Given the absence of scientific sampling, the results should be viewed with a fair modicum of caution. In a more recent investigation utilizing a traditional written survey, Hinduja and Patchin questioned a random sample of about 2,000 middle school students from a large school district concerning experiences with cyberbullying, both as victims and purveyors. Estimates from this study were substantially more conservative than those from the online survey, yet appreciably more reliable. As shown in Table 1.8, approximately 17 percent of the students reported having been the victim of cyberbullying, and an almost identical percentage admitted to having cyberbullied another. Also, 12 percent had been both perpetrator and victim at one time or another, while as many as 77 percent denied involvement in cyberbullying in either role. Importantly, of the 23 percent having any experience with cyberbullying, more than half are both givers and takers of online abuse.

Table 1.8
Prevalence of cyberbullying victimization and offending

Offending	Victimization		
	Nonvictim	Victim	Total
Nonbully	77.1%	5.3%	82.4%
Bully	5.6%	12.0%	17.6%
Total	82.7%	17.3%	100.0%

Source: Adapted from Hinduja and Patchin, "Cyberbullying Fact Sheet," http://www.cyberbullying.us/cyberbullying_fact_sheet.pdf.

Effects and Response

Whatever the level of prevalence in the aggregate and whatever the form (physical or psychological, online or interpersonal), for the individual victims of bullying, the impact can be devastating, as demonstrated by the following:[23]

- In a study done in Australia, 6 percent of boys and 9 percent of girls reported staying home to avoid being bullied.[24]
- In a review by British researchers of 10 studies of bullying, every one of the investigations found higher levels of depression among young people who were bullied by their peers.[25]
- A study of bullying in the elementary grades found that children who were repeatedly victimized were more likely to exhibit a host of health-related problems, including sleep difficulties, bedwetting, depression, and frequent headaches and stomachaches.[26]
- An analysis of data from the National Longitudinal Survey of Youth found that adolescents who had been the victims of repeated bullying before the age of 12 had significantly greater adjustment problems later on during adolescence, including depression, academic struggles, and difficulties getting along with peers.[27]
- A study of over 16,000 Finnish school children, ages 14 to 16, found significant associations between bullying victimization and both depression and suicide ideation. Boys who were frequently bullied were over five times more likely to be moderately to severely depressed, and four times more likely to be suicidal than those who were not bullied; girls who were often bullied were over three times more likely to be moderately to severely depressed, and eight times more likely to be suicidal than their nonvictim counterparts.

If there is any silver lining to the tragedies that befell schools during the 1990s, it may be the increased awareness and concern over the age-old problem of school bullying. In response to the perceived crisis, various anti-bullying intervention programs have been implemented in school districts across the country, some featuring character development and others focusing on peer-mediation and conflict resolution processes (see Appendix C).

For example, the Olweus Bullying Prevention Program, the oldest and best-known comprehensive curriculum, not only includes interventions specific for bullies and for victims, but also addresses the important role of peer bystanders.[28] The Committee for Children in Seattle sponsors two age-specific anti-bullying curricula.[29] The Steps to Respect program, which is designed for younger children, emphasizes friendship skills and empathy for victims of teasing and intimidation. The group's Second Step curriculum promotes empathy, impulse control, and anger management for children up through the 8th grade.

Despite the range of promising tools for bullying suppression, there are significant hurdles to their successful application in school settings. Most of all, the school climate must be amenable to changing norms surrounding intimidation and aggression. Intolerance for acts of bullying must be the perspective widely embraced and shared by both faculty and students.

Demaray and Malecki argue that social support or the lack thereof, as perceived by bullies and/or their victims, is a critical factor in determining whether the behavior is encouraged or discouraged in the prevailing school culture.[30] They contend, furthermore, that successful prevention efforts must turn social support decidedly against bullying. In reviewing the more popular anti-bullying programs, however, they failed to find a sufficient social support component in most.

Unfortunately, even when students and teachers appear, at least superficially, solidly unified against bullying, certain deeply rooted prejudices that favor bullies over victims remain somewhat resistant to change. In their study of perceptions and attitudes among middle school students and teachers, Crothers and Kolbert found relatively weak confidence in the utility of anti-bullying curricula and role-playing strategies.[31] Rather, both groups seemed to prefer an approach that encourages victims to be more assertive and to stand up for themselves. Indeed, the long-standing "blame the victim" viewpoint, suggesting that victims are in some way responsible for their mistreatment, remains somewhat impenetrable.

Unnever and Cornell's survey of over 2,400 students drawn from six middle schools adds to the discouraging outlook on bullying prevention. When asked about how commonly their peers and teachers attempt to prevent bullying at school, the responses reflected significant degrees of indifference: 20 percent indicated that teachers almost never attempted to prevent bullying and 40 percent reported the same lack of effort on the part of their fellow classmates. Conversely, only 6 percent and 24 percent perceived that other students and faculty, respectively, tried almost always to prevent bullying.[32]

Regardless of the approach to prevention and change, it remains extremely challenging to convince bullies that their actions are disadvantageous for themselves, besides being injurious to the targets of their abuse. All too often, bullies gain from their use of power over weaker classmates. Not only do they often acquire some tangible outcome, such as their victim's lunch or personal property, but they are typically admired for their strength and supremacy. Based on responses from nearly 400 middle school students in Virginia, Thunfors and Cornell observed that bullies were, based on peer nominations, overwhelmingly considered to be the more popular students in class.[33]

Moreover, the personal gratification experienced by bullies and brutes may not just be social, but appears to have a biological basis as well. A University of Chicago study compared brain scans from teenage boys with aggressive conduct disorders along with a matched group of nonaggressive adolescents as they watched a video clip of someone inflicting pain on another person. The aggressive subjects responded with increased activity in the pleasure-sensing portion of the brain, while the comparison group showed no such reaction.[34]

The problem of bullying and its solution goes well beyond the walls of little red schoolhouses. In our competitive culture, bullies frequently win. We worship athletes who taunt their opponents. In the workplace, managers are often rewarded for manipulating subordinates. And many of our political leaders capture votes by bullying ("challenging") their rivals with tough-sounding, "bring it on" rhetoric. Efforts to combat school bullying will be feeble so long as we admire brutes and pity pushovers.

ON TO COLLEGE

On April 16, 2007, nearly eight years after the Columbine massacre, an intro-verted and deeply troubled undergraduate student at Virginia Tech's Blacks-burg campus shot and killed 32 students and faculty members, and wounded 17 others, before turning the gun on himself. The massacre actually involved two separate shooting sprees, spaced some two and one-half hours apart.

That frigid and windy Monday morning near the end of his senior year would be the last for Seung-Hui Cho, a Korean national who had moved with his family to the United States at the age of 8, living briefly in Maryland before settling in Virginia. Just before 7 a.m., with a gun hidden inside his coat, Cho walked a short way across campus and snuck into Ambler Johnston Hall, a large co-ed dormitory for undergraduates. After reaching the fourth floor of the high-rise, Cho shot and killed Emily Hilscher, who had just returned to her room after visiting her boyfriend, and then fatally shot Ryan Clark, a resident advisor who lived next door and had checked to see what the noise was all about.

Responding to a 911 call received just after 7:15 a.m., the campus police assumed, based on the apparent circumstances, that the early morning double-murder had resulted from an isolated domestic quarrel and that the campus community was in no further danger. In fact, they proceeded to inter-rogate Hilscher's boyfriend, a known gun enthusiast, as a person of interest. Given the usual context of campus violence, the domestic quarrel theory would have been reasonable. The authorities would soon learn, however, that the most plausible explanation could not have been further from the truth.

After taking a break from his deadly mission to carry out an important errand at the post office, Cho returned to campus and struck again. Shortly after 9:30 a.m., the 23-year-old gunman walked through the main entrance of Norris Hall, which housed the School of Engineering, and chained-locked the doors behind him. To discourage any interruptions, Cho positioned a note inside the door warning that a bomb would explode if the lock and chains were removed. Once inside the building, the assailant climbed the stairs onto the second floor. After scoping out the location and peeking into classrooms, he barged into an Advanced Hydrology class. Without saying a word, he started shooting, managing to kill the instructor and 9 of the 13 students in the classroom. Cho then moved on to other targets—first in a classroom directly across the hall and then elsewhere within the building. By the time the police arrived and Cho took his own life, he had fired nearly 200 rounds from his two semiautomatic handguns over a time span of just about 10 minutes. The death toll at Norris Hall was staggering: 25 students and 5 faculty members were fatally shot and 23 others were injured, either by gun-fire or from jumping out of windows in an attempt to escape.

This exceptionally violent episode was not the first indication of Cho's emo-tional and behavioral problems. Cho's act of carnage had roots that started forming years earlier. As a child, Cho was diagnosed with selective mutism, an anxiety-based inability to speak. Apparently his difficulty mastering the Eng-lish language, combined with his extreme shyness, was enough to make him the daily object of ridicule and scorn throughout his middle and high school years. By the time he had moved on to college at Virginia Tech, Cho was filled with hatred and resentment—toward his peers, Americans, or perhaps all of humankind. His isolation from family and classmates continued on through high school and into college. While at Virginia Tech, Cho's depression grew deeper. Although diagnosed with a mood disorder, Cho failed to receive much in the way of treatment for his worsening mental health.

Cho's adjustment issues and his fascination with violence were well-known around the Virginia Tech campus, although arguably no one could have anticipated the full extent of his dangerousness. In December 2005, after a brief overnight stay at a local mental health facility, Cho was referred to the campus counseling center for follow-up. The counselor's observations hardly indicated much concern: "[Cho] denies suicidal and/or homicidal thoughts. Said the comment he made was a joke. Said he has no reason to harm self and would never do it."[1]

Cho may also have worried some of his teachers with his behavior and his violence-laden prose, but could anyone have expected that he was capable of murder, let alone mass murder? In 2005, Cho had been accused of stalking two young women and was ordered by the court to receive outpatient mental health services. More recently, one of his instructors had urged him to seek counseling when he wrote violent passages in some of his creative writing assignments.

The scope of the Virginia Tech massacre may have been unprecedented, but the idea of a college student opening fire on his peers was hardly unforeseen. It was only a matter of time that shootings associated with middle and high school students would graduate to the college level. Many of the miseries suffered by students long before they matriculate continue to distort their thinking about peers and about themselves. The emotional scars suffered by a student who felt bullied or harassed throughout the early years of schooling (or other psychological risk factors) do not necessarily dissipate or heal later in life.

Cho had many of the characteristics discovered in younger school shooters. He was extremely isolated socially, had virtually no one on whom he depended for encouragement and support, felt profoundly rejected, blamed all of his problems on others around him, and had access to semiautomatic weapons. He also had a model for his massacre in the legendary Columbine slayings. Though the massacre at Columbine High had occurred several years earlier, Harris and Klebold had remained heroic icons in the minds of alienated and marginalized students around the country—including Cho.

In between his two killing sprees on campus—the double-homicide in the residence hall and the massive slaughter in a classroom building hours later— Cho anticipated his own demise. During his brief respite from mayhem, he mailed a package of materials—his writings, photographs, and a videotaped "manifesto"—to NBC News in New York. The photographs showed Cho aiming his firearms in a menacing pose. They depicted the killer as a powerful man who could not easily be ignored. The videotape consisted of a rambling, incoherent, and disjointed message in which he sought to justify his rampage as a rational response to those who had destroyed his life. The wrongdoers had had many chances to change their ways, Cho indicated, but they chose not to do so. Therefore, the victims of his shooting spree were, in the mass killer's mind, actually responsible for the mass murder. Regrettably, executives at NBC released both the photos and the videotape, ensuring that Cho's image would carry on in infamy and that the potential of a copycat effect would remain for years to come.

CAMPUS HOMICIDE

The massacre of 32 victims on the otherwise bucolic campus of Virginia Tech sent shockwaves through college and university communities across America. Not only was it the most devastatingly violent episode ever to occur at an institution of higher learning, it was the largest mass shooting of any kind in our nation's history. The sense of serenity and security that characterized most campuses was suddenly shaken by the Virginia Tech tragedy. And when, in February 2008, another seemingly random shooting at the hands of a former student claimed the lives of five students at Northern Illinois University, college administrators everywhere had to confront a new reality in which the risk of campus rampage was not to be ignored. One massacre may have been considered an aberration, but two in less than a year seemed more like an emerging trend.

Notwithstanding the high-profile shootings at Virginia Tech and Northern Illinois University and the resulting potential for copycats, it is important to maintain perspective on the actual level of risk. Based on data gleaned from the FBI's Uniform Crime Reporting program and the U.S. Department of Education's records on campus crime at four-year colleges, as well as detailed media reports gathered from searching electronic newspaper databases, 76 homicides were reported on college campuses nationwide between 2001 and 2005. Leaving aside cases involving faculty, staff, or other nonstudents as victims, the count of undergraduates and graduate students murdered at school numbered 51, an average of about 10 per year. As reflected in Table 2.1, of these homicides, many involved intimate partners, friends, or acquaintances, or stemmed from drug deals gone bad, not rampaging shooters. When

Table 2.1
Patterns of college campus homicide in the U.S., 2001–05

Characteristic	Percent
Weapon	
Gun	52.2%
Knife	11.6%
Personal	21.7%
Other	14.5%
Sex of Victim	
Male	61.3%
Female	38.7%
Victim Role	
Student	57.3%
Faculty	9.3%
Staff	9.3%
Child	5.3%
Other	18.7%
Sex of Offender	
Male	90.8%
Female	9.2%
Offender Role	
Student	35.5%
Former student	5.3%
Outsider	32.2%
Undetermined	27.0%
Victim/Offender Relationship	
Partner	12.5%
Friend	28.3%
Acquaintance	6.6%
Stranger	27.6%
Undetermined	25.0%

Note: Includes only four-year colleges and universities.

compared with virtually any metropolitan area, a student's chance of dying by homicide actually decreases once he or she steps onto campus.

Any life cut short is tragic, of course. In light of the nearly 20 million college students in the United States, however, the chances of being murdered on campus are about as likely as being fatally struck by lightning. The real dangers on campus lie elsewhere: Each year, more than 1,000 college students commit suicide, and at least as many die in alcohol-related incidents such as binge drinking. Rather than focusing on these "not my son or daughter" concerns, many parents obsess instead about Virginia Tech-type shootings and demand that college administrators focus on upgrading security and protecting their children from armed assailants.

The Grad School Phenomenon

The issues that motivate campus shooters and their younger counterparts tend to be vastly different. Shootings at middle schools and high schools are frequently precipitated when students feel bullied or persecuted by their classmates and/or teachers.[2] However, the perpetrators of mass shootings at colleges and universities are often graduate students—older individuals who turn to violence in response to what they perceive to be unbearable pressure to succeed or the unacceptable reality of failure. Indeed, the most striking fact pattern among campus shootings is the disproportionate involvement of graduate students as perpetrators. Of the 13 fatal multiple shootings at colleges in the United States from 1990 through 2008, shown in Table 2.2, eight were committed by current or former graduate, law, medical, or nursing students, compared to three by more traditional undergraduates and two by outsiders.

Unlike undergraduates, students in graduate and professional programs often lack balance in their personal lives, narrowly focusing on academic work and training to the exclusion of other interests and other people in their lives. They may even work in the lab to all hours of the night, subsisting on cold pizza and junk food, thereby jeopardizing their health and well-being. Students who had been at the top of their class through high school and college may come to find themselves struggling to get by with just passing grades. No longer supported financially by parents, they experience great pressure to juggle assistantship activities or outside employment with coursework and thesis research, with little time for attending to social networks. At some point, their entire lifestyle and sense of worth may revolve around academic achievement. Moreover, their personal investment in reaching a successful outcome can be viewed as a virtual life-or-death matter. This perception can be intensified for foreign graduate students from certain cultures where failure is seen as shame on the entire family. Foreign students experience additional pressures because the academic visas allowing them to remain in this country are often dependent on their continued student status. Indeed, a recent study of student mental health at the University of California reported that both graduate students

Table 2.2

Shootings involving multiple fatalities on college campuses in the U.S., 1990–2008

Date	School	Shooter, Age	Role at School
Nov 1, 1991	University of Iowa	Gang Lu, 28	Graduate student
Dec 14, 1992	Simon's Rock College	Wayne Lo, 18	Undergraduate student
Jan 26, 1995	University of North Carolina	Wendell Williamson, 26	Former law student
Aug 15, 1996	San Diego State University	Frederick Davidson, 36	Graduate student
Jun 28, 2000	University of Washington	Jian Chen, 42	Medical student
Aug 28, 2000	University of Arkansas	James Easton Kelly, 36	Former graduate student
May 17, 2001	Pacific Lutheran University	Donald Cowan, 55	None
Jan 16, 2002	Appalachian School of Law	Peter Odighizuwa, 42	Former law student
Oct 28, 2002	University of Arizona	Robert Flores, 40	Nursing student
Sep 2, 2006	Shepherd University	Douglas Pennington, 49	Parent of students
Apr 16, 2007	Virginia Tech	Seung-Hui Cho, 23	Undergraduate student
Feb 8, 2008	Louisiana Tech	Latina Williams, 23	Undergraduate student
Feb 14, 2008	Northern Illinois University	Steven Kazmierczak, 27	Graduate student

and international students are particularly vulnerable to mental health problems due in large part to their increased levels of stress.[3]

For all of these reasons, it is important that graduate admissions committees look beyond grades and test scores to discern evidence of possible academic or disciplinary problems in the backgrounds of recruits. A record of attendance at multiple institutions without completing a degree, for example, may warrant inquiry into the reasons for such transiency. In addition, faculty advisors and academic standing committees should be wary of retaining a marginal student when the prospects for degree completion begin to appear remote. Mentors and advisors must be alert to situations in which a student's dignity and entire sense of self-worth are on the line, with nothing left to lose.

It is a well-worn yet importantly true statement that campus violence is everyone's concern. And in response to heightened alarm following the Virginia Tech shooting, many segments of college communities have been corralled in an attempt to reduce the risk. College officials have convened high-level strategic planning groups; threat assessment and management teams have been assembled with skilled professional staff members; technology departments have strived to upgrade campus-wide communication tools for handling emergencies; students and residence hall advisors have been briefed on dangerous situations; and, of course, campus police departments have focused on training and emergency readiness. However, one key sector of the campus community has been comparatively absent from the multifaceted response: the faculty. Other than encouraging instructors to report suspicious behavior in their students, the vital role of faculty in promoting a healthy campus climate has been relatively ignored.

Faculty have tremendous influence over the lives and ambitions of students, undergraduate and graduate alike. Regrettably, not all faculty members are sensitive to this enormous and often unrestrained power. Although skilled in their own academic discipline and in imparting knowledge to students and advisees, they may not be particularly concerned about those aspects of their students' lives that go beyond but still affect academic progress.

Some academics choose to pursue the scholarly life because of its solitude. They are comfortable with books and ideas, but not necessarily with people. Moreover, the protections of academic freedom and tenure make it difficult for senior administrators to encourage faculty to change in this regard, even when there are indications of unfairness in either grading practices or interactions in or outside of the classroom. With a few exceptions, this does not arise from mean-spiritedness, but only from lack of awareness regarding their profound impact on students—positive or negative. Furthermore, many academics perceive their primary professional allegiance to be to the "community of scholars," while neglecting or dismissing their connection to the campus community as just a "part-time" activity a couple of days per week.

Compounding the problem is the fact that faculty mentors, the gatekeepers to success, may be oblivious to the range of pressures confronted by their students from academics, work or assistantship duties, extra-curricular interests, and, of course, family and friends. Faculty sometimes see their own classes and homework assignments as the most important thing in their students' workloads, without regard for other academic and nonacademic demands. At the extreme, some faculty may even seek to maintain an oppressive relationship with students, perhaps perpetuating the power imbalance that they themselves endured during their years in graduate school. If a faculty member treats a student unfairly, there is often little that administrators can do to intercede, except in the most egregious cases related to sexual harassment or other forms of clear-cut discrimination.

In confronting these problem situations, deans and department chairs have been known to "reward" bad behavior by removing faculty from certain class assignments (e.g., required courses or large undergraduate sections) and placing them in small graduate classes despite the enhanced significance of the faculty-student role at that advanced level. At least, the reasoning seems to be, graduate students are older, wiser, and less vulnerable. Although this may be true, the stakes are higher and the consequences of mistreatment potentially deadly. To combat the all-too-frequent dilemma of how to utilize burned-out or dispirited senior faculty, college officials should use whatever leverage they may have (e.g., merit pay raises) to persuade faculty to contribute positively to a climate of fairness and student-centeredness. Whether or not it makes the difference in preventing some angry student from avenging perceived mistreatment, it is the right thing to do.

In light of these conditions, the following set of strategies would be appropriate and advisable, particularly for those universities with sizable graduate student populations:[4]

- Enhance the screening of graduate school applicants to identify signs of academic or personal adjustment issues.
- With a thorough system of assessment for academic progress, be prepared to withdraw students whose chance of success in a reasonable amount of time appears remote.
- Train faculty members to deal effectively with problem students and to be aware of the appropriate limits of their power over the lives of students. Assessments of student-faculty interactions need not be limited to just course evaluations.
- Provide faculty members with information on available referral resources for students whose concerns go beyond what can be addressed within the faculty-student relationship.
- Encourage and support graduate-student organizations that have a focus extending beyond academic and professional matters. Strive not to set unreasonable expectations for graduate and professional students that would force them to abandon or ignore other important aspects of their lives.
- Ensure that graduate and professional students have adequate mental-health-insurance coverage. These students may be especially in need of access to counseling services through an on-campus facility or a contractual arrangement with an outside provider.

CAMPUS VIOLENCE

Of course, issues of violence and violence prevention extend well beyond the few widely publicized crimes that are featured in the news. But even in the broader context of campus violence, the incidence is rather low, and the risk of serious victimization is typically far lower than in the areas adjacent to most campuses.

Table 2.3 displays rates of violent crime on college campuses based on the 6,651 two- and four-year schools, representing a combined enrollment of over

Table 2.3
Violent crime rates at colleges and universities, 2006 and 2007

| Offense | Two-year colleges (1,721 schools with 12 million enrollment) | | | | Four-year colleges (2,593 schools with 18 million enrollment) | | | |
| | 2006 | | 2007 | | 2006 | | 2007 | |
	Number	Rate per 100,000	Number	Rate per 100,000	Number	Rate per 100,000	Number	Rate per 100,000
Homicide	0	0.00	1	0.01	7	0.04	42	0.23
Forcible rape	129	1.07	137	1.13	2,228	12.38	2,191	12.18
Robbery	247	2.04	254	2.10	1,038	5.77	1,038	5.77
Aggravated assault	455	3.76	418	3.46	1,841	10.23	1,720	9.56
Total violent crimes	831	6.87	810	6.70	5,114	28.42	4,991	27.74

Source: Based on data from U.S. Department of Education, http://ope.ed.gov/security.

30 million students, that submitted complete data reports to the U.S. Department of Education. The rates for 2006 and 2007 are remarkably similar—and exceptionally low in contrast to the overall rates for the nation (for 2007, for example, the U.S. crime rates per 100,000 population were 5.6 for homicide, 30.0 for forcible rape, 147.6 for robbery, and 283.8 for aggravated assault). The only noteworthy shift between the years is for homicide, completely owing to the Virginia Tech incident that drove the number of homicides among four-year schools from 7 cases in 2006 to 42 in 2007. Overall, the several thousand victims of campus violence among the millions of college students translates to a rate per 100,000 students that is a small fraction of the corresponding U.S. figure, even taking into consideration the fact that with their lengthy winter and summer breaks college students are typically on campus for not much more than half the year.

Not only do college campuses have remarkably low rates of violence, but the campus location (urban/suburban/rural), a factor that typically correlates with general crime rates, does not emerge as an important variable based on empirical analyses of campus crime. Contrary to the concerns of many parents (particularly those residing in comfortable and safe suburban communities) about sending their children to college in some "dangerous big city," campuses in urban centers do not tend to have higher rates of victimization than do those in remote, rural locations. This surprising fact points to the unattractiveness of a college campus as a potential crime target relative to its surrounding areas. In urban centers, at least for property crimes, there tend to be far more desirable crime targets off campus, where far greater wealth can be found.

The relatively low prevalence of criminal activity on college campuses—urban and rural—also stems from the fact that most schools maintain their own campus police or public safety departments, which do much more than supplement whatever municipal, county, or state law enforcement resources that exist. Moreover, schools in areas considered to be most at-risk for violence (based on neighborhood characteristics) typically maintain larger police and security forces to provide adequate protection for the campus community. For example, among the 100 largest colleges that responded to the 2004–2005 BJS Survey of Campus Law Enforcement, the 44 urban schools employed on average 3.2 officers per 1,000 students compared to an average of 2.6 per 1,000 students for the 56 schools in nonurban settings.

Based on an analysis of more than 220 college campuses, Fox and Hellman found that crime rates correlate most strongly with the percentages of students who attend full-time and who live in campus housing.[5] Both of these factors increase the overall level of exposure to crime on campus. These are indeed partially the reason that urban schools in general do not have higher crime rates—that is, urban schools tend to have greater percentages of students who commute from home to school and thus are less exposed to campus crime.[6]

THE CLERY ACT

The fact that college students spend considerable time off campus may have been at least partially responsible for the overly broad, unreasonable, and impractical scope of the campus crime data collection protocol prescribed by the U.S. Congress in the Student Right-to-Know and Campus Security Act of 1990 (see Appendix D). This legislation mandated that colleges and universities participating in federal student aid programs "prepare, publish, and distribute, through appropriate publications or mailings, to all current students and employees, and to any applicant for enrollment or employment upon request, an annual security report" outlining campus security policies and campus crime statistics for that institution.[7]

This legislation is more widely known as the "Clery Act," named for the Lehigh University freshman who was brutally murdered on April 5, 1986 in her dormitory room. In fact, a 1998 amendment to the bill officially changed its name to the Jeanne Clery Disclosure of Campus Security Policy and Campus Crime Statistics Act.

Nineteen-year-old Jeanne Ann Clery had been raped, sodomized, beaten, and strangled by a fellow student who later bragged to his friends of his vicious assault on the beautiful blond-haired co-ed. While attempting to cope with their daughter's murder, Connie and Howard Clery were outraged when university officials revealed that there had been 38 violent offenses reported on the Lehigh campus during the three-year period prior to the incident. This was precisely the kind of information that they—and other parents of college students—would have wanted to know when choosing the right school for their sons and daughters. The Clerys banded together with other victims of campus crime and convinced the U.S. Congress to enact legislation compelling colleges to be more forthcoming.

Prior to the legislation, over 300 campus police agencies were already submitting crime statistics to the FBI as part of the Uniform Crime Reporting program, a strictly voluntary crime reporting mechanism for law enforcement agencies around the country—including campus police. Concerned that this represented a small share of the more than 8,000 community colleges, four-year colleges, and universities, Congress mandated that all schools collect and disseminate, to all students or prospective students as well as the U.S. Department of Education, annual tabulations of murder, rape and other sex offenses, robbery, aggravated assault, burglary, motor vehicle theft, and arson. Conspicuously absent from the requirements was larceny, the offense category that, according to the FBI statistics, includes over 80 percent of reported campus crimes.

Though larceny was excluded (significantly reducing the volume of data to report), the act required campus officials to collect information on various other offenses. These included not only incidents that occurred on campus and were reported to the campus police, but student victimization taking place in the areas surrounding campus. Information on student victimizations at off-campus locations such as fraternity and sorority houses, whether these events were reported to the campus authorities or the local police, was also to be collected. In addition to the offense tallies, campus officials were also required to report data on hate crimes and all arrests and disciplinary actions associated with liquor, drug, and weapons violations.

There is no doubt that the Clerys and others who pushed tirelessly for this legislation were well-intentioned. However, the reporting requirements of the bill, particularly compared with the FBI's voluntary crime reporting program for local police agencies, can be so onerous that important resources may need to be drawn away from critical enforcement and crime prevention initiatives. In addition, the rules are so complex and the required training so extensive that the resulting Clery crime data are of dubious reliability and validity.[8]

For 2006 and 2007 combined, for example, the University of California's Davis (UC Davis) campus, with an enrollment of nearly 30,000 students, reported through the Clery system as many as 79 forcible rapes. The other nine campuses of the University of California system, with a combined student population of almost a quarter million, reported only 99. The dubious distinction that UC Davis holds with regard to rapes on campus cannot be explained by any characteristic of the school or the student population that would produce more sexual assaults. Rather, the school has long prioritized the disclosure and prevention of sexual assault partially by encouraging students to come forward to report victimization. "The students know where to go, and the people they go to know where to send them," said Jennifer Beeman, director of the school's Campus Violence Prevention Program, to a reporter from *The Chronicle of Higher Education.* "If we're doing our job, the numbers are going to be higher."[9]

The UC Davis campus rape numbers are hardly the only anomaly emerging from the Clery data reports. For example, Ohio State University reported 53 rapes in 2006 and then 65 in 2007. These figures may not be unusually high for a campus of over 50,000 students, of which nearly 49 percent are female. However, that the school reported not a single aggravated assault for either year is more than curious.

Ironically, whereas the rape and murder of Jeanne Clery was the incident that helped launch the campaign for required crime reporting by colleges and universities, neither the murder nor the rape figures in the Clery data reports are particularly informative. Murder is so rare, and yet so newsworthy, that the Clery reporting mechanism is hardly needed to keep track of these incidents. As far as rape data are concerned, the figures say much more about victims' willingness to come forward than any level of safety on campus. Yet without these two crimes, the time-consuming and expensive Clery initiative most likely would not have been implemented; surely the move toward data collection would not have been prompted solely to measure burglary and auto thefts, even though these two offense categories represent fully three-quarters of all reported crimes on campus.

As college campuses generally strive toward inclusiveness and encourage tolerance for diversity in gender, race, ethnicity, religion, nationality, and sexual orientation, concern for violence associated with prejudice is particularly acute. For students and faculty at Connecticut's Wesleyan University, it was tragic enough when 21-year-old junior Johanna Justin-Jinich was murdered on May 6, 2009, at a popular student bookstore near campus, prompting a two-day lockdown of the school. But news that the suspected gunman had targeted Justin-Jinich specifically for her religious affiliation and had written in his journal "I think it okay to kill Jews and go on a killing spree at this school," made the crime all the more insidious and horrific.

Consistent with the special concern for hate crime, the Clery data program also requires schools to report tallies of incidents on campus that are motivated by various forms of bigotry and prejudice. While there is no question that acts of violence and intimidation related to race, ethnicity, gender, and other categories of bias have devastating impacts on the entire campus community, the volume of Clery reports of such episodes is incredulously low. For 2006 and 2007 combined, the entire group of over 8,000 schools that participate in the Clery program reported fewer than 100 incidents. As an indication of how unreliable these data may be, of the 27 students reported in 2006 to have been victims of aggravated assault in a bias-motivated episode, as many as 10 were linked to the same university, a large southern public institution. In addition, of the 23 reported cases of hate crimes involving bodily injury reported in 2007, seven came from one small private college in Ohio. And six of the seven hate-motivated forcible rapes reported in 2006 were submitted by one school, a modest-size satellite campus of the University of Wisconsin system, possibly reflecting the tendency for that particular school official to interpret sexual assault as an expression of gender bias or the inclination for officials from other colleges not to view sexual assault in this way.

Overall, it is hard to justify the time and expense needed to report and disseminate crime data that has such low reliability and therefore little utility. They certainly shouldn't be seen as an accurate gauge of school safety or levels of crime victimization. Perhaps the resources would be far better directed toward crime prevention or student counseling services. The Clery law does provide the U.S. Department of Education some teeth to enforce the reporting requirements, but apparently there has not been much more than a nibble of enforcement. Since 1990, only five schools have been assessed any fines for noncompliance, penalties that by law may range up to $27,500 for each violation. At the extreme, Eastern Michigan University (EMU) was compelled to pay $357,500 to the U.S. Department of Education as penalty for 13 counts of Clery noncompliance, including failure to alert students about an apparent homicide on campus. After discovering 22-year-old Laura Dickinson dead in her dorm room in December 2006, EMU officials, presumably in an attempt to avoid panic, stated in a written announcement to the campus community, "At this point, there is no reason to suspect foul play. We are fully confident in the safety and security of our campus environment."[10] Regardless of the extent of culpability, in general, it is hard to imagine the established scale of penalties carrying much weight whatsoever.

RAPE AND SEXUAL ASSAULT

The notion that official crime statistics need to be approached with a healthy degree of skepticism and caution is not new or surprising. Criminologists have long been wary of placing too much stock in police-reported crime levels. Apparently, the problems of reliability and validity with these crime data are especially apparent when college data are concerned.

In the general area of crime measurement, researchers have found victim surveys—questioning random samples of individuals regarding their experiences of crime victimization, whether or not they chose to report them to the police—to be a useful vehicle for understanding crime patterns and trends. Unfortunately, there has not been assembled a routine process of victimization research with college students (the NCVS school crime supplement pertains only to students in middle and senior high schools). The private nature of many colleges, as well as the overriding concerns for protecting human subjects, would likely prohibit any such government-sponsored ongoing survey program. Other methodological issues, such as the difficulty in building a sampling frame from which to select student respondents, also limit the prospects for this alternative measuring strategy.

However, given the significant concern on college campuses regarding sexual assault and the suspiciousness of the official crime reports, Krebs and several colleagues undertook in 1996 a one-time online survey of random samples of undergraduates at two large universities, obtaining completed responses from 5,446 females and 1,375 males.[11] Focusing their analysis on the female respondents (very few of the males reported having been victimized), the researchers discovered prevalence rates for sexual assault among the female students to be hardly trivial: 13.7 percent had been victims of at least one completed sexual assault since entering college. Moreover, 4.7 percent were victims of physically forced sexual assault, and 11.1 percent were sexually assaulted while intoxicated. Over two-thirds of the substance-facilitated cases occurred while the victim had voluntarily used drugs or alcohol, while a small percentage involved victims who had been drugged without their knowledge or consent. Despite the gravity of these offenses, the reliability of some of the prevalence estimates was not especially strong in light of the limited number of cases reflected in the low percentages. At the extreme, the 0.6 percent of women who reported having been attacked after unknowingly being drugged into submission would translate to only a few dozen respondents. Any attempt to generalize such an unreliable estimate to the entire population of college women nationally would be overly speculative due to the operation of sampling error.

Concerned about the possible idiosyncrasy embodied in studies of one or a couple of schools and the limits of generalizing from such small samples, Fisher and colleagues surveyed a nationally representative sample of women attending a two- or four-year college or university during the 1996–1997 academic year.[12] A total of 4,446 female students were interviewed over the telephone about their experiences related to various forms of sexual assault. The focus of the questions was quite broad, including completed, attempted, or threatened sexual assaults; unwanted sexual contact ranging from vaginal or anal penetration to fondling or kissing; and levels of coercion ranging from brute force to verbal pressuring. Overall, the survey addressed twelve specific areas—from threats of sexual contact without force to completed acts of forcible rape.

The results with regard to the most serious form of assault—forcible rape, both completed and attempted—are shown in Table 2.4. Although the percentages of students reporting rape victimization may appear low, the rate of 27.7 per 1,000 female students is about four times that reported among similarly aged females in the NCVS for that same year. Notwithstanding the concern for reliability of any statistic based on a limited yield of cases (123 for the whole sample), the relatively elevated rate of rape among college women may have much to do with the campus environment (e.g., co-ed residence halls with limited supervision). When expanding the focus to the full range of incidents, all the way down to unforced yet unwanted sexual contact, the total number of victims and incidents reported in the survey reached 568 and 1,161, respectively.

Serial Predators

Despite their exceptionally low risk of violent crime at most college campuses, or perhaps because of it, college students have been known to be choice targets for serial predators. Many serial killers, for example, have exploited the trusting nature and naïveté of young men and women who are busy enjoying

Table 2.4
Rape victimization of female college students

	Victims			Incidents	
Offense	Number	Percent	Rate per 1,000	Number	Rate per 1,000
Completed rape	74	1.7%	16.6	86	19.3
Attempted rape	49	1.1%	11.0	71	16.0
Total	123	2.8%	27.7	157	35.3

Note: The number of incidents exceeds the number of victims because of some women experiencing repeat victimization.

Source: B.S. Fisher et al., *The Sexual Victimization of College Women.*

the freedom of campus life after having escaped from the watchful eyes and supervisory control of their parents.

In August 1990, for example, the city of Gainesville, Florida, shortly after having been named by *Money* magazine as one of America's most livable cities, was rocked by the vicious murders of five college students—four from the University of Florida and one from local Santa Fe Community College—over a period of just a few days. Several of the victims had been raped and sexually mutilated, and one was decapitated and then eviscerated from neck to pubic bone. Fortunately for the community, the string of murders stopped almost as quickly as they had begun, although the perpetrator would not be identified until over four months later. The assailant, 36-year-old Danny Rolling, was an unemployed drifter who had drifted into town enjoying—and exploiting—the hospitality of an open campus. It was orientation week at the University of Florida, which meant frequent partying among strangers soon to become best friends. Rolling moved freely and inconspicuously about the area, including clusters of off-campus student housing, enabling him to select his targets without arousing suspicion.

Decades earlier, infamous serial killer Theodore Bundy culminated his multi-year, multi-state killing spree by invading the Chi Omega sorority house on the campus of another large public institution in the Sunshine State—Florida State University. In the pre-dawn hours of January 15, 1978, Bundy viciously assaulted four sorority sisters as they slept in their beds, killing two of them. For several years, Bundy had felt most comfortable on college campuses, blending in exceptionally well among the student populations and finding sufficient numbers of trusting co-eds to satisfy his lust for killing. His frequent ploy, which he perfected while a student at the University of Washington in Seattle, was to ask some attractive young woman to assist him in carrying a pile of books to his car strategically parked at a remote lot on campus. Wearing a cast and sling, Bundy pretended that his arm was broken; many women agreed to assist the seemingly helpless, handsome charmer and died violently as a result.

Even though college students have been prime targets for Bundy, Rolling, and many other serial predators, there is little cause for students to be overly and unnecessarily guarded. The number of such episodes is small, and the odds are exceptionally low that some stranger in need of assistance is actually a deadly rapist/murderer. Encouraging college students to be constantly vigilant, beyond a reasonable modicum of common sense, would only breed a sense of cynicism and unnecessarily detract from the full enjoyment of campus life.

3

BLAMING AND SCAPEGOATING

Whether occurring at school or in some other setting, serious acts of violence by juveniles or young adults invariably raise difficult questions about causation. Certain forms of youth violence—for example, those involving robbery, those associated with gang activity, and those arising out of conflict over drugs or romantic entanglements—are fairly straight-forward to comprehend based on familiar motives such as profit, loyalty, and jealousy. Other, more unusual episodes of youthful aggression, especially but not exclusively school shootings, are substantially more perplexing and beg for plausible explanation.

There is no shortage of hypotheses and speculations from which to choose when struggling to make sense of seemingly senseless murder and mayhem—perplexing cases range from Charles Whitman's mass shooting high above the University of Texas campus in 1966 to Seung-Hui Cho's murderous rampage at Virginia Tech four decades later.[1] For these as well as the less dramatic instances, the more common targets of responsibility include:

- The media that desensitizes young people to violence
- Peer groups—especially gangs—that promote bad behavior
- Parents that do a poor job of raising and supervising their children
- Massive schools that do not allow students to bond with pro-social role models
- Oppressive school climates that alienate children with disrespectful treatment
- Bullying that pushes victims of intimidation and harassment to the brink of violence
- An educational system that fails to teach important life skills including cooperation and self-control

- Psychiatric conditions that predispose certain children and adolescents to violent behavior
- Lax gun laws that give students easy access to powerful weapons

However, each contributor has its limitations in accounting for aberrational behavior. It is not difficult to cite example after example in which these elements are present. But given the relative infrequency of serious school violence—especially in comparison to the prevalence of any of these suspected causal forces in any population of juveniles or young adults—it would be foolish to suggest that one factor can explain the phenomenon.

It may be a reflection of human nature or just cultural tradition, but society typically seeks to assign blame for hideous and senseless acts of violence that we find unfathomable. Moreover, our desire to identify, and perhaps scapegoat, various external forces is intensified for those cases in which the perpetrator has committed suicide or is killed by the police, and is therefore no longer around to absorb the public scorn. Someone or something must be held accountable, if not the perpetrator himself.

BLAMING PARENTS

In April 2000, fully one year following the Columbine massacre, the Pew Research Center surveyed 1,000 adults, including 283 parents with school-age children, about the causes of and solutions for school violence.[2] By a healthy margin, poor upbringing by parents was cited as the leading cause of school violence. As shown in Figure 3.1, 45 percent of all respondents nominated poor parenting as the major cause, compared to, for example, only one-quarter who indicated that violent entertainment was the primary factor. Although the respondents who, themselves, had school-age children were somewhat less critical of parental upbringing than others in the survey, they still tended to place the greatest weight on the role of parents, with 38 percent selecting poor parenting as the primary cause, just ahead of the 35 percent who focused most on violent media.

These survey results are hardly surprising, as there is a long tradition in our society of faulting parents for their children's misbehavior, and this is especially true when it comes to extreme acts of mayhem. A widely held view is that if the parents weren't directly responsible for having created the "monster" that their child had become, then at least they should have seen the warning signs and intervened.

In many instances, parents are easily criticized for lapses in judgment. At the egregious extreme, both the informal court of public opinion and the formal court of law were decidedly critical of Michele Cossey, 46, of Norristown, Pennsylvania, who confessed to having assisted her troubled and bullied 14-year-old son assemble a cache of weapons to boost his self-esteem. Apparently, the boy, who had been relentlessly teased over his obesity, was enthralled

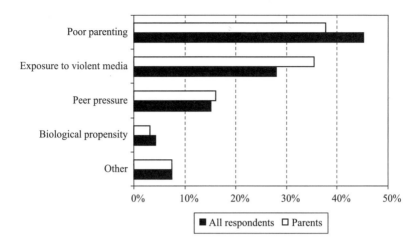

Figure 3.1 Perceived leading causes influencing school shooters
Source: Based on Pew Research Center, "A Year after Columbine: Public Looks to Parents More Than Schools to Prevent Violence."

with the Columbine murders and had plans to avenge his mistreatment at his former school. With therapy, the youngster's mental health improved remarkably, while his mother was sentenced to serve time for child endangerment.

In truth, bad judgment by parents of young offenders is often not so different from the kinds of mistakes that virtually any good parent will make from time to time. But when the outcome involves something as devastating and catastrophic as a schoolyard attack by one's child, then the full history of parenting decisions comes under close scrutiny and poor choices are highlighted. For example, Bill and Faith Kinkel, whose 15-year-old son Kipland fatally shot two classmates and wounded 25 others at Thurston High School in Springfield, Oregon, were severely condemned—after the murderous fact—for having relented to his persistent appeals to buy him guns, even while knowing of his long-standing emotional and developmental problems. On balance, however, the Kinkels were deeply devoted parents, as well as highly regarded school teachers, who tried virtually everything imaginable to help their troubled son. Just before his armed assault at school, Kip executed his parents to spare them the shame of what he was about to do (and perhaps also in response to some pent-up feelings of anger and resentment).

Days after learning about the devastation caused by her son at Columbine, Susan Klebold made a quick trip to Hour Star Images, a beauty salon within sight of the school, ostensibly to be presentable for the hoards of media that were hovering about town. This seemingly odd step was seized on by the press without regard for whatever positives there had been to her parenting. She and her husband Thomas were quite generous toward their son Dylan, at least in terms of material items. In fact, one such purchase for Dylan was the black BMW (which he had wired with explosives) found in the school parking lot.

In his richly documented and detailed examination of 10 school shooters, psychologist Peter Langman concluded that abuse and neglect suffered by several
assailants, particularly at the hands of their parents, were important keys to understanding their extraordinary acts of rage.[3] According to Langman, 16-year-old Evan
Ramsey (who killed two and wounded two others at Bethel Regional High School
in Alaska), 13-year-old Mitchell Johnson (who joined with a friend to murder five
and wound 10 more at the Westside Middle School in Jonesboro, Arkansas), and
16-year-old Jeffrey Weise (who shot and killed seven victims at his high school in
Red Lake, Minnesota, as well as his grandfather and his grandfather's girlfriend at
home) all suffered the effects of post-traumatic stress disorder (PTSD). Langman
reasoned that the PTSD, although linked to childhood traumas, was exacerbated
by other stressors (modeling of family violence, harassment at school, rejection,
conflict with the school administration, and peer influence to commit murder).

The "cycle of violence" hypothesis does indeed have considerable empirical
support, at least for understanding more broadly the inter-generational transmission of aggression. Violent parents often raise violent children, by a combination of biological predisposition and social learning. Moreover, when the
parent's aggression is directed against the child, the psychological effects go
well beyond learning and imitation. However, the abuse/PTSD explanation is
incomplete at best when applied to Ramsey, Johnson, and Weise, as the levels
of victimization that they each reportedly endured were neither unique nor,
by unfortunate standards, extraordinary. Although perhaps a contributor,
abuse/PTSD alone will generally not produce the extreme levels of rage and
despair common in episodes of school shootings.

ALCOHOL, DRUGS, AND MEDICATIONS

Another major area of focus—and blame—surrounds drug and alcohol use.
Although substance abuse by children and adolescents is problematic for many
reasons and may indicate profound emotional problems that warrant clinical
attention, it has not played a significant role in serious episodes of school violence.
None of the major cases of school shootings involved an intoxicated assailant. To
the contrary, the level of planning and methodical action typically found in such
crimes would be compromised were the perpetrator not stone cold sober.

However, several case histories of school shooters include the use of prescribed medication, typically antidepressants and stimulants—a fact that has
not escaped the attention of advocacy groups campaigning against the alleged
over-prescribing of psychiatric medications such as Prozac and Ritalin. Associated with the Church of Scientology, the Citizens Commission on Human
Rights (CCHR), a well-known activist organization whose mission is to expose
human rights abuses by the psychiatric profession, has identified a number of
school shootings involving assailants who were taking or had recently taken
antidepressants.[4] Most prominent on the CCHR list are these reported cases
and medications:

- Kip Kinkel (Springfield, OR—5/21/98): Prozac
- Eric Harris (Littleton, CO—4/20/99): Luvox
- Jeff Weise (Red Lake, MN—3/21/05): Prozac
- Seung-Hui Cho (Blacksburg, VA—4/16/07): Undisclosed antidepressant
- Steven Kazmierczak (Dekalb, IL—2/14/08): Prozac, Xanax, and Ambien

While it may be tempting to blame these medications—as has been done through lawsuits against the "deep pocket" pharmaceutical manufacturers brought on behalf of surviving victims of school shootings—there is little hard evidence of a causal link between school violence and the adverse side effects of psychotropic prescription drugs. If there is any violence-triggering effect at all, it may just be that the medications lift the paralysis of depression enough to enable the user to act, which may include getting even for real or perceived mistreatment.

It is hardly probative that a select handful of perpetrators had used psychiatric drugs prior to their murderous rampages. The homicidal and suicidal tendencies exhibited by these assailants may be linked, not to the drugs they were prescribed, but to the psychological conditions—such as depression—that warranted their psychopharmacological regimen. Given the large numbers of children and young adults who are prescribed antidepressants, a certain few could be expected to act violently merely by virtue of the overall base rate of such violence in the general population. In addition, were it not for the availability of these medications and their therapeutic benefits, arguably there would be a higher prevalence of violence. Finally, notwithstanding the concern that certain medications may produce sudden and episodic outbursts of violence, most of the school massacres in recent years reflect long-term planning and deliberation, not the sudden explosion of rage.

PEER EFFECTS

Further complicating a narrow perspective on individual characteristics of offenders, be it their family backgrounds or their psychiatric histories, is the fact that adolescents are particularly influenced by peers and social expectations. Thus, focusing exclusively on the individual offender to find an answer to persistent questions regarding causation ignores the fact that students often act in group contexts far differently than when they are alone. To understand the course of events surrounding those shootings that implicated more than one person either as accomplice or accessory, we must examine the interactions among co-conspirators as closely as we scrutinize their personal backgrounds and individual pathologies. To children, the expectations and approval of close friends can be all-important, especially when parents and other adults are not around.

In October 2007, shortly after fatally stabbing his mother, 16-year-old Luke Woodham killed his ex-girlfriend Christina Menefee and her friend and wounded several others during an early morning shooting spree at his high school in Pearl, Mississippi. Once in custody, Woodham insisted that a pal,

Grant Boyette, had urged him to assault his mother and former girlfriend during a lengthy telephone conversation on the day before the murder spree. Boyette and several others, suspected to be members of a cult-like group that called itself "the Kroth," were charged with conspiracy.

It is also arguable, if not probable, that Columbine's Dylan Klebold would not have responded quite so violently to his own personal troubles and frustrations if it were not for the strong influence of his buddy Eric Harris. Harris's background and behavior revealed much hostility and a wide array of psychopathic features, as clearly reflected in the rants and raves of his diary and Internet postings. By contrast, Klebold was generally quiet, shy, intelligent, and well-behaved—a good student who was highly regarded by his teachers. But Harris brought out the very worst in him. Thus, an understanding of Klebold's uncharacteristic violent behavior must include the interpersonal dynamics of his relationship with his accomplice. In cases of killing teams like that of Klebold and Harris, where one member follows the lead of another, typically the leader enjoys his role of commander and the follower enjoys being praised for his loyalty. Murder can then become a perverted stage for teenage male bonding—a symbiotic display of manly power.

EXPOSURE TO VIOLENT ENTERTAINMENT

If the series of school rampages that took place in the years following the 1999 watershed event at Columbine High is, at least to some extent, a reflection of imitation (a concern discussed in depth in Chapter 5), whereby so-inclined adolescents find encouragement to kill in the acts of their predecessors, then how was the contagion of homicide and threats of violence first launched? Given how popular culture saturates the daily experiences of children and teenagers, many observers have blamed violent television, movies, and especially video games for inspiring extreme acts of youth violence. In fact, some—including former U.S. Attorney General John Ashcroft—condemned video games for literally teaching children to kill and, more generally, for making simulated mayhem both realistic and singularly pleasurable.

The presumed link between violent entertainment and school shootings apparently resonated with many Americans, liberals and conservatives alike. Within two days of the Columbine High School shooting, the Gallup organization launched a telephone survey of some 650 adults, questioning them about the factors that they believed to be responsible for school shootings like that at Columbine. Prompted with a series of possible causes, respondents ranked media violence third on the list of potential culprits, following closely behind ineffective parents and easy access to guns. Overall, 49 percent of respondents indicated that entertainment violence carried a "great deal" of responsibility for school violence, and 79 percent indicated it carried at least a moderate amount of responsibility.[5]

It is tempting to implicate the media for hideous acts of youth violence at school and elsewhere. After virtually all of the major school shootings, news stories surfaced concerning some young assailant's keen interest in violent entertainment—reports that have been eagerly exploited by various media watchdog organizations looking to fault Hollywood for its lack of restraint.

As part of a special report on school violence published in the aftermath of the Columbine massacre, *TIME* magazine assembled an inventory of common factors to the half-dozen major school massacres that had occurred in America during the previous three years.[6] Under the label "cultural influences," the magazine identified the entertainment favorites—music, movies, and games—of each of the perpetrators. Luke Woodham of Pearl, Mississippi, and Dylan Klebold and Eric Harris of Littleton, Colorado, reportedly enjoyed listening to music by the controversial heavy metal rocker Marilyn Manson. Manson was so offended by the implied link between the Columbine shooting and his music that he vigorously disputed the allegation in an essay for *Rolling Stone* magazine.[7]

Heavy metal music was just one of the many entertainment scapegoats highlighted in the special report. For instance, *TIME* noted that the video games *Doom* and *Mortal Kombat* were favorites of various school shooters. In addition, the special role that Oliver Stone's 1994 film, *Natural Born Killers*, may have played in inspiring 14-year-old Barry Loukaitis's rampage at his junior high school in rural Washington State was not lost on the magazine's reporters. During Loukaitis's trial for the murders of his math teacher and two classmates, a friend testified that the defendant had remarked how much fun it would be to mimic the escapades of the film's lead characters—Mickey and Mallory, a young pair of bored outcasts who celebrated their love with a brutal killing spree.

Author Joseph Lieberman extended the film's condemnation in commenting on its impact on Eric Harris and Dylan Klebold: "The code letters for their Columbine attack were *NBK*, standing for the title of their favorite movie, *Natural Born Killers*. Eric wrote in his journal, '*NBK* comes too quick. Everything I see and hear relates to *NBK* somehow. Sometimes it feels like a goddamn movie.'"[8]

Fourteen-year-old Michael Carneal, who killed three classmates and wounded five others at Heath High School in West Paducah, Kentucky, was more a fan of *Basketball Diaries*—a 1995 film in which a high school hoops star, played by Leonardo DiCaprio, daydreams of shooting up his high school class. Carneal also enjoyed playing violent video games, including *Doom* and *Quake*. Within months of the shooting spree, the parents of the three slain children filed a $130 million lawsuit naming the producers and distributors of *Basketball Diaries*, as well as computer game companies and two Internet pornography sites, for their alleged role in causing Carneal's violent outburst. The legal long-shot fizzled in August 2002, when a Federal appeals court in Cincinnati dismissed the case, ruling that it was "simply too far a leap from shooting characters on a video screen to shooting people in a classroom."[9]

Whatever the strength or weakness of the causal connection, an FBI research group, after thoroughly studying dozens of school shooters, identified "fascination with violence-filled entertainment" as one in a rather long list of warning signs:[10]

> The student demonstrates an unusual fascination with movies, TV shows, computer games, music videos, or printed material that focus intensively on themes of violence, hatred, control, power, death, and destruction. He may incessantly watch one movie or read and reread one book with violent content, perhaps involving school violence. Themes of hatred, violence, weapons, and mass destruction recur in virtually all his activities, hobbies, and pastimes. The student spends inordinate amounts of time playing video games with violent themes, and seems more interested in the violent images than in the game itself. On the Internet, the student regularly searches for Web sites involving violence, weapons, and other disturbing subjects. There is evidence the student has downloaded and kept material from these sites.

LINKING MEDIA AND AGGRESSION

Notwithstanding anecdotal evidence concerning the influence that media violence may have had in inspiring the school shooters of our time, scientific research into the linkages between violent media in its many forms and youth violence and aggression has a long history dating back to the early days of television and the popular emergence of comic-book superheroes. Over the past half-century, social and behavioral scientists have studied in detail the extent to which entertainment violence affects the attitudes and actions of impressionable youth.

Some of the earliest work was contributed by experimental psychologists interested in the dynamics of the learning process. For example, Bandura and colleagues staged a variety of controlled experiments showing that young children tend to imitate violence viewed on film.[11] Despite the evidence that children often mimic violence—particularly when it is rewarded—this body of research was criticized on methodological grounds, in that experimentally induced behavior observed in artificial laboratory settings may not generalize to real-world situations. A further criticism was that the apparent impact of television or film violence on behavior could be short-term and transient.

Although controlled research designs have many methodological strengths, the need for generalizing beyond the laboratory encouraged a number of survey designs that attempted to correlate viewing habits with aggressive behavior. The vast majority of empirical studies have found that those students who, by their own account or according to parents and teachers, were class bullies or aggressive in other ways generally had the greatest exposure to violent entertainment.

In one of the earliest efforts, for example, McIntyre and Teevan surveyed over 2,000 junior and senior high school students about their favorite television programs and their engagement in aggressive behavior, from fighting in school to serious delinquency. As expected, preferences for violent television content were associated with greater proclivity toward aggressive behavior.[12] More recently, a cross-national study of some 30,000 adolescents found a significant correlation between heavy viewing of violent television programming and verbal aggression and bullying.[13] While impressively suggestive of a link between viewing preferences and aggression, these and similar research studies have struggled with the "chicken-and-egg" ambiguity: Did viewing televised violence influence aggression or were aggressive children simply drawn to violent entertainment? Or, are both symptomatic of some other factor?

An answer to this causation conundrum eventually came from longitudinal research that followed subjects from childhood through adolescence and into adulthood, measuring, at several points along the way, their aggressiveness and their consumption of violent entertainment. In what many consider the most rigorous investigation to date, Eron and colleagues found that not only were viewing and behavior correlated, but that viewing choices tended to predict future aggression, while aggression did not predict future viewing habits.[14] At a minimum, preferences for violent entertainment and aggressiveness may be mutually reinforcing: Violent entertainment may stimulate violent activity, and violent activity may be affirmed as appropriate by habitual consumption of violent media content.

Desensitization to Violence

Taken all together, concern for the effects of violent entertainment on the emotional and social development of children is not unwarranted, although the exact nature of the impact is not completely clear. To some extent, children may indeed mimic what they see on the screen—be it on television, in the theater, or in an action game. Just as plausible, however, is the rival hypothesis that violence impacts viewers not so much through imitation and learning, but by the process of desensitization, a general numbing of the adverse emotional responses to violence. Certainly, there has been at least some evidence produced over several decades suggesting that a steady diet of media-depicted violence can help to desensitize young people, distorting their perceptions of social reality, and even inspiring heinous, brutal crimes. The average child grows up observing tens of thousands of murders and more than 100,000 acts of violence on TV.[15] Cumulatively, this has an effect, although the exact size and nature of the effect have been debated for almost as long as television has existed.

In a series of experiments on the desensitizing impact of "slasher films" (movies that combine themes of sex and violence), psychologist Daniel Linz and colleagues observed that watching sexually violent entertainment over a period of weeks caused college-age students to become callous and nonempathic to the suffering of rape victims.[16] The impact, however, was transient, as subjects' sensitivity to victims of sexual violence returned in a matter of days.[17] This begs the question, however, of what effect a steady and constant diet of such material could have on the attitudes and behaviors of adolescents.

VIDEO GAMES

In some respects, violence in television and film, which has been the focus of most of the academic research and public debate, is relatively tame. It represents a passive form of entertainment, as compared to the more active participation provided by video games. Rather than just lying on the living room couch and witnessing a movie massacre on DVD, children can cybernetically kill on demand—and learn to enjoy it—through one of many violent action games available to them in computer gaming stores or on the Internet. Moreover, the intrinsic incentives and rewards of these games—such as accruing a top score from killing, advancing through game levels while developing homicidal mastery and defeating an opponent in an Internet-based competition—reinforces the will to kill, at least in the game setting. Although these games are fantasy, the use of multimedia sound and advanced graphics can make the line between virtual reality and stark reality become rather thin. Finally, role-playing games and the 360-degree perspective of more recent game consoles have taken yet another step toward realism.

Concern and outrage over violent games such as *Grand Theft Auto* have been articulated everywhere from local parent groups to the U.S. Congress. Although less well-known than the *Grand Theft Auto* editions, a collection of titles in the *Postal* series turns killing into sport. At each level, the player is challenged with new mass murder opportunities. The killing sprees in this game are so extensive that *Postal* has been subject to distribution bans in certain parts of the globe.

Other video games have direct relation to the issue of school violence. Produced by the same group as *Grand Theft Auto*, the 2006 release of *Bully* simulates classroom chaos at a fictional academy whose motto, "Canis Canem Edit," translates to "Dog Eat Dog." Advertisements for the title clearly appeal to a certain type of young audience: "As a troublesome schoolboy, you'll stand up to bullies, get picked on by teachers, play pranks on malicious kids."

It has been a challenge for youth development scholars to keep their research agenda up to pace with the fast-changing world of gaming technology. Even so, the weight of the evidence, derived through a wide range of methodological approaches, suggests that frequent playing of violent video games tends to impact negatively on an adolescent's attitudes, thinking, and behavior.

A recent experimental study from the Indiana University School of Medicine discovered that playing video games with violent themes can even alter the gamer's brain activity. The researchers compared two randomly formed groups of adolescents who were instructed to play video games for a half-hour period of time, with one group playing violent video games and the other group playing nonviolent titles. MRI scans indicated significantly greater activity in the area of the brain responsible for emotional arousal among those in the violent game playing group compared to those in the nonviolent game playing group.[18]

Reviewing the results of dozens of research studies on the effects of playing violent video games, psychologist Craig Anderson reported a statistically significant link between exposure to such games and increases in aggressive behavior, aggressive thinking, aggressive affect, and cardiovascular arousal, as well as decreases in helping behavior.[19] Whatever the psychological or physiological dynamics, the potential problems associated with video games will likely be debated for years, at least until some new, more powerful entertainment technology emerges to grab the attention of America's youth.

CONTROLLING ENTERTAINMENT

To whatever extent empirical evidence can implicate a causal connection between violent entertainment in its many forms and aggression, there remains deep concern, both in Congress and in American living rooms, over the long-term impact of this thriving and largely unregulated industry. No matter what the nature or strength of the correlation, millions of Americans believe—rightly or wrongly—that those who profit handsomely from producing and distributing violent entertainment, particularly to eager and impressionable youngsters, need to be more responsible in their business practices. Worried parents and politicians alike insist the First Amendment guarantee of free artistic expression stops when innocent lives are sacrificed.

Within a month of the Columbine massacre, the Gallup Organization polled 1,014 adults about what changes they viewed as necessary to reduce the likelihood that similar acts would occur in the future. Respondents were asked, specifically, whether they thought that the federal government should take steps to regulate violent media content. A majority—or close to it—indicated a desire to see government intervention with regard to the Internet (65 percent), video games (58 percent), television (56 percent), movies (49 percent), and music (48 percent).[20]

Of course, efforts to control the exposure and impact of violent entertainment of all forms on impressionable children are hardly new. As early as the 1960s, parents and child advocates were alarmed about exposing young viewers to unrealistic images of "sanitized violence"—portrayals of aggression absent of grim reality. That is, because television programs and motion pictures of the day failed to depict the more destructive aspects of punching, stabbing, and shooting, youngsters were growing up believing that violence didn't have strong and lasting consequences. To placate anxious parents (as well as to avoid threatened government interference), a voluntary code of the motion picture industry—movie ratings—was then established to assist parents in monitoring their children's viewing choices.

Eventually the problem of sanitized film violence was replaced by a much more troubling phenomenon. To lure young people to the box office, producers frequently gave them exactly what they wanted—more graphic sex and violence. The movie rating system soon became a media version of "forbidden fruit"—more a guide for children in determining what they really "must see" than a guide for parents on what their children must not see. Experimental studies of the factors influencing viewer choice have found that teenage boys, in particular, prefer programs and films with an *R* rating or a parental warning, regardless of their content.[21] From the perspective of a young viewer, if you're not part of the "mature audience," then you must be part of the "immature audience," and what self-respecting, red-blooded American adolescent wants to be labeled that?

Parental warnings and violence ratings have since been extended to television shows and video games under the assumption—or rather hope—that they will aid parents in selecting age-appropriate entertainment options for their children. But as with films, the more mature ratings tend to boost the desirability of proscribed material among immature youngsters who are eager for adulthood.

Rather than provide creative alternatives to parental supervision, politicians and entertainment industry leaders have sought to develop a method for allowing parents to continue working full-time at the office while still having remote control over their children's access to violent television. Through legislation that became effective in 2000, all new TV sets (with at least 13-inch screens) had to be equipped with a V-Chip (V for violence), with which parents can theoretically filter out the most offensive programs from their children's after-school viewing options.

It may be naïve, however, to expect that unsupervised teenagers—left alone in front of their V-Chip-controlled TV sets—will instead tune into *National Geographic*, read Shakespeare, or take up playing chess. More likely, they will bypass their parents' attempts at absentee censorship by renting a grotesque film on DVD, playing a violent video game, or listening to the hate-filled lyrics of some heavy metal band on their iPod. Or, they might just go over to a friend's house whose parents don't use a V-Chip. The lesson is clear: Technology cannot adequately substitute for genuine attention and involvement from parents and other significant adults in the daily lives of children.

In the final analysis, even with enhanced rating systems and parental controls, it is important not to let the entertainment industry off the hook for its willingness to pander to and profit from the darker side of human nature. At the same time, we should be careful not to place inordinate blame on the industry for the unacceptably high levels of youth and school violence in America. We should be similarly wary of single-issue critics, who contend that the problem with kids today is the media, plain and simple. If anything is simple, it is the fallacy of such a simple-minded point of view. As the polling data clearly suggest, the media has often been exploited as a convenient scapegoat, and censorship as an easy solution. Public concerns, political considerations, self-interests, and fear have often encouraged us to point fingers at a profitable industry, while ignoring some of the fundamental causes of violence that are much more difficult to resolve.

THE GUN DEBATE

By the fall of 1991, after having failed in repeated efforts to have a perceived injustice reversed, Gang Lu knew that his best and last resort was a firearm—"the great equalizer," as he called it. For this 28-year-old graduate student, things had changed dramatically from the point in time when he was widely considered a rising star. In 1985, Gang Lu had been chosen for a coveted doctoral fellowship in Physics at the University of Iowa. But achievement never came easy for Gang Lu, as he had toiled hard in school throughout his life, painstakingly preparing for national science tests given by the Chinese government to identify the academic elite. Unfortunately for Gang Lu, within a year after entering the program at the University of Iowa, a brighter doctoral prospect arrived in the department who was also from his homeland of China—a younger, handsome, charismatic rival for whom everything—not just academics—came easily. It didn't take long for Linhua Shan, the new arrival, to eclipse Gang Lu in his pursuit of excellence. For Gang Lu, the final straw came when Shan was nominated by the department for outstanding doctoral dissertation. Unable to think objectively, Gang Lu couldn't accept that Shan's thesis was brilliant, while his own was just competent and workmanlike—nothing that would turn the scientific community on its ear. Gang Lu's disappointment was only part of the problem. Failure to win the D.C. Spriestersbach dissertation prize would deny him a significant advantage in seeking a tenure-track post in the tight job market. He felt his work had been judged unfairly by the department chair and other professors who had the power to nominate the prize winner. From Gang Lu's perspective, they would have to pay for destroying his chances, ruining his life, and causing him shame.

After several attempts to appeal the decision up through the University's administrative hierarchy, Gang Lu saw only one way to even the score. On November 1, 1991, after months of anguish and detailed planning, he launched his all-out assault during the regular Friday afternoon Physics Department seminar held in Room 309 of Van Allen Hall. Gang Lu removed from his briefcase a .38-caliber revolver and without saying a word—words were unnecessary, as everyone was already painfully aware of his grudge—started blasting away. He killed Professors Christoph Goertz and Robert Alan Smith, both of whom were members of his dissertation committee, and shot and seriously wounded Linhua Shan, his "successful" rival for the prize.

Gang Lu next traveled down the hall and killed department chair Dwight Nicholson. He then returned to the seminar room to pump a few more rounds into Shan to finish the job he had started. With that accomplished, the gunman went across campus to confront T. Anne Cleary, Associate Vice President for Academic Affairs, with whom he had filed an appeal. He killed Cleary and also wounded her receptionist, who was little more than an impediment along his murder route. By the time the police arrived, Gang Lu had only to execute one final element to his plan: suicide.

In advance of his massacre, Gang Lu had written to his sister in China out-lining his funeral wishes, sending along the contents of the bank account he shortly wouldn't need. He also wrote a letter to the media outlining his griev-ance against the Physics Department and describing how his gun would help to right the terrible wrongs that had been done to him. "Private guns make every person equal, no matter what/who he/she is," he wrote. "They also make it possible for an individual to fight against a conspired/incorporated organi-zation such as Mafia or Dirty University officials."

In the wake of virtually any large mass shooting, significant debate surfaces about the role of firearms in facilitating a bloodbath. Of course, guns didn't make Gang Lu lose out to his rival countryman, nor did they encourage his desire to kill those whom he blamed for ruining his life. However, for Gang Lu, the gun was a necessary instrument to achieve his desired outcome, and it was likely the only weapon that would do. Certainly, knives or other objects would not have made it possible to execute his entire hit list without being subdued. Explosives, on the other hand, might have provided a means of mass destruction—much like what occurred in Bath, Michigan, on May 18, 1927, when Andrew Kehoe detonated a cache of explosives hidden in the basement of a local school, killing 38 children, five adults, and himself. However, Gang Lu's plan was not to kill just anyone, but selectively only those intended tar-gets for his payback. A firearm was his only logical choice.

Even more than with homicides generally, guns are implicated in the vast majority of school homicides. Of the nearly 400 victims killed in elementary and secondary school-related homicides between 1992 and 2008, 72 percent were shot to death. Although "only" 52 percent of homicides at college cam-puses between 2001 and 2005 involved a firearm, all the campus slayings since 1990 that claimed at least two lives were committed with handguns or rifles.

Shootings by children and teenagers typically involve weapons that they have taken or stolen from others, often their parents or other relatives. As criminologist Gary Kleck has noted, for example, six of the seven multiple-vic-tim school shootings that occurred in the 1997/1998 and 1998/1999 school years involved firearms that the perpetrators had "borrowed" from others; only one assailant used his own weapon—a hunting rifle.[22] Given the typical "beg, borrow or steal" source for weaponry, it is questionable that many of the gun control proposals raised in the aftermath of high-profile school shoot-ings (e.g., closing the "gun show loophole") would have averted a tragedy.

Although not a mass shooting, one of the most extreme and tragic exam-ples of the unauthorized use of another person's gun involved the February 29, 2000, shooting at the Buell Elementary School in Mount Morris Township near Flint, Michigan. Using his uncle's .32-caliber handgun that he found lying around the house, 6-year-old Derrick Owens shot and killed a classmate, Kayla Renee Rolland, days following a fight between the two out on the play-ground. The diminutive assailant was too young to be charged criminally, but Uncle Jamelle James, age 20, pled no contest and served over two years in prison for involuntary manslaughter, stemming from his negligence in not having securely locked away the gun that ultimately was used by his nephew to kill Kayla Rolland.

The Buell Elementary School case prompted new proposals for parental (and family) responsibility laws. In fact, the state of Michigan looked to increase the punishment for any adult whose negligent handling or storage of a weapon resulted in its use by an underage child against a friend or classmate. Moreover, the American public is generally supportive of holding parents accountable; an April 2000 Gallup Poll found that nearly 7 of 10 respondents favored holding parents legally responsible if their children use their guns to commit a crime.[23] Although well-intended, this rush to legislate fails to recognize that unsafe keeping of a firearm has a far more powerful, intrinsic punishment, one very close to home. A child who discovers a loaded gun in the home is more likely to use it against himself, a sibling, or a parent than to take and fire it at school or play outside the home.

Many gun control advocates had anticipated that the numerous and widely publicized school shootings of the late 1990s would have promoted their cause. In fact, based on a content analysis of print and electronic news commentary in the aftermath of the Columbine school shooting, Lawrence and Birkland found that inadequate gun control was identified as a problem in 42 percent of the media reports, ranking it first, well ahead of the next leading concern, popular culture, at 28 percent.[24] Despite the media's frequent calls for tightening gun laws, public sentiment, apparently, was not so easily persuaded. A series of Gallup opinion polls taken over the past two decades, including several in the months following the Columbine shooting, suggest that support for stricter gun control measures is on the wane. As shown in Figure 3.2, there was a modest yet transient spike in public support for gun control in the immediate wake of Columbine.[25] Overall, Columbine and the cluster of other mass shootings at schools across the country did nothing to alter the downward trend in support for stricter gun laws and the complementary increase in the percentage of Americans who see the existing set of gun laws as appropriate.

Commenting on the overall downward trajectory in support for stricter gun controls despite the frequent media focus on lax gun laws, Birkland and Lawrence pointed to the resistant segment of the population with conservative, pro-gun attitudes.[26] An alternative interpretation of these data would suggest that Americans were indeed increasingly supportive of tighter gun restrictions, but were satisfied with the expanding controls on firearms implemented during the 1990s, including the 1993 Brady Law and the 1994 assault weapons ban.[27]

ARMING FACULTY AND STUDENTS

Even while some Americans argued for stricter gun control in the aftermath of school shootings, others took the exact opposite stance: to allow certain individuals to carry concealed weapons on school grounds so they might mount a counter-attack against an armed assailant and thereby protect human life. Gun advocates often point to the mass shooting in Pearl, Mississippi, in which the school's assistant principal went to retrieve his gun from his car and overcame the shooter. Unfortunately, by that time, two students were already dead. On the other hand, critics have questioned the fact that the assistant principal had chased down the assailant as he was attempting to drive away.

Just as the U.S. Congress empowered airline pilots to carry guns to thwart future hijackings of commercial planes, there have been several attempts in states like Georgia, Colorado, and Texas to pass similar provisions for school teachers and administrators—concealed weapons laws for the faculty. In fact, the local school board in the tiny town of Harrold, Texas, voted in August 2008 to allow teachers to carry concealed firearms in that community's one school, serving grades K–12. With a total enrollment of just over 100 students, the strident initiative will likely have little effect except to have made national headlines for the obscure hamlet near the northern state border.

Supporters of initiatives to allow faculty to carry concealed weapons argue that ever since the early 1990s when the U.S. Congress established schools as gun-free zones, an armed assailant—intruder or insider—would be assured to face little opposition. The belief is that arming teachers and administrators might serve as a powerful deterrent.

Notwithstanding the Pearl, Mississippi, episode, some determined offenders might instead welcome a violent shoot-out; after all, many expect to commit suicide or to be gunned down by police SWAT teams. For most educators, especially the ones who are frustrated when dealing with the belligerent bully seated in the back of the classroom, marksmanship should just be about A's and B's, not guns and ammo.

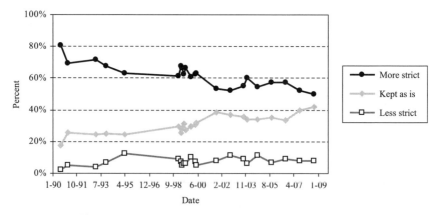

Figure 3.2 Public opinion of preferred level of restrictions on firearms sales
Source: Based on Lydia Saad, "Shrunken Majority Now Favors Stricter Gun Laws," *Gallup News Service.*

Supporters of initiatives to arm school officials and train them in marksman-ship skills may be vociferous, but they are far from the majority. In an April 2005 national poll conducted by the Gallup organization, only 22 percent of respondents thought that arming teachers would make schools safer, while nearly three-quarters indicated that such an approach would make schools more dangerous. By contrast, 62 percent of the same respondents were in favor of the move to arm airline pilots.[28]

The same pro-gun arguments, only louder, have been heard in response to shootings on college campuses, where much of the student population (as well as the staff) may be accomplished shooters. Ironically—and unfortunately, at least in the minds of some observers—at the time of the Virginia Tech massa-cre, a bill was stalled in the Virginia General Assembly that would have empowered licensed gun owners to carry concealed weapons on the Blacks-burg and other campuses in the state.

The U.S. Congressional legislation described in Chapter 1 concerning guns in schools pertained only to elementary and secondary schools, and not to college campuses. Rules and procedures related to gun possession at two-year and four-year colleges and universities are instead regulated by individual states. As of 2008, only one state—Utah—granted students with license to carry concealed weapons the absolute right to do so at any public or private post-secondary school. However, many states leave the decision to the individual colleges, while about half the states strictly prohibit anyone other than sworn law enforcement personnel from carrying guns—concealed or not—on their campuses.

The Virginia Tech massacre also gave the national grassroots organization Stu-dents for Concealed Carry on Campus (SCCC) ammunition for its campaign to change state laws around the country. SCCC contends that the carnage at Vir-ginia Tech would have been considerably lessened had students other than the gunman been armed and ready to retaliate. On the other hand, in such situa-tions, one must wonder how it would be possible for anyone to distinguish the "good guys" dressed in denim and toting backpacks from the "bad guy" dressed in denim and toting a backpack. In addition, there is evidence that even trained gun owners, when suddenly immersed in a chaotic shooting scene, may not have the special skills needed to respond without making matters worse.[29]

As part of its campaign, SCCC has promoted "National Empty Holster Days" in which students protest their campus gun bans by wearing empty holsters to class, symbolic of disarmament. Whether or not effective in advancing the cause, the sight of students wearing holsters, even if empty, has tended to unnerve many students and faculty. Out of concern for negative repercussions stemming from possible confusion, the Dean of Students Office at one university at least felt it necessary to disseminate throughout the campus this warning:[30]

> During the week of April 21–25, 2008, IUPUI students will participate in the Sec-ond National Empty Holster protest here on campus. These students are members of the Students for Concealed Carry on Campus (SCCC) and will attend classes

wearing EMPTY holsters. This symbolic protest is a result of state laws and campus policies that prohibit concealed weapons on college campuses in the hands of
law-abiding citizens, and more specifically, concealed weapons permit holders. Students participating in this protest will be wearing EMPTY holsters that are to be
fully visible. Protestors will go about their daily activities and should not create
any unnecessary disturbance. Please be advised that these students pose no threat
to campus safety and are not carrying weapons.

It is difficult to predict what changes might occur in the years ahead with
respect to permitting concealed weapons on college campuses, or, for that
matter, in public schools at all grade levels. Gun enthusiasts were bolstered by
the Supreme Court decision in *District of Columbia v. Heller* that struck down
a long-standing handgun ban in the nation's capital and reaffirmed the sanctity of the Second Amendment.[31] In the wake of this case, pro-gun forces are
setting their sights on challenging various state and local gun restrictions
around the country. In the end, the debate about concealed weapons on campus may be resolved more by political posturing than by practical efficacy.

CONSPIRATORIAL THINKING

The late 1990s cluster of school shootings, seven of which involved multiple
victims, prompted a strong response from President Bill Clinton. One week after the Columbine massacre, the President pushed for a series of gun control
initiatives designed to avert such tragedies. At the political fringe, The Cutting
Edge Ministries, a far-right Christian-based extremist organization, condemned the Clinton administration for its gun control response. Cutting Edge
released a map, reproduced in Figure 3.2, displaying the major school shootings that had occurred during Clinton's presidency.

Curiously, the locations virtually formed two straight lines, the intersection
of which pinpointed Hope, Arkansas—Clinton's birthplace. Based on this evidence, Cutting Edge suggested that the President was involved in an unholy
conspiracy to disarm America. As further proof, Cutting Edge inferred from
the timing of the shootings that there had been a deliberate attempt to obfus-
cate the plot: "[T]he plan was drawn up before the first school shooting
occurred. If Edinboro had been followed by Paducah, then by Jonesboro, for
example, in a straight timeline, someone would probably have spotted the
connection. But, if each successive school shooting were random as to time,
then the chance of discovery would be far less."[32]

Clinton's successor in the Oval Office had a very different posture concerning
gun restrictions, particularly in relation to school safety. In the fall of 2006, President George W. Bush's alliance with the gun lobby was tested when a series of four
school shootings occurred over a period of two weeks, the last of which claimed
the lives of five young girls inside a one-room schoolhouse in the quiet Amish
community of Paradise, Pennsylvania. Bush hastily convened an invitation-only

Figure 3.3 Cutting Edge Ministries' map of school shootings during the Clinton administration

Source: Adapted from "School Shootings Have a Pattern that Implicate the President and his Government," http://www.cuttingedge.org/news/n1344.cfm.

White House summit on school violence, to which no gun control advocates—particularly representatives of the Brady Campaign against handgun violence—were welcomed. President Bush, First Lady Laura Bush, and other members of the cherry-picked panel made no mention of the common thread among the events that precipitated the summit—guns. No matter what each of the speakers believed with regard to the role of guns in episodes of school shootings, it was noteworthy that the topic was conspicuously absent from the discussion.

4

RISK FACTORS, WARNING SIGNS, AND PREDICTION

For more than a century, criminologists have endeavored to identify the psychological, biological, and sociological correlates of criminal behavior, in part as an avenue toward predicting criminality and the propensity toward violence. Then came the April 1999 Columbine High School massacre, prompting the Clinton Administration and the U.S. Congress to order a comprehensive report on the causes and prevention of youth violence.

The requested document, *Youth Violence: A Report to the Surgeon General*, included, among other things, a chapter reviewing the extensive research literature on the varied risk factors associated with youth offending.[1] As summarized in Table 4.1, risk and protective factors, both early- and late-onset, can be classified into several domains spreading out from the individual to the wider community.[2] Such attributes as being male, being poor, coming from a single-parent home, having delinquent peers, having experienced significant head trauma, having struggled academically, and living in a neighborhood plagued with high levels of gang activity and illicit drug use are all widely held risk factors that increase the likelihood of aggression. Moreover, the combination of many such factors would magnify the tendency toward violence.

Notwithstanding the validity of these conclusions, there are few combinations of risk factors that make serious violence a likely outcome—violence simply becomes *more* likely than in the absence of these risk factors. Therefore, predicting violence, even in the presence of multiple risk factors, would have a significantly high percentage of false positives—that is, individuals who do not act violently despite the confluence of several factors that places them at risk. Moreover, the false positive percentage tends to increase as the prevalence of the behavior decreases. For especially rare events—such as school shootings—the false positive problem is prohibitively large, regardless of the number of risk factors present.

As an example from another sphere, it would seem logical that the likelihood of a plane crash increases with such risk factors as pilot inexperience, small plane size, and especially poor weather conditions. Although these may be reasonably strong correlates in the aggregate, it would be absurd to predict that a small plane being flown by an inexperienced (but licensed) pilot in unfavorable weather conditions will crash. That is, the vast majority of flights are uneventful no matter how many unfavorable risk factors exist. Simply put, it is virtually impossible to predict rare events—like plane crashes or school shootings—regardless of the amount of data or the sophistication of the research. In the case of serious school violence, it is unlikely that a juvenile will commit murder—let alone a massacre—even if several risk factors are present, and even if he or she announces a plan to do so.

FALSE POSITIVES

In any area of decision-making, including the attempt to predict violent behavior, two types of error—false positives and false negatives—can arise. Whereas false positives represent those instances where a particular outcome does not result despite a prediction that it would, false negatives involve cases in which an outcome does result despite a prediction that it would not.

The extent of the false positive problem depends on three parameters—the percentage of the population of interest that will exhibit a particular outcome (known as the "base rate") and the percentages of those with and those without the outcome who have X, the characteristic(s) used to make a prediction. It might be tempting to adopt some prediction strategy if most violent students have X while few nonviolent students do. However, the percentage of false positives (nonviolent students among those exhibiting X) will be substantial whenever the base rate—the overall percentage who are violent—is small.

Suppose that we wished to predict serious violence among students in middle school, the grade levels at which rates of victimization are highest. According to the 2007–2008 School Survey on Crime and Safety, there were 1.9 incidents of serious violence (defined as rape, sexual battery other than rape, physical attack, or fight with a weapon, threat of physical attack with a weapon, and robbery with or without a weapon) for every 1,000 middle school students.[3] Although no data are available for offending rates, we might estimate it to be about 2.0 per 1,000, since there generally tend to be more perpetrators of school violence than victims. Thus, the base rate is 0.2 percent, indicating that serious violence is extremely limited in the overall population of students. This low base rate may be a good thing for the safety of schools, but not for the prospects of reliable prediction.

Suppose, hypothetically, that research had determined that some characteristic (X) was present among as many as 99 percent of middle school students

Table 4.1
Typology of risk and protective factors

Domain	Risk Factors	Protective Factors
Individual	Being male Low IQ Medical/physical ailments Antisocial attitudes Hyperactivity/restlessness Difficulty concentrating Substance abuse Exposure to media violence Risk taking Intolerance toward deviance	Being female High IQ Positive social orientation Perceived sanctions for misbehavior
Family	Low SES/poverty Antisocial parents Poor parent-child relations Broken home Abusive or neglectful parents	Supportive relationships with parents Parental mentoring Parents' positive view of peers
School	Poor attitude Poor performance Academic failure	Commitment to school Recognition for conventional behavior
Peer group	Weak social ties Antisocial peers	Friends engage in conventional behavior
Community	Neighborhood crime and drugs Neighborhood gang activity Neighborhood disorganization	

Source: Adapted from Box 4-1: Early and late risk factors for violence at age 15 to 18 and proposed protective factors, by domain, in U.S. Department of Health and Human Services, *What You Need To Know About Youth Violence Prevention* (Rockville, MD: U.S. Department of Health and Human Services, Substance Abuse and Mental Health Services Administration, Center for Mental Health Services, 2002): 60.

who had committed serious acts of school violence, but was present among only 5 percent of nonviolent students. With these prevalence rates applied to a total middle school population of 18.6 million, the association of serious violent offending (O) and the risk factor (X) would be as given in Table 4.2. Even though nearly all offenders possess X, very few of those who possess X are offenders. The percentage of false positives—that is, the percentage of nonoffenders having X—is as high as 893,172/930,000 = 96 percent, an unacceptably large figure. Finally, the false positive problem would be far worse if the

Table 4.2
Effect of low base rate on false positives

Committed serious act of violence (O)	X present		
	Yes	No	Total
Yes	36,828	372	37,200
No	893,172	17,669,628	18,562,800
Total	930,000	17,670,000	18,600,000

attempt was to predict some behavior that occurs at an even lower base rate—for example, school shootings.

Because of the low base rate associated with serious violent offending, the prospects for reliable prediction are slim. The only circumstance when the false positive percentage might be low enough to make prediction feasible would be for the risk factor(s) to be exceptionally rare in the general population while exceptionally commonplace in the offender group. However, there are few, if any, attributes or telltale behaviors that distinguish offenders and nonoffenders with such clarity.

WARNING SIGNS

In the aftermath of virtually any high-profile episode of school violence, much of the focus (and finger-pointing) surrounds the warning signs that were reportedly missed or ignored by parents, teachers, peers, and law enforcement officials. Why weren't the assailant's parents aware of his deepening depression, if not of his arsenal of guns and ammunition? Why didn't classmates alert teachers or school officials when the assailant made threatening remarks? Why didn't the teachers intervene when the assailant was repeatedly victimized by a group of bullies? And why didn't the police take action following complaints about the violent content on the assailant's *Facebook* page?

Parents and politicians alike have urged, and even demanded, concerted efforts to identify the would-be perpetrators—the "few bad apples" who are rotten to the core—before they wreak havoc on their classmates. However, there are very many apples in the orchard that are not quite perfect in color, size, or shape, but are fine just beneath the surface. That is, lots of teenagers look, act, or dress consistent with our image of the schoolyard shooter—they might wear black trench coats, have scary tattoos, or don gang headgear. Yet very few of them will translate their deviant adolescent attitudes into dangerous acts of violence. The few accurate predictions will be far outnumbered by the many false positives.

In addition, an attempt to single out the potential troublemakers could do more harm than good by stigmatizing, marginalizing, and traumatizing already troubled youth. "Don't play with Johnnie—he's a bad apple." Already ostracized and harassed by his peers, Johnnie will sense that the teachers and the administration are also against him. The "bad apple" label could eventually become a self-fulfilling prophesy, encouraging doubly-alienated children to act out violently.

Despite the severe limitations in foretelling violence, a host of prediction tools have been widely disseminated in response to various episodes of school violence. Of course, warning signs and checklists play well in the popular media, from newspaper sidebars to on-screen graphics for daytime TV talk shows. It is routine for news analyses of school violence to promote an inventory of "things to look out for."

In August 1998, hoping to prevent a repeat of the previous academic year that had featured a cluster of well-publicized shootings, the U.S. Department of Education (DOE) distributed to schools across America a manual highlighting 16 warning signs of violence.[4] This broad-ranging collection of red flags included children who bully classmates, as well as children who are bullied by their classmates. Another telltale sign warns of students having minimal interest in academics. Just these three flags would capture significant shares of most middle-school populations. In an attempt not to miss a single potential troublemaker, the net widens to include nearly everyone. While there is little doubt that many items in the list of warning signs would indicate an at-risk child—such as violent ideation reflected in stories, poetry, and other written material—these are more "yellow flags" that figuratively only turn red once the blood has spilled on them.

To be fair, it was only with some reluctance that the DOE packaged and promoted its warning signs inventory. Indeed, the fuller document contained reasonable and important cautions against taking an oversimplified approach to violence prediction: "It is important to avoid inappropriately labeling or stigmatizing individual students because they appear to fit a specific profile or set of early warning indicators."[5] Unfortunately, much of the context fell on deaf ears and blind eyes in the rush to promote a sense of preparedness amid a seemingly growing epidemic of bloodshed.

At least some education officials and security consultants were apparently eager to have available a brief summary guide to violence prediction, one not so overloaded with cautionary notes about profiling violence-prone students. After all, danger was potentially lurking inside every classroom and behind every locker door. To fill this need, the American Psychological Association (APA), in conjunction with the MTV network, produced a pocket-size pamphlet appropriately named "Warning Signs," perfect for anyone wanting a quick answer regarding the dangerousness of the rowdy student in the back row of the class.[6]

Although the concern about school violence may have reached a fever pitch following several mass shootings during the late 1990s, the school violence problem was a significant issue over a decade earlier. In 1981, President

Reagan's Working Group on School Discipline compiled its findings and recommendations regarding matters of school discipline in a report titled "Chaos
in the Classroom: Enemy of American Education." As part of his overall push
for improved school safety, Reagan directed federal funding to establish the
National School Safety Center (NSSC), a private organization located in his
home state of California that opened its doors in 1984.

Among many other activities and programs, the NSSC promotes its own
checklist of 20 warning signs for school violence:[7]

- Has a history of tantrums and uncontrollable angry outbursts
- Characteristically resorts to name calling, cursing, or abusive language
- Habitually makes violent threats when angry
- Has previously brought a weapon to school
- Has a background of serious disciplinary problems at school and in the
  community
- Has a background of drug, alcohol, or other substance abuse or
  dependency
- Is on the fringe of his or her peer group with few or no close friends
- Is preoccupied with weapons, explosives, or other incendiary devices
- Has previously been truant, suspended, or expelled from school
- Displays cruelty to animals
- Has little or no supervision and support from parents or a caring adult
- Has witnessed or been a victim of abuse or neglect in the home
- Has been bullied and/or bullies or intimidates peers or younger children
- Tends to blame others for difficulties and problems he causes himself
- Consistently prefers TV shows, movies, or music expressing violent
  themes and acts
- Prefers reading materials dealing with violent themes, rituals, and abuse
- Reflects anger, frustration, and the dark side of life in school essays or
  writing projects
- Is involved with a gang or an antisocial group on the fringe of peer
  acceptance
- Is often depressed and/or has significant mood swings
- Has threatened or attempted suicide

Whichever collection of violence predictors one chooses to adopt, they all
seem to overlap considerably and to share the same limitations—that they
are inclined to over-predict and produce many false positives. They also tend
to include some items that have not been empirically supported, and others
that are so obvious so as to insult the intelligence of any school official who
might be tempted to follow their direction. Even so, the pervasive levels of
fear surrounding school violence—as high today as back in the 1980s—
encourages many otherwise sensible people to accept the prescriptions
uncritically.

It is rather challenging to verify empirically any given set of warning signs since the number of violent outcomes is so few and the base rate so low. The vast majority of students whose background and behavior exhibit various risk factors will not act in a malicious and threatening manner. Despite these limitations, Verlinden and her colleagues carefully assessed the accuracy of the DOE, APA, and NSSC checklists by comparing them to 10 school rampage shooters from 1996 through 1999.[8] Whereas the NSSC model included 13 of the 17 most common elements among the 10 cases, the other two checklists included fewer than half of the common traits. Regardless of these results, this post-hoc search for warning signs does not address the matter of prediction.

In September 1999, with concern over school violence at a high point and school administrators desperate for guidance, the FBI produced a school shooter profile based on an analysis of six school rampages.[9] Despite the FBI's reputation for offender profiling (as in assembling a profile of an unidentified offender from characteristics of the crime scene), the 20-item offender profile of school shooters, reproduced in Figure 4.1, would hardly be useful in trying to find a few dangerous needles within a huge haystack of countless students who would exhibit many of the profile traits. In addition, some of the profile elements—such as feeling powerless—would be impossible to apply given how difficult they are to observe. Other items—such as showing no remorse after killing—would have no predictive value whatsoever because of the reversed temporal order.

Whereas the model presented earlier in Table 4.1 was designed to describe youth violence in general, the elements and precipitants of school violence—especially rampage shootings—are considerably different.[10] Moreover, offender profiles and the warning signs checklists, besides having practical limitations for prediction, tend to be somewhat atheoretical. By contrast, Katherine Newman developed a theoretical model of rampage shooters based on common elements in their backgrounds and circumstances.[11] Specifically, Newman postulated that five factors were necessary—but not sufficient—conditions:

1. Marginality—limited involvement with peers or bullying victimization
2. Individual vulnerabilities—psychological conditions or family problems
3. Cultural scripts—imitation of real or fictional avengers
4. Under the radar—not exceptionally worrisome to others
5. Access to guns—ability to borrow or steal a deadly weapon

It is arguable whether these five factors are necessary conditions or just likely ones. The lack of sufficiency, on the other hand, is incontrovertible. As Newman rightly cautioned, the model may help to identify a large pool of adolescents in need of some form of intervention, but cannot reliably predict such a violent outcome as a school rampage. That is, these factors may be likely in known cases of school shooters, but a school shooting is not likely given the known presence of these factors. The most that can be said is that a school shooting is more probable with these factors present than without them.

The suspects involved in the six school shootings that the FBI reviewed displayed similar traits. While any one of these characteristics alone may not describe a potential school shooter, taken together, they provide a profile that may assist law enforcement, schools, and communities to identify at-risk students.

- The suspects were white males, under 18, with mass or spree murderer traits.
- They sought to defend narcissistic views or favorable beliefs about themselves, while, at the same time, they had very low self-esteem.
- They experienced a precipitating event (e.g., a failed romance) that resulted in depression and suicidal thoughts that turned homicidal.
- They lacked, or perceived a lack of, family support. Two of the suspects killed one or both of their parents.
- They felt rejected by others and sought revenge or retaliation for real or perceived wrongs done to them.
- They acquired firearms owned by a family member or someone they knew.
- They perceived that they were different from others and disliked those who were different (i.e., self-loathing). They needed recognition, and when they did not receive positive recognition, they sought negative recognition.
- They had a history of expressing anger or displaying minor acts of aggressive physical contact at school.
- They had a history of mental health treatment.
- They seemed to have trouble with their parents, though no apparent evidence of parental abuse existed.
- They were influenced by satanic or cult-like belief systems or philosophic works.
- They listened to songs that promote violence.
- They appeared to be loners, average students, and sloppy or unkempt in dress.
- They seemed to be influenced or used by other manipulative students to commit extreme acts of violence.
- They appeared isolated from others, seeking notoriety by attempting to copycat other previous school shootings but wanting to do it better than the last shooter.
- They had a propensity to dislike popular students or students who bully others.
- They expressed interest in previous killings.
- They felt powerless and, to this end, may have committed acts of violence to assert power over others.
- They openly expressed a desire to kill others.
- They exhibited no remorse after the killings.

Figure 4.1 FBI Offender Profile
Source: Stephen R. Band and Joseph A. Harpold, "School Violence: Lessons Learned," FBI Law Enforcement Bulletin 68 (September 1999), 14.

THREAT ASSESSMENT

As Marisa Reddy and her colleagues emphasized, there is a vast difference between dangerous acts and dangerous people, and between making a threat and posing a threat.[12] While profiles of school shooters and associated lists of warning signs strive—albeit unsuccessfully—to help identify those who pose a threat, threat assessments attempt to guide an appropriate response if and when a student jeopardizes the safety of classmates, teachers, or staff.

While rejecting the notion of profiling as a flawed strategy plagued by the false positive dilemma, the FBI later shifted (or clarified) its focus to evaluating those students who go as far as to articulate threats against the school or their classmates.[13] The FBI assessment approach is predicated on a four-class typology of threats: direct, indirect, veiled, and conditional. Direct threats are those in which specific targets and specific actions are identified, whereas indirect threats suggest an unambiguous desire to cause harm but without any clear indication of how, when, and against whom. Veiled threats only intimate the possibility of violence but do not specify a plan to harm others. Finally, a conditional threat, like a veiled threat, indicates only a possibility, but establishes that potential as leverage for some desired outcome.

The FBI threat assessment approach also outlines three levels of risk, generally predicated on how detailed and how plausible the threat appears to be.[14]

> *Low Level of Threat:* A threat that poses a minimal risk to the victim and public safety.
> - Threat is vague and indirect.
> - Information contained within the threat is inconsistent, implausible, or lacks detail.
> - Threat lacks realism.
> - Content of the threat suggests person is unlikely to carry it out.
> *Medium Level of Threat:* A threat that could be carried out, although it may not appear entirely realistic.
> - Threat is more direct and more concrete than a low-level threat.
> - Wording in the threat suggests that the threatener has given some thought to how the act will be carried out.
> - There may be a general indication of a possible place and time (though these signs still fall well short of a detailed plan).
> - There is no strong indication that the threatener has taken preparatory steps, although there may be some veiled reference or ambiguous or inconclusive evidence pointing to that possibility—an allusion to a book or movie that shows the planning of a violent act, or a vague, general statement about the availability of weapons.
> - There may be a specific statement seeking to convey that the threat is not empty: "I'm serious!" or "I really mean this!"
> *High Level of Threat:* A threat that appears to pose an imminent and serious danger to the safety of others.
> - Threat is direct, specific and plausible.
> - Threat suggests concrete steps have been taken toward carrying it out. For example, statements have been made indicating that the threatener has acquired or practiced with a weapon or has had the victim under surveillance.

Of course, defining the type and level of some threat is one thing; deter-mining whether the particular student in fact poses a significant risk of vio-lence is quite another. For the purpose of evaluating the likelihood that a threat will be translated into a violent act, the FBI proposed a four-pronged assessment model that, as it happens, is somewhat similar to the general typology presented in Table 4.1 at the outset of this chapter:[15]

- *Personality of the student* (e.g., poor coping skills, failed love relationship, depression, narcissism, pathological need for attention, exaggerated sense of entitlement, inappropriate humor, alienation, dehumanization of others, lack of empathy, lack of trust, rigid and opinionated, poor anger management, unusual interest in sensational violence, fascination with vi-olence-filled entertainment)
- *Family dynamics* (e.g., turbulent parent-child relationship, access to weap-ons, lack of intimacy, student "rules the roost," no monitoring of TV)
- *School dynamics and the student's role* (e.g., low attachment to school, school tolerates disrespectful behavior, inequitable school discipline, inflexible culture, pecking order among students, code of silence among students, unsupervised computer access)
- *Social dynamics* (e.g., peer groups supportive of violence, drug or alcohol use, lack of outside interests, copycat effect in wake of highly publicized incident)

Even if the emphasis is on threat assessment rather than profiling, in practical terms the FBI approach reduces to a checklist of indicators applied to students who have made threats rather than to the general student population. Although this may reduce the low-base-rate/high-false-positive problem discussed earlier, the prospects for reliably identifying violence-prone youth remains unproven. Much of the FBI assessment tool is based on hunch rather than empirical research. And, as conceded within the report, there is no empirical guidance for determining which of the four prongs is more important in predicting violence, or which of the specific indicators should carry more weight than others.

The most extensive analysis of school shooters to date was accomplished as part of a joint effort of the U.S. Secret Service and the DOE.[16] The so-called "Safe School Initiative" focused specifically on "targeted school violence," defined as episodes in which a current or recent student, with a deliberate choice of the school as location, assaulted a victim(s) at his or her school using a lethal weapon. Consistent with these parameters, 37 incidents involv-ing 41 attackers were identified in the United States from 1974 through 2000. Analyzing extant data on all cases and in-depth interviews with 10 of the assailants, the study team concluded:[17]

- Incidents of targeted violence at school rarely are sudden, impulsive acts.
- Prior to most incidents, other people knew about the attacker's idea and/or plan to attack.

- Most attackers did not threaten their targets directly prior to advancing the attack.
- There is no accurate or useful profile of students who engaged in targeted school violence.
- Most attackers engaged in some behavior prior to the incident that caused others concern or indicated a need for help.
- Most attackers had difficulty coping with significant losses or personal failures. Moreover, many had considered or attempted suicide.
- Many attackers felt bullied, persecuted, or injured by others prior to the attack.
- Most attackers had access to, and had used, weapons prior to the attack.
- In many cases, other students were involved in some capacity.
- Despite prompt law enforcement responses, most shooting incidents were stopped by means other than law enforcement intervention.

Beyond these general findings based on the collection of school shooters, the researchers urged against profiling of potential school shooters and, quite reasonably, in favor of a deliberative, team-based approach to evaluation, not based on a checklist of indicators or warning signs but involving a case-specific qualitative review of the student's history and circumstances. Threat assessment, as described, should be "a fact-based investigative and analytical approach that focuses on what a particular student is doing and saying, and not on whether the student 'looks like' those who have attacked schools in the past."[18]

Arguably, school shootings may be viewed as part of a more generic class of targeted violence, a cluster that would include workplace homicides, mass murders, and political assassinations. Subsequent to the "Safe School Initiative" report, members of the study team attempted to build on intelligence derived from Secret Service efforts to identify would-be assassins.[19] Working under the assumption that those who threaten targeted violence—including school shooters—were similar in motive and approach to those who target political officials, Borum and colleagues adapted and modified a list of questions that could guide a threat assessment and investigation, including one conducted by a team of school administrators, law enforcement officials, and school psychologists, to determine the level of risk associated with a student threat:[20]

Question 1: What motivated the subject to make the statements or take the action that caused him or her to come to attention?

Question 2: What has the subject communicated to anyone concerning his or her intentions?

Question 3: Has the subject shown an interest in targeted violence, perpetrators of targeted violence, weapons, extremist groups, or murder?

Question 4: Has the subject engaged in attack-related behavior, including any menacing, harassing, and/or stalking-type behavior?

Question 5: Does the subject have a history of mental illness involving command hallucinations, delusional ideas, feelings of persecution, etc., with indications that the subject has acted on those beliefs?

Question 6: How organized is the subject? Is he or she capable of developing and carrying out a plan?

Question 7: Has the subject experienced a recent loss and/or loss of status, and has this led to feelings of desperation and despair?

Question 8: What is the subject saying and is it consistent with his or her actions?

Question 9: Is there concern among those who know the subject that he or she might take action based on inappropriate ideas?

Question 10: What factors in the subject's life and/or environment might increase/decrease the likelihood of the subject attempting to attack a target?

Despite the growing acceptance of the threat assessment paradigm, especially over the more mindless concept of profiling, school officials may still not be sufficiently equipped, in terms of having precise guidelines and practical training, to carry though with the assessment process. As Dewey Cornell has argued, "[t]he available literature on threat assessment generally advises schools on what principles to follow, but not on how to put them into practice."[21] Responding to this need, Cornell's group at the University of Virginia refined a practical assessment model, moving from the theoretical domains reflected in the FBI and Secret Service contributions to an applied strategy for threat evaluation and response. As illustrated in the detailed flow-chart in Figure 4.2, the Virginia Threat Assessment Model involves a step-by-step process, critically dependent on the determination of whether a threat is transient (e.g., a temporary fit of anger) or substantive (e.g., sustained intent to harm others). Importantly, an empirical comparison of the Virginia Model to assessments accomplished in less formal or informal ways, confirmed the advantages of implementing and training in a structured and guided approach.[22]

The move away from red-flag counting and toward contextual assessment of threats has certainly been a major advance. Still, the value of any threat assessment effort depends most critically on the training, knowledge, and skills of those engaged in the process. Regardless, the ability to validate empirically this or any other threat assessment model remains out of reach. A successful outcome generally signifies a nonevent. Therefore, endorsements of any assessment activity can really only come from those involved in performing these difficult tasks.

High-Tech Assessment

While various government agencies and study groups were developing strategies and tools for preventing school shootings, the Bureau of Alcohol, Tobacco,

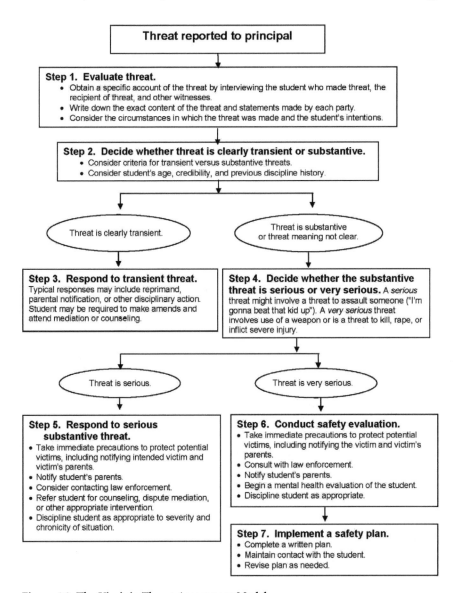

Figure 4.2 The Virginia Threat Assessment Model
Source: Reprinted with permission from Sopris West Educational Services, from *Student Threats of Violence*, by Dewey G. Cornell and Peter L. Sheras © 2005.

and Firearms (BATF) was looking to go high-tech. The goal was to automate the tasks of prediction and threat assessment by adapting a computerized approach called MOSAIC, originally designed by a California firm to screen and evaluate threats against public officials. The computer program takes a school official through a series of questions about the threat and threatener, eventually producing an evaluative report concerning risk.

In late 1999, with blessing and assistance from the BATF, the student-focused tool—Method for Assessment of Student Threats (MAST)—was field-tested at 25 volunteer schools across the country. However, given the proprietary nature of the instrument, little is known about its design or its effectiveness. Regardless, the program has been resoundingly criticized by many skeptics and various advocacy groups concerned about student privacy issues. Whatever its value or lack thereof, MAST has hardly revolutionized the student threat assessment enterprise.

Years later, following high-profile shootings at college campuses, interest in computerized threat assessment surfaced once again. A State of Missouri task force study of the issue of campus violence undertaken in the wake of the 2007 Virginia Tech massacre went so far as to recommend that "each institution should thoroughly evaluate the viability and appropriateness of using assessment tools (e.g., MOSAIC) designed to identify individuals with the potential for violent behavior."[23]

Whatever the objective—be it profiling, prediction, or threat assessment—the value of indicator-based approaches remains unclear. First, some indicators, although perhaps logical, have not been verified empirically, or have even been contradicted. For example, few observers might question the role of alcohol and drugs as symptomatic of a troubled child who may indeed require individual or family counseling. However, there is no evidence that alcohol or drugs has been implicated in previous violent attacks at schools. And even if there had been some substance abuse in the assailant's background, there have been very few involving a substance-impaired perpetrator.[24] To the contrary, school shooters tend to be clear-headed, deliberate, and methodical.

In addition, as noted previously, there is no research evidence concerning the relative importance or optimal weights that should be assigned to each of the profile/prediction/assessment characteristics, nor is there any sense concerning how many of the risk factors must be present to establish a risk significant enough to warrant intervention. It is hard to believe that any student who makes a threat would have none of these traits, even if the threat is all talk and no action.

SCHOOL SIZE AND CLIMATE

The overriding theme of this discussion is not that violent behavior is completely unpredictable, but that prediction devices, from simple checklists to automated query systems, are inadequate for this purpose. The most important and useful strategy would be to have smaller schools to reduce student-teacher ratios and caseloads of guidance counselors.[25] As of the 2006/2007 school year, the national average for students per guidance counselor stood at 475, nearly twice the standard load recommended by the American School Counselor Association (ASCA).[26] Although the basis for the ASCA prescription is not entirely clear, there certainly is much room for improvement in terms of providing ample assistance to children at risk academically or emotionally.

It is critical that school personnel, those who spend hour upon hour with students, be in the position to know them sufficiently enough to notice changes in mood or behavior. Smaller classes and increased staffing would allow school personnel to observe even the subtle signs of trouble, which cannot be easily determined from a simplistic checklist. More important, the focus should not necessarily be on the potentially violent child, but on the unhappy child (although at times these may be one and the same). Warning signs may be superficially useful, but only so far as to reach troubled youngsters long before they become troublesome. Waiting until a student has murderous intentions—until he carries a weapon to school or makes overt threats of violence (two of the most obvious items in many checklists)—is waiting perilously too long.

Increased staffing needs also extend to school psychologists and social workers. Given the challenges that children and adolescents face in an increasingly toxic culture, all of which contribute to a wide array of emotional and behavioral problems, from depression and eating disorders to violence and suicide, students in elementary and secondary schools could greatly benefit from increased availability of mental health professionals and counseling services. For this purpose, the DOE established in 2000, as part of its Safe and Drug Free Schools initiative, an annual grant program to assist schools in upgrading their level of service and training. In 2009, for example, a total of $21 million was awarded to 63 school districts in 28 states. Although the funds should go far in responding to the mental health needs of students in these districts, the magnitude of mental health concerns in school across the nation clamors for significantly greater funding and a broad-based strategy.

To whatever extent warning signs and threat assessment systems are valid and useful, a heavy emphasis on how to identify characteristics of the individual troublemaker lets schools off the hook. By turning the problem of schoolyard violence into a lesson in abnormal psychology, the blame is deflected entirely outside of the school setting. From this perspective, students have to change, not the schools. A recent study of city schools suggests that elementary-level administrators who have failed to institute anti-violence policies and programs are especially likely to take the "abnormal psychology" approach.[27] They tend to regard their students as victims of inadequate upbringing, family conflict, excessive exposure to media violence, and parental abuse and neglect. Under such circumstances, anti-violence programs in the schools would be mistakenly considered a waste of scarce economic resources. Perhaps the goal should be to develop warning signs to identify dangerous school environments rather than dangerous students, and then to work toward improving the climate for learning and for living.

One of the more important observations concerning the factors underlying many episodes of school violence is the fundamental role that alienation plays in facilitating aggressive or destructive behavior. Students at risk for such conduct often feel little attachment to teachers, other students, and the school in general. Although certainly not the only contributor, large school size tends to work against the development of an emotional attachment to classmates as valued peers and teachers as supportive mentors. When a student feels like no one knows his or her name, and no one at school really cares, then the likelihood of violence is magnified. Moreover, as suggested earlier, it is far too easy in a massive and depersonalized school setting for a troubled student to fall through the cracks of supervision and observation.

In the wake of the massacres at Columbine High, a school that had an enrollment of nearly 2,000 at the time of the shooting, then-Vice President Al Gore blasted the practice, "herding all students . . . into overcrowded, factory-style high schools [where] it becomes impossible to spot the early warning signs of violence, depression or academic failure."[28]

The evidence linking student alienation/disconnectedness and conditions found in large schools—like Columbine High and others (e.g., Pearl High School in Mississippi and Thurston High in Springfield, Oregon) that had witnessed a mass shooting—is more than just anecdotal. Based on a nationally representative sample of over 500 public schools, Haller found that school size was significantly related to problems of disorder and truancy, even after controlling for racial composition, percentage of disadvantaged students, student achievement levels, and location type.[29] As Haller concluded, "[b]oth theory and evidence suggest that large schools are more disorderly than small ones."[30]

Regrettably, during the 1950s and 1960s push to expand school capacity to accommodate the educational needs of the massive babyboom cohorts, it was believed that a few large schools would be more cost-effective than many small ones. In addition, economies of scale were expected to enable large schools to offer a wider array of curricular and extra-curricular options.

Regardless of the programmatic and cost advantages, not every adolescent can thrive in a large school environment. In addition, certain functions and opportunities that a large school might offer are not necessarily available to all. For example, a high school enrolling thousands would still have a limited number of positions on athletics teams or open spots on the cast of a school play.

Along these same lines, the emphasis of recent education reform on test scores and school accountability has had negative, unintended consequences on the very richness of offerings that large schools can offer. Encouraged, if not pressured, by the test-score proficiency focus of the No Child Left Behind Act of 2001, school systems have altered their curricula, expanding on the basics of English, math, and science, while dispensing with "the frills" such as drama, music, or sports. For many students, particularly those who may struggle academically, these extra-curricular options were vitally important in allowing them to excel in other areas and to make school meaningful. Moreover, there have been numerous reports of marginal students being counseled to leave school or transfer, rather than to take on and perhaps fail the proficiency test, thereby lowering the school's overall results. "No child left behind" at times has become "some children pushed out."

Finally, other than size, another important feature related to school climate involves the level of respect that teachers and school administrators show their students. An authoritarian and punitive disciplinary approach in which students are—or perceive that they are—treated unfairly, fosters a climate in which violence of many forms is especially likely. Instead, a disciplinary process in which students understand their rights, and have a full hearing of grievances and disputes, goes a long way to empower students without making them feel the urge to seize power in a ruthless or violent manner.

A Major News Media Event

April 16, 2007, was Patriots Day in history-rich Boston, Massachusetts, an occasion highlighted by the 111th Boston Marathon. Despite the ominous weather forecast that nearly forced an unprecedented cancellation of the longest-standing event of its kind, a record number of more than 2,000 officially registered runners from around the globe competed in the 26-mile race through Boston's western suburbs to the finish line in Copley Square.

For the Boston media, nothing comes close to the annual marathon in terms of breadth and depth of coverage. While the local television stations focused their cameras on Boston's famous foot race and lamented that no new time records should be expected given the weather conditions, the national networks, especially the 24-hour cable news channels, featured their own marathon coverage—of the "Massacre at Virginia Tech," which occurred that same morning. As usual, the television news outlets devoted full attention to every possible detail, complete with special on-screen graphics and somber music interludes leading in and out of commercial breaks. As the day wore on, networks played over and over again a grainy video clip—complete with sounds of gunfire—that had been captured by cell phone, as if viewers needed to see and hear what it was like during those frightening moments on campus.

With seemingly much enthusiasm, the on-air anchors at CNN, MSNBC, and the FOX News Channel tracked the rising death toll in Blacksburg, Virginia. When the carnage reached 20 dead, reporters proclaimed this as a new record for school shootings—a breaking development embellished by streaming and screaming alerts on the screen.

The Virginia Tech shooting had, indeed, eclipsed Charles Whitman's infamous 1966 tower-top shooting at the University of Texas, a murderous mark of distinction that had survived for more than four decades despite the bloody episodes at Columbine High School and elsewhere. The TV anchors, talk-show hosts, and various pundits all seemed to be quite impressed, if not obsessed, with the enormity of the Virginia Tech carnage. Within hours, as the death toll climbed higher and higher, there was more "breaking news." With over 30 victims dead at two locations on Virginia Tech's campus, the record for the largest mass shooting in the United States of any type and at any venue— which previously stood at 23 victims killed by George Hennard during his 1991 massacre at the Luby's Restaurant in Killeen, Texas—had been shattered.

For the remainder of the day and evening, viewers were told repeatedly that the massacre at Virginia Tech had been the "biggest," the "bloodiest," the "absolute worst," the "most devastating," and any other superlatives that came to mind. Notwithstanding the cruel absurdity of treating human suffering as any sort of achievement worthy of measuring in such terms, there is little positive that can be derived by highlighting such records. But there is one significant negative: Records are made to be broken. Of course, the overwhelming majority of Americans who watched the news would have identified with the pain and suffering of the victims, their families, and the entire campus community. However, a few would instead have identified with the power of the perpetrator. Therein lies the danger. For the rare few who view Seung-Hui Cho, the Virginia Tech shooter, as an inspirational role model, the records touted by the news can be misinterpreted as a spine-chilling challenge. Empathizing with the frustration and hostility that likely led to the Virginia Tech rampage, and seeing Cho as a hero who had the guts to take matters— and guns—into his own hands and strike back against injustice, these individuals may be encouraged by the media's coverage of the massacre to do something similar, or worse.

The television news desks were not the only ones driven to excess. The headlines in daily papers on the following morning shamelessly highlighted the magnitude of the event. The *Boston Herald*, in typical tabloid fashion, featured this new American record for mass shootings by setting the number "32" in 4-inch-tall type on its front page. The tabloid's simple, striking headline was obviously meant as an attention grabber. And news outlets across the country, both print and electronic, were in fierce competition for attention, a potential sales or ratings bonanza. But what about this horrible saga did *not* capture America's fascination with violence and murder? Was the shooting not sensational enough without the gimmicks, the sound effects, and, most of all, the obsession with the record body count? Whatever the appropriate level and tone of news coverage, modern communications technology was as responsible as the gunman himself for making the Virginia Tech rampage the big media event that it was—one that, for years, will have an impact on the nation's consciousness.

THE CHANGING NATURE OF NEWS TECHNOLOGY

For those who live in Austin, Texas, and often pass by the 307-foot tower that landmarks the sprawling campus of the state's flagship university, the name Charles Whitman is all too recognizable.[1] Of course, back in August 1966, when Whitman climbed out to the structure's observation deck and turned the campus below into his own personal shooting gallery, killing 14 and wounding dozens of others (in addition to murdering his wife and mother the day before), all of America was familiar with Whitman's name and what was then called the "Crime of the Century." The University of Texas mass shooting—the largest in history at that time—was covered extensively by the media. *TIME* magazine placed Whitman on its cover, replacing the wedding of President Lyndon Johnson's daughter; and *Life* magazine featured a dramatic photo of the tower from the vantage point of a cluster of bullet holes through a windshield. TV stations also showed taped footage of the event— that is, after the many hours it took for the material to be relayed around the country.

Despite the uniqueness of the crime in that era and the national media coverage, for most Americans, the Texas Tower shooting was just some crime that occurred at someplace far away from their hometown. Were that shooting to have happened today, however, the coverage and the impact would have been qualitatively different. It is not that people today are more fascinated with crime and would pay closer attention to the story. After all, decades ago, detective magazines were the equivalent of today's murderer biographies shown on the *A&E* television network and elsewhere. Truman Capote's *In Cold Blood* was as popular then as Thomas Harris's series focusing on fictional killer Hannibal Lecter is today. America's taste for blood and gore is no greater today than decades ago, but the news media's capacity to satisfy the appetite has, with the help of technology, expanded tremendously.

The 1999 shooting at Columbine High School, for example, lasted for well over an hour, as the first responders to the scene waited on the periphery for the SWAT unit to arrive. In the meantime, since the school was a just a few miles south of the heart of Denver, it took only minutes for media crews to arrive on the scene and beam live images from their mobile microwave satellite trucks. As a result, Americans witnessed the drama unfold "first-hand" on their television screens. They watched students climb out of upper-story windows and jump to safety as the shooters—off screen—stalked the hallways of the school. The shooting may have occurred hundreds of miles or more away from their homes, but thanks to technology, it felt like it was happening just down the street.

Of course, technology would not make such a big difference if media outlets were not so ready and willing to broadcast breaking stories through extended live coverage. Not only was this type of saturation not possible in Charles Whitman's day, but there likely would not have been the great urge to use it. The three networks at that time (NBC, CBS, and ABC) had their afternoon soaps, and the idea of cutting away from *Another World* or *Days of Our Lives* for anything more than a few moments to broadcast a news bulletin may have been considered too risky a decision in light of the millions of soap opera devotees. Only for a news development as historically significant as the assassination of a president would pre-empting regular programming seem unequivocally like the correct move.

The nature of television news changed, however, with the development of cable television and the emergence of 24-hour news channels. Outlets like MSNBC and CNBC were finding it rather difficult to boost ratings in the early years, when most viewers had little interest in seeing the same news stories repeated hour after hour. But with the 1995 trial of O.J. Simpson, the former football player and Hollywood celebrity charged with brutally killing his estranged wife and her friend—combined with the judge's willingness to allow cameras in the courtroom—the cable channels found something provocative to fill their 24-hour news cycles that Americans would dial in to watch. In the years since the most closely watched trial ever, the cable channels have found live and continuing coverage of breaking stories—plane crashes, natural disasters, and multiple murders—to be a high-ratings staple. In fact, the traditional networks have often followed the lead of their cable cousins by featuring the same type of pre-emptive coverage of the most significant episodes such as Columbine and the Virginia Tech massacre. The end result is that American viewers are glued to the TV, watching real-life crises, from car chases to hostage standoffs and, of course, school mass murder.

COLUMBINE DÉJÀ VU

The images and sounds of the massacre at Virginia Tech were hardly new to the audience of millions who tuned in to the continuing coverage of the crime and its aftermath of collective grieving. It recalled the horrific string of school shootings—in middle schools and high schools, rather than college campuses—that marked the latter half of the 1990s with tragedy.

The sudden barrage of schoolyard bloodshed during the late 1990s was baffling to most Americans. The apparent surge in school violence was particularly astounding in that it emerged just as rates of homicide among the nation's youth were declining from the peak years of the early 1990s. During the first part of the decade, the "epidemic" of youth violence had become a national obsession, as countless adolescents and young adults, particularly in urban areas, were deeply entrenched in gang subcultures and heavily armed. These youths' behaviors were so fundamentally different from earlier conceptions of waywardness and delinquency that the term "super-predator," coined by Princeton University professor John J. DiIulio to characterize a generation of ruthless, fatherless, Godless, impoverished hoodlums, was embraced by the mainstream news media.[2]

However, then crime rates fell throughout the 1990s, particularly among the nation's youth population. In fact, by the time that Americans were reading headlines about two killers at Columbine High School, the nation's murder rate had plummeted to a 30-year low, largely as a result of the sharp down-turn in youth violence.

But, of course, the Columbine shooting was not just an isolated incident that could be explained away as a bizarre aberration, as well as a complete abomination. Rather, it had been preceded and was followed by mass shoot-ings at schools spanning the country, from Arkansas to Alaska. Unable to account for the sudden and untimely surge in school violence, experts and laypeople alike seemed perplexed, asking "what's the matter with kids today?"

In many respects, however, adolescents today are not fundamentally differ-ent from earlier generations. There have been alienated adolescents for as long as there have been teenagers, and the problem of schoolyard bullying has existed for as long as there have been schools. However, earlier generations of disgruntled and dispirited youth responded in less violent ways. They might have conceived of some silly prank to get even, or picked up a rock and smashed some windows. But the idea of opening fire on their classmates would never have crossed their minds. Times have since changed: The climate is different; the role models and the weapons are different as well. Unlike years ago, angry, alienated kids today see that there are options; one of the possibil-ities that may cross their minds—perhaps several times—is the idea of a school shooting. Indeed, the image of school massacre is never very far from students' minds. The seed has been planted in their imaginations, and through media saturation and public fascination surrounding these crimes, that seed continues to be well-watered.

The nature and context of the schoolyard massacres were radically different from the gang-related warfare over crack cocaine markets that had plagued major American cities years earlier. The young mass shooters in Littleton, Col-orado; West Paducah, Kentucky; and Pearl, Mississippi, were hardly expressing gang ideation or establishing their turf. Many school shooters wore black clothing or accessories reflecting "goth" culture, but these were nothing akin to gang colors or symbols. Although they may have been influenced in a very general way by the nation's obsession with the youth crime problem, their in-spiration was far more direct. They influenced each other through messages across the mass media and the Internet. If there is one thing that absolutely characterizes the behavioral tendencies of adolescents, it is the tendency to take cues from each other.

THE COPYCAT EFFECT

The clustering of several school massacres within a few years of each other is clearly more a reflection of copycatting—or contagion—than any funda-mental and lasting shift in adolescent behavior patterns. In other words, expo-sure to massive media coverage of shootings and their aftermaths can potentially encourage imitators. Not only are children and adolescents exposed to the idea of getting even for perceived injustices through violence, but they are taught that such violence can earn them celebrity status. Indeed, more than the media coverage itself, it is the notoriety that popular culture showers on school shooters that teaches our youth—especially alienated and marginalized teenagers—a lesson about how to get attention and how to be in the spotlight.

This so-called copycat effect, while widely accepted in the popular media, has had only limited attention in scholarly research, and mostly in the area of suicide. Sociologist David Phillips of the University of California at San Diego gave the popular copycat theory more than a modicum of credibility with a series of studies related to the publicity surrounding suicides and subsequent increases in attempted or completed suicides. The application of the copycat theory seemed plausible, if only by extension, with regard to highly publicized school shootings.

Kostinsky, Bixler, and Kettl provided some solid empirical support for the imitative effect spurred by the Columbine High School shooting.[3] They used incident reports pertaining to threats of violence against students, faculty, or the school that were submitted to the Pennsylvania Emergency Management Association (PEMA) in compliance with a directive to all schools statewide prompted by the Columbine episode. Analyzing the distribution of daily counts of all threat reports during the several weeks that remained in the school year following the April 20, 1999, shooting, the researchers noted a sharp spike immediately afterward, with a peak of nearly 45 threats on day 10, and a gradual decline thereafter. As shown in Figure 5.1, the graph closely resembles a pattern with a skewed-right tail, interrupted only by zero counts coinciding with weekends. Although comparable data were not collected prior to the Columbine shooting, interviews of school officials overwhelmingly suggested that threats had previously been a much rarer occurrence.

Despite the methodological sophistication reflected in the analysis of these post-Columbine threat data, the interpretation is confounded by the interaction of student action and administrative reaction. The extent to which the dramatic jump in the daily reports indicates a genuine increase in threatening acts or an increased readiness of school officials to alert state authorities is not at all clear. Just as students might have been more inclined to make threats following the lead of the two Columbine shooters, school personnel would have been much more likely to interpret virtually any level of threat as a significant sign of danger. Furthermore, as the weeks passed beyond the Columbine date, students may have been distracted by other issues, from studying for finals to preparing for the prom, and school administrators may have learned to be less skittish in dealing with routine disciplinary matters.

The copycat effect, therefore, can influence both the one who makes a threat and the one who receives and responds to it. That is, whatever the intent underlying some remark, be it menacing or harmless, previous events

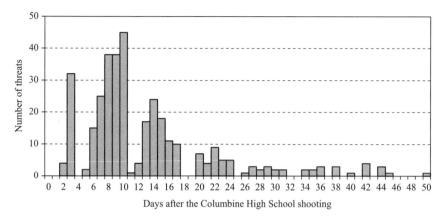

Figure 5.1 Daily number of school violence threats in Pennsylvania after Columbine
Source: S. Kostinsky, E.O. Bixler and P.A. Kettl. "Threats of school violence in Pennsylvania after media coverage of the Columbine High School massacre." *Arch Pediatr Adolesc Med.* 2001; 155:994–1001. Copyright © 2001 American Medical Association. All rights reserved.

can radically impact how it will be interpreted. This lesson in context was painfully and appropriately learned by 43-year-old graduate student Reza Hussain from the events that followed his December 1, 2005, telephone complaint to the Office of the Provost at the University of Iowa.

Hussain had not had an easy time pursuing his doctoral degree. Before enrolling in the chemistry program at the University of Iowa, he had confronted various personal and academic challenges at several other universities. In one case, it was an incompatibility between his own concentration area and the particular strengths of the department. In another instance he had bitter conflicts with his faculty advisors, dooming his chances of finishing his degree. Hussain's academic troubles were especially stressful because of the great success that his father and sisters had achieved in medicine and law. For Hussain, failing once again would be devastating. Unfortunately, after several terms at Iowa, Hussain's academic standing was in jeopardy. He had failed his comprehensive examination and was panicking about whether he was ready for the upcoming retake. Unable to convince his faculty advisor, the department chair, or the dean to postpone the exam retake, he decided to call the Provost's Office as a last resort.

Not long into the conversation, the receptionist had reason for concern. The caller, who refused to give his name but whose phone number appeared on the caller ID, made mention of guns and a mass shooting that had traumatized the campus a decade earlier. There was little doubt that the angry student on the phone was referring to the 1991 massacre of five members of the campus community by disgruntled graduate student Gang Lu. Hussain's reference to some of the details related to the Gang Lu shooting spree suggested the distinct potential for copycat behavior. There were many similarities between Hussain and Gang Lu: Both were doctoral students in the hard sciences at the University of Iowa; both felt discriminated against or slighted by the faculty; and both felt that the perceived unfair treatment could have strong negative impact on their academic careers. Thus, whether or not he meant to alarm campus officials, Hussain's words were reasonably interpreted as a threat and he as a potential copycat of Gang Lu. Hussain was arrested within hours and eventually withdrawn from school by University officials.

A Close Copy

The April 2007 shooting at Virginia Tech, a tragedy that sent shockwaves throughout the country, reverberated much like Columbine in terms of copycat threats of violence. Within a day of the news from the Blacksburg campus, threats, often with specific references to the Virginia Tech shooting, prompted lockdown or evacuation procedures to be initiated at college or high school campuses in as many as 10 states.[4] As if the enormity of the massacre wasn't newsworthy enough, NBC chose to release the menacing photographs and video that Seung-Hui Cho had mailed to the network's New York offices on the very day of his shooting. In fact, Cho took time away from his campus assault, between the double-murder in his dormitory and the slaughter of dozens in a classroom building later in the morning, to mail the package containing his personal dossier. It didn't take very long for Seung-Hui Cho, posthumously, to become as big as the Columbine duo of Klebold and Harris in terms of undeserved celebrity. However, although Cho's image likely had even greater exposure than did the Columbine shooters, the fact that he was Korean, rather than Caucasian like the majority of Americans, actually limited the extent to which he would challenge Klebold and Harris as an iconic role model for others.

The contagion effect is much more profound when the imitator shares similarities with the role model. It is not sheer coincidence that the string of multiple shootings at middle and high schools in the late 1990s almost exclusively involved white youths in small towns or rural areas. Of course, the high incidence of school shootings in small-town America may have had much to do with the lack of security preparedness in rural areas as well as the fact that, as Katherine Newman hypothesized, it is more difficult to escape the shame and humiliation of failure in a environment where everyone seemingly knows everything—especially the dirt.[5] However, copycatting would also help to explain the small-town thread.

When a 15-year-old white student from a small town is publicized throughout the media after shooting up his high school in response to constant bullying by classmates, some other white 15-year-old from small-town America may think to himself, "I understand exactly what he was going through because that's my world." In contrast, a black student living in the inner-city is less likely to empathize in the same way because that isn't anything like his experience; even if his own experiences did include taunting and intimidation, he would not so easily see himself in the position of the rural white student. Confirming the similarity factor, Kostinsky and his colleagues noted in their analysis of reported threats throughout Pennsylvania after the Columbine shooting—perpetrated by two suburban white males—the predominance of cases involving schools in suburban and rural areas serving student populations that were overwhelmingly comprised of white children.[6]

Some scholars have suggested that the "rural white kid" image relative to school shooters reflects more the way in which the news media "frames" the school violence problem. Menifield and his colleagues content-analyzed newspaper coverage of six episodes of school violence, three involving white rural teenagers and three implicating urban black youth.[7] As expected, the three rural shootings received substantially greater attention in terms of number, length, and placement of newspaper stories. However, the three rural cases were all multiple homicides, while the three urban assaults were either nonfatal or involved a single victim. To a large extent the difference in news focus surrounded victim count and degree of harm committed rather than locale or even race. Even so, a further observation stemming from this research was that the rural perpetrators were often described in a sympathetic light—for example, as the victim of bullying and harassment—whereas the urban assailants were often characterized as ruthless and reprehensible.

Social psychologists who specialize in imitation and reinforced learning point out that we are far more likely to model the behavior of others if we perceive their acts as reaping some reward. Many rational adults would question, therefore, how compelling Dylan Klebold and Eric Harris could be as role models when, at the end of the school day, they were found lying dead on the floor from self-inflicted gunshot wounds. However, teenagers would often interpret the outcome very differently from their parents. To an unhappy, alienated adolescent, the two gunmen could be seen as heroes: Not only had they avenged the bullying, intimidation, and acts of ostracism that are commonplace in sprawling high schools like Columbine, but they were famous for it. When *TIME* magazine placed the gunmen on their cover with the headline "The Monsters Next Door," most readers saw the "cover boys" as just that—monsters. A few like-minded teenagers saw them as celebrities who had the courage to get even, to claim a victory for bullying victims everywhere.

The role of folk hero was clearly reflected in the popular culture surrounding Columbine and, to a lesser degree, the other shooters that preceded and followed the 1999 shooting. The Web site *www.blackplague.org* (since shut down) launched a tribute to the collection of school shooters with admiring stories of their bravery. In a widely criticized initiative motivated by profit, attention, or both, game-maker Danny Ledonne developed and marketed "Super Columbine Massacre RPG," a role-playing game set in the context of

Columbine High School, mixing animated targets for a make-believe school shooter with digital images from the actual episode.

ADULT COPYCATS

The late 1990s was not the only time when schools were under siege by armed assailants. A decade earlier, the fears of parents and school officials were focused on school intruders—adults, not children—who used students as surrogate targets to exact a measure of revenge against society. From the assailant's perspective, what better way to have an impact than to terrorize society's most cherished and defenseless members?

In September 1988, 19-year-old James Wilson of Greenwood, South Carolina, went on a shooting spree at a local elementary school, killing two innocent children. When the police searched his home, they discovered that Wilson had pinned to his wall a photo of his hero taken from the cover of *People* magazine. His idol was 30-year-old Laurie Dann, a woman who a few months earlier had committed a similar crime at an elementary school in Winnetka, Illinois. Dann had suffered a long history of mental illness and assaults against others. In the years leading up to the school shooting, she had attempted to murder her husband with an ice pick, poisoned sorority members at Northwestern University, and mailed poisoned items to many other people. At the school, Dann shot and killed an 8-year-old boy and injured five others. She escaped by foot through the woods and conned her way into the home of Ruth Andrew, holding her and her 20-year-old son Philip at gunpoint. The intruder shot and wounded Philip as he ran from the house. When police arrived and surrounded the house, Dann walked upstairs and into a bedroom where she took her own life.

After the armed assaults by Laurie Dann and subsequently by James Wilson, several other schools were targeted, seemingly at random, by adult assailants. Although most of the episodes, fortunately, did not result in any fatalities of students or faculty, it appeared to be open season on schools and schoolyards. After several months and many shootings, the killing season came to a dramatic and tragic end, when 24-year-old Patrick Purdy set sight—literally—on the Cleveland Elementary School in Stockton, California, to vent his anger. Although Purdy had attended the school as a child, his reason for selecting the target was more the fact that the student population had become overwhelmingly comprised of children of Southeast Asian descent. He blamed Southeast Asians for all of his problems; in Purdy's mind, they had taken over the neighborhood and the jobs.

While the late 1980s saw a cluster of armed assaults in which adult outsiders perpetrated multiple-victim school shootings, that offender pattern all but disappeared in the subsequent years—at least for almost two decades. But then, on September 27, 2006, 53-year-old Duane Roger Morrison took siege of the Platte Canyon High School in Bailey, Colorado, only some 30 miles from the site of the Columbine shootings. Armed with a revolver and a semi-automatic pistol (plus a backpack that he falsely claimed contained a bomb), Morrison seized six female student hostages whom he sexually assaulted. He later released four of the hostages but killed one girl when she tried to escape. The day of terror eventually ended when Morrison shot and killed himself.

Only a week later, in another incident having a sexual motive, 32-year-old local milkman Charles Carl Roberts IV, the married father of two, took hostages at a one-room Amish schoolhouse in Lancaster County, Pennsylvania. Roberts sent the male students and adult females away but kept control of 10 young Amish girls who remained in the schoolhouse. Roberts had a shotgun and handgun, tools and equipment for binding the girls, barricade equipment, and candles, toilet paper, and other supplies indicating he planned to be there for awhile. Roberts had also brought tubes of sexual lubricant. He phoned his wife from the scene and confessed to her that he had been dreaming about molesting girls for years. Police swarmed the schoolhouse sooner than Roberts had anticipated. He did not get the chance to molest any of the girls, but shot all 10 at close range, killing 5 of them.

A CONTAGION OF COPYCAT THEORY

A thorny but all too frequent quandary for educators occurs when two students submit homework papers with remarkably similar answers. Does it suggest that one pupil copied from the other? Or, could it instead reflect just a similar understanding of the class material? The same type of question applies to assessing copycat behavior: Does similarity in the actions or words of two distinct school shooters, for example, support the copycat thesis, or are we perhaps misled by coincidental resemblance?

In his detailed book, *School Shootings: What Every Parent and Educator Needs to Know to Protect Our Children,* Oregon-based journalist Joseph A. Lieberman discusses several cult-hero icons who appear to have influenced Virginia Tech shooter Seung-Hui Cho, as support for the contagion hypothesis.[8] Cho's admiration for the two Columbine shooters was clearly reflected in both his writings and recordings. But Lieberman draws some fascinating, yet tenuous, connections between Cho and Kimveer Gill, a 25-year-old who opened fire at Dawson College in Montreal in September 2006, killing 1 and wounding 19 before taking his own life.

In explaining Gill's homicidal behavior, Lieberman gives considerable weight to the impact of photographs and videos that Cho had made of himself and sent off to the NBC network, images that were indecently plastered across TV screens and the pages of newspapers everywhere. Lieberman makes special note of the likeness between Cho's materials and those that Gill recorded prior to his deadly attack. Lieberman comments, for example, on the similarity of poses: Both Cho and Gill are shown brandishing weapons, as well as aiming their guns straight at the camera lens. However, in the YouTube era, where young adults routinely take and upload video clips of themselves, is it that unusual for two young campus killers both to chronicle their violent potential in this way? And how exceptional would it be for someone who is posing with guns for the camera to aim the weapon menacingly at the lens? We might question, therefore, whether Cho had been influenced by Gill, or whether they both had just coincidently been motivated by the same desire to document their path to murder.

Given the tendency to exaggerate, if not fabricate, potentially causal connections between violent events, attempts to prove the copycat effect through anecdotal evidence can lead to uncritical acceptance of some tidbit or factoid without verification. Many fine scholars and careful researchers have, for example, fallen deep into this trap with regard to a widely repeated tale about the 1996 multiple shooting by 14-year-old Barry Loukaitis and the novel *Rage*, published two decades earlier by a youthful Stephen King using the pseudonym Richard Bachman. In King's fictional account, high school senior Charles Decker takes his algebra class hostage at gunpoint after fatally shooting two teachers, and then turns class time into an introspective discussion of adolescent identity issues. Loukaitis did indeed own the book and, by virtue of its tattered appearance, had likely read it—even studied it—more than a few times. On February 2, with a fair degree of planning, the Decker-wannabe entered his fifth period class dressed in a long trench coat, inside of which he had concealed two pistols, dozens of rounds of ammunition, and a high-powered rifle. After turning the classroom into a true "dead zone," Loukaitis exited with a grin, and said dryly "This sure beats algebra, doesn't it?"—a line *reportedly* lifted straight from the pages of *Rage*.

It was an intriguing story of copycatting, albeit a false one. Although Loukaitis did, according to witnesses, make the remark, no such line appears in King's story. The closest is when Decker quips, "This sure beats panty raids." As rumors and legends often develop, the curious connection was first reported in a national news story published in *The New York Times*, generally believed to be authoritative in its coverage. Since that time, apparently, many others have told the tale of "sure beats algebra," without checking the actual text of *Rage*. Those who have perpetuated this myth do enjoy some level of excuse, however. Because of sharp criticism of the book, including allegations that it may have recklessly helped to inspire a crime wave of school shootings, Stephen King directed his publisher to take *Rage* out of print.

AVERTING THE COPYCAT PROBLEM

In *The Copycat Effect*, Loren Coleman concludes his detailed study of imitation by advancing a set of recommendations for how the news media might change the context and style of coverage given to high-profile tragedies, like school shootings, to lessen the contagion effect.[9] He sensibly argues that the print and electronic media should strive to avoid stereotypes, clichés, and sensationalism.

However, some of his suggestions may have unintended implications. For example, Coleman would have the news media focus less on the background characteristics that humanize the perpetrator and more on the grim after-effects. By this logic, should we commend rather than condemn *The National Enquirer* for having published photographs of Klebold and Harris lying dead at the Columbine crime scene? Although this may have been done in questionable taste, could journalistic practices of this type reduce the glamour sometimes associated with evil-doers?

Coleman's seemingly sound recommendation that the news media focus more on the sadness and grief of the surviving loved ones could also be counter-productive, at least in terms of the copycat effect. Media coverage of frightened students jumping out of school windows, of tearful classmates consoling each other, and of victims' funerals and memorial services may resonate with the vast majority of Americans who identify with the victims. Yet those few who admire the villains might view these images of sadness in a very different—even positive—light. That is, from their perspective, they might welcome the opportunity to turn their school into a bloody crime scene, perceiving the grim and sorrowful aftermath as a validation of their ultimate power over the lives of countless people.

Teenagers have always sought to be the first on their block to try out a new fad. In the 1930s, they were swallowing goldfish. In the 1950s and 1960s, they went on cramming themselves and all their friends into phone booths and Volkswagen Beetles. School shootings represent a deadly version of the same phenomenon. We certainly should not ignore the problem of school violence. However, we must attempt to respond without gratuitously calling so much direct attention to it. Rather than giving over so much of our attention during prime time or school time to reminding children of recent classroom tragedies, we should be doing more to enhance the quality of life and learning for all of our students. The contagion of school shootings, like other fads, will dissipate eventually, but only if we let it.

6

HYPE, FEAR, AND OVER-RESPONSE

The string of school shootings that marked the late 1990s changed the face of public education, and had many Americans questioning their faith in the notion that schools were safe places for children to grow intellectually and socially. Each episode of schoolyard terror—at least those that were highlighted, if not hyped, by the national media—incited widespread fear, dread, and anxiety. Each recurrence of the seemingly same old story of some alienated adolescent running amok in the hallways of his school intensified concerns that school shootings were not just an occasional and frightening aberration, but a new and persistent crime wave that should place schools everywhere on high alert.

In reaction to the latest crime trend, the Gallup polling organization, which routinely measures the social and political pulse of Americans, incorporated school violence and safety as a regular theme in its ongoing program of survey research. Gallup had not examined the issue since 1977, when a quarter of parents surveyed across America indicated a concern for their children's safety at school.[1] Twenty years later, Gallup was compelled by the series of multiple-fatality shootings that occurred during the 1997/1998 school year—from the October 1, 1997, episode in Pearl, Mississippi, to the May 21, 1998, killing spree in Springfield, Oregon—to resurrect the topic for its June 1998 national survey. Gallup then repeated its scan of public opinion related to school violence in three surveys fielded within a month after the appalling Columbine massacre. Since Columbine, Gallup has routinized its questioning regarding school violence and safety in surveys coinciding with the start of each school year, as well as at exceptional points in time, such as immediately following the March 2000 school shooting in Santee, California.

Figure 6.1 summarizes the overall results of the sequence of Gallup polls related to a question presented to parents about whether they fear for the

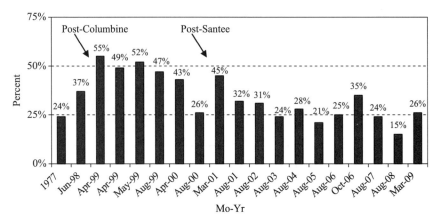

Figure 6.1 Percentage of parents fearful for oldest child's safety while at school
Source: Based on Linda Lyons, "Parents Concerned About School Safety," *Gallup News Service.*

safety of their oldest child while he or she is at school. Clearly, the Columbine shooting had a strong effect on the respondents' sense of security for their children, as the majority of respondents (55 percent) surveyed on the day following the April 20th murder indicated being afraid.

As Americans faced new challenges during the decade after Columbine (precipitated by the 9/11 attack on America), the school-related fears of parents gradually subsided, despite a spike of 45 percent in the survey taken immediately after the multiple shooting at Santana High School in Santee, California.[2] By the late 2000s, as the level of panic and media hype dissipated, the percentage of parents worried about their child's safety settled back to 26 percent, just about the same level as decades earlier.[3]

The available data pertaining to how students responded emotionally to the tragic school shootings paint a different picture from those that characterize their parents' concerns. Lynn Addington compared data from the National Crime Victimization Survey School Supplement collected just before and just after the Columbine episode.[4] Examining this contrast, Addington found only a marginal increase in fear in terms of both breadth and magnitude. Specifically, the percentage of students, ages 12 to 18, who indicated feeling apprehensive about safety while at school rose by only 4 percent. And for those who did report heightened concern, the extent of increase was rather modest. Overall, the level of fear among students prior to Columbine was fairly low, and after Columbine it was just not quite so low. Moreover, there was virtually no difference in the percentage of students reporting fearfulness while traveling to and from school, an activity unrelated to a Columbine-style event.

To some extent, fear stems from a belief that a dreaded event has some reasonable likelihood of occurring. In a nationally representative survey conducted by Gallup within a year of the Columbine shooting, three out of

10 American adults indicated that they believed it was indeed likely that a similar incident would take place in their own community.[5] Specifically, among adults with school-aged children, 40 percent reported that they were more concerned about their child's safety at school than they had been prior to the Columbine shooting. Finally, when asked about the security response from their child's school in the aftermath of Columbine, nearly three-quarters perceived there to have been an increase in security, yet over one quarter were still not satisfied with the school's level of preparedness.

Six years later, following a mass shooting at a school on an Indian reservation in Red Lake, Minnesota, Gallup once again polled Americans concerning school shootings—specifically, whether respondents felt it was likely that such shootings could occur in their community. As shown in Figure 6.2, the results were virtually the same—as least within the range of sampling error—as those obtained by the poll fielded immediately after Columbine. In both surveys, nearly one in three Americans felt that a similar school shooting was very likely to occur in their own community, and over two-thirds believed that such an incident was at least somewhat likely.

The similarity in poll results reflects more a stability in fear level than the impact of media coverage. The Red Lake episode received a mere fraction of the national attention and media exposure given to Columbine. The relative lack of coverage surrounding Red Lake partly reflected its location—an Indian reservation, with which few Americans could relate or identify. Moreover, the shooting was eclipsed by another major national news story (specifically, the "right to die" debate surrounding the Terri Schiavo case).[6]

Thus, no matter what the statistics suggest, the American public appears either to be unaware or else unconvinced of the low likelihood of school shootings. This exaggerated view of the risks not only has had negative effects on

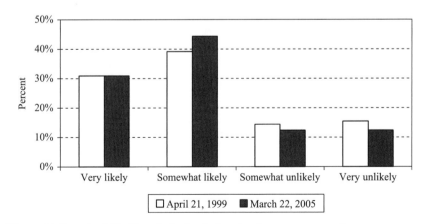

Figure 6.2 Perceived likelihood of school shooting in own community

Source: Heather Mason Kiefer, "Public: Society Powerless to Stop School Shootings," *Gallup News Service.*

the public's level of trust in school safety, but has also opened the doors for all sorts of extreme and unnecessary steps to protect children from an unspeakable—and unlikely—horror.

BULLET-PROOFING

It is not especially clear when or how State College, Pennsylvania, earned the nickname "Happy Valley." Official sources at Penn State University, the large public institution situated in the heart of the region, attribute the popular usage to sportswriters covering the school's exceptionally successful football program.[7] The early morning hours of Tuesday, September 17, 1996, started out exceptionally happy in Happy Valley, despite the overcast skies and cold drizzle, as the beloved Nittany Lions had trounced Northern Illinois 49-0 before a home crowd of nearly 100,000 at Beaver Stadium. But the afterglow of victory in Happy Valley would vanish in a violent instant.

At about 9:30 a.m., 19-year-old Kerry Butler, a sophomore from suburban Philadelphia, was rushing to her creative writing class by way of the grassy commons near the "HUB," the popular name on campus for the Hetzel Union Building, when shots rang out. The sound of gunfire sent her, and countless other students, scurrying for cover. In a particularly extreme case of "town-gown" conflict, Jillian Robbins, a 19-year-old high school drop-out from State College and former army reservist, had ventured onto campus to wreak havoc, and possibly to commit suicide on a public stage. Stopping in front of the busy student center, Robbins spread a tarp beneath a cluster of trees that decorated the lawn. She then removed a 7-mm Mauser rifle from under her long, duster-style coat, took aim through the scope, and started shooting at randomly chosen human targets.

The shooting spree ended moments later, as suddenly as it had begun. Robbins had only managed to fire off five rounds before senior Brendon Malovrh bravely darted from behind a tree to wrestle the gun away from her. Robbins then grabbed her backup weapon—a hunting knife with a 7-inch blade—waving it at Malovrh so erratically that she ended up only stabbing herself in the leg.

Unfortunately, Malovrh's heroic act came too late for Melanie Spalla, a 21-year-old journalism major who was fatally struck by one of the bullets while walking toward her dorm some 130 feet from the shooter. Another projectile wounded 22-year-old Nicholas Mensah in the abdomen.

One of the remaining few bullets was headed straight for Kerry Butler, but she never felt much of an impact. In fact, she wasn't really sure what was happening at the time, nor did she recognize the fallen student as a shooting victim. Having just recently gotten out of bed to take her second period exam, Butler was pretty much in a sleepy daze, and any thoughts that ran through her head were focused on the upcoming test. Nearly two hours later, after

successfully completing the exam unaware and unfazed by the reality of what
had just happened to her, Butler and her classmates learned about the shooting spree. Stunned by the news, she called the campus police to volunteer herself as a witness to the crime, not knowing that she was actually a victim.

Not until the next day, while preparing her blue canvas backpack for class,
did Butler notice its contents—shredded books and papers, as well as pieces
of the slug lodged inside the pages of a thick statistics text, just millimeters
away from where her spine would have been. Statistics may not have been
Butler's favorite class, but in the end it was potentially a life-saver.

It was surely a miraculous stroke of backpack luck that spared Kerry Butler.
But in the years since Butler's close brush with death, the barrage of fatal
shootings at schools of all levels inspired a wide array of entrepreneurs to turn
protection into profit.

Two fathers of school-aged children from Massachusetts seized the opportunity to market "My Child's Pack," a bullet-resistant backpack lined with a protective "BulletBlocker" shield made of sturdy, yet nonmetallic material so as
not to set off electronic screening devices at school or in an airport. According
to the MJ Safety Solutions' promotional material, this must-have back-to-
school item provides "safety with style." Its downloadable video ad (complete
with news footage of campus massacres and the musical refrain, "Four Dead
in Ohio," from Crosby, Stills, Nash, and Young's 1970 gritty song *Ohio* about
the fatal shooting of student protesters at Kent State University) claims that
97 percent of school shooting victims could have been spared had they used
the company's product.[8] So successful was the commercial venture in terms of
both publicity and sales that MJ Safety Solutions soon expanded its product
line to include a bulletproof safety seat for teachers and a complete classroom
safety and survival kit.

A competitor of MJ Safety Solutions, Backpackshield Manufacturing of Austin, Texas, markets a portable bullet-resistant shield—a semi-rigid, antiballistic
panel originally designed for military use. Available in a wide variety of attractive colors to coordinate with most any school bag, the lightweight insert can
easily fit inside most conventional school backpacks and computer bags.

The Spero Group, an organization dedicated to providing water and other
nutritional/health-related essentials to undeveloped areas around the world,
moved far-afield from its core mission when it made a splash in the secure
backpack marketplace. Spero claims to sell the *original* bullet-resistant backpack, noting that in product tests, the item stopped a 9-mm full metal jacket
and a .44-magnum. The backpack comes in three colors, with styling that is
"sophisticated, modern, urban yet rugged enough to last, with affordable protection."[9] Perhaps to avert any possible criticism for its side venture, the firm
stipulates that a share of its profits goes to charitable initiatives in Africa.

Years before the bullet-shielding inserts became available, and before shootings on college campuses were widely publicized, another e-commerce outfit
sold backpacks with metal strips in the shoulder straps, intended to cover a

youngster's vital organs in case a classmate started shooting. The hope was that the victim would be fortunate enough to have the bullet hit the strap and be deflected. The advertisement recommended that students fill their backpack with heavy books (notwithstanding the negative impact on posture), based on the idea that these tomes may slow down the bullet—as occurred with Kerry Butler's statistics text. The reality, however, is that should there, in fact, be a school shooting, the best thing a student might do is drop the 40-pound backpack and run as fast and as far as possible.

Looking back at her experience after many years, Kerry Butler still feels lucky to have survived the Penn State shooting in such a bizarre manner. Still, if she had it to do all over again, even after her close call with death, she would opt not to purchase and wear a bullet-resistant accessory.[10] She understands the exceptionally low likelihood of such an event at a usually peaceful campus like Penn State's.

PRACTICAL TRAINING

Protection and preparation include not just personal forms of self-defense, such as bullet-resistant backpacks, but institutional responses as well. In the wake of mass shootings at Virginia Tech and Northern Illinois University, colleges and universities were forced to confront the grim reality that they were not immune to the risk of random gun violence. Unlike middle schools and high schools that could look to access control—e.g., guarded entrances and weapons checkpoints—as a primary strategy for prevention, the openness of most institutions of higher education required school officials to consider student orientation and preparedness training as a more feasible move toward promoting campus safety.

In the months following the high-profile campus massacres, the ever-popular "College Survival Guides" shifted focus from tips on how to study for a midterm to advice on where safely to sit while taking the midterm. Even the well-known "Complete Idiot's Guide" series published a volume on campus safety. Those who, by virtue of their choice in reading material, seek easy-to-understand advice are instructed, for example, to run or hide on hearing the sound of gunfire.[11]

In 2008, a new security DVD, *Shots Fired on Campus: Student Version*, demonstrating tips and techniques on how to survive an "active shooter" attack on campus, became a widely popular curriculum for new student orientation. Apparently, many colleges bought the message, quite literally. According to the Center for Personal Protection and Safety, the security consulting company in Spokane, Washington, that produced and distributes the DVD, dozens of colleges and universities around the country preordered the 20-minute instructional video at $495 per copy and spent an additional $1,000 for a campus intranet site license, even before its release. Once available, hundreds more institutions placed orders in time for the September start of classes.[12]

The *Shots Fired on Campus* video opens with a dramatization of a class-room full of students who are baffled and confused by a startling series of loud popping sounds that only some recognize as gunfire. A voice-over urges students not to take chances in such a situation, to presume that the sound is gunfire rather than any number of alternative explanations for the noise. Over the course of the video, students are encouraged to develop a "survival mind-set," and are taught when to run and when to hide, as well as how to confront an armed assailant when there is no escape possible. While the natural response would be to huddle together for protection, viewers are advised instead to spread out so as to make it that more difficult for an armed assail-ant to target his victims.

The video urges students always to think defensively. For example, when entering a classroom or lecture hall, students are encouraged to be aware of all escape routes—both doors and windows—and to be ready to run if neces-sary. Students are instructed to avoid seats in the middle of a row in the lec-ture hall, as sitting in this location would delay any attempt to flee. Notwithstanding the question of whether this approach is reasonable, such strategic planning could, as a down side, result in a classroom with students all seated near the aisle or back row, but no one in the middle sections. Safer or not, the professor would find it quite challenging to lecture to a class with such an unusual seating arrangement.

As of April 2009, Northern Michigan University (NMU), by decision of its president, required all faculty and other university employees to view a set of online training materials regarding active shooters. These resources included the *Shots Fired on Campus* video, as well as a PowerPoint presentation sum-marizing the major points and providing some localized information, such as emergency contact numbers.

The NMU training materials recommend these specific steps for securing an area in the event of an active shooter incident:[13]

- Lock and barricade doors.
- Turn off lights.
- Close blinds.
- Block windows.
- Turn off radios and computer monitors.
- Keep occupants calm, quiet, and out of sight.
- Keep yourself out of sight and take adequate cover/protection (i.e., con-crete walls, thick desks, filing cabinets), which may protect you from bullets.
- Silence cell phones.
- Place signs in exterior windows to identify the location of injured persons.

Despite the healthy sales to college campuses around the country, the popular *Shots Fired on Campus* DVD does have its detractors. Loren Coleman, author of *The Copycat Effect,* said in a newspaper interview with London's *Independent,* "It's a graphic demonstration of fear marketing, and it gives away all the countermeasures law enforcement, psychologists, and negotiators can use. For $1,500, schools would be far better off getting a counselor to speak to vulnerable students and prevent this kind of thing happening in the first place."[14]

The no-nonsense *Shots Fired on Campus* DVD, despite containing repeated statements that active shooter events are quite rare, implicitly puts students on alert. When a college or university places the video on its intranet for students to view, the subtle message to them becomes: "The risk is sufficiently high for us to recommend (or compel) you to watch and be prepared."

An alternative approach to campus safety uses humor to make the lessons more palatable. At the flagship campus of the University of Illinois in Urbana-Champaign, the Dean of Students Office sponsored a light and lively 15-minute instructional video on safety and security. The program, hosted by a student/actor as "Sam Safety," takes a decidedly playful look at several aspects of crime prevention and risk reduction.[15] Despite the annoying laugh-track, the show is produced to look like a TV news report, with anchorman Sam and field reporters Sally Sassafras and Dave Defense offering some extraordinarily elementary tips on campus safety. Students are given advice on how to avoid being the victim of assault, including pointers such as: "Don't travel alone when it's dark"; "If you must go out alone, use well-lit sidewalks"; and "Never walk through alleys or parks at night." The video also instructs students to lock their dorm rooms at all times so as to prevent theft and to look both ways while crossing the street. Students are required to watch the instructional video and then to complete a 12-item test of their safety smarts. Included in the test are such "brain-teasers" as:

> Which of the following is an important factor in preventing burglaries?
> a. Surround your door with garlic
> b. Assume your roommate has common sense
> c. Ensure your door is locked
> d. All of the above
>
> What should you do to avoid being a victim of assault?
> a. Walk in groups
> b. Stay in well lit areas
> c. Avoid deserted areas
> d. All of the above

Notwithstanding the utter simplicity—after all, these are students who have been admitted to the state's finest public institution of higher education—the test is not actually graded. Also, the interactive online questions are repeated until a student provides the correct response to each item in the sequence.

The light-hearted style of the University of Illinois video would likely cause some security professionals to cringe. After all, security is hardly a laughing matter. Yet, laughter can be an effective defense mechanism, helping people to deal with issues that they find frightening. Unlike the University of Illinois' low-key approach, the widely distributed *Shots Fired on Campus* video leaves little to the imagination. Its attempt to be exhaustive results in a long list of do's and don'ts for dangerous situations. Unless students opt to review and study the messages intensely, which for the vast majority of college students is highly unlikely, few would calmly recall the video's step-by-step recommendations in the midst of a terrifying episode months, if not years, later. Students need not be treated like security trainees. When it comes to presenting them with useful information about campus safety, less is more.

DRILLING STUDENTS

The recent commercial ventures described above were hardly the first to exploit fear, particularly the widespread concerns of parents that a shooter could strike their son's or daughter's school without warning. Shortly after the Columbine episode, a security consulting group calling itself "Escape School" produced and marketed a video designed to teach children in secondary schools how to react in the event of a shooting episode. In the video, security consultant Bob Stuber lectures kids on how to find safe refuge behind a barricaded door, and how to "outsmart a bullet" by running in a zigzag pattern, making it difficult for a shooter to take steady aim. Whereas public schools are often restricted in their attempts to educate young minds about safe sex and how to avoid sexually transmitted diseases, apparently instruction on avoiding a barrage of gunfire is acceptable, if not encouraged.

In addition to marketing the training video, Stuber took his school safety curriculum on the road, offering his survival skills training to any school willing to invest the time, the resources, and the children. Part of Stuber's tactical exercise involves a somewhat disturbing role-playing activity in which he chases girls and boys up and down the corridors and from classroom to classroom, pointing his large flashlight as if it were a firearm and shouting "bang-bang!" or "boom, you're dead, get down!"[16] Although it is only a test of their preparedness, student participants testify to the realism, which may account for their frequent and intense screams.

Whereas Stuber offers his "Safe Escape" course as an outside consultant, many schools and school districts around the country have chosen to stage their own so-called "Columbine drills," in which a scene reminiscent of the infamous high school massacre is reenacted, involving teachers, students, and sometimes the local police.

Just as schools have traditionally staged fire drills to ensure a quick and orderly evacuation in case of a blaze, a newer type of drill has been implemented in many schools in the form of a staged lockdown. South Brunswick High School in New Jersey, for example, introduced a student preparedness drill to simulate a shooting incident on campus.[17] Schools in several other states have been urged, if not required, to follow similar practices. In fact, at a post-Columbine statewide conference, the Massachusetts Department of Education adopted a specific guideline regarding training drills. The advisory prescribed that schools in the state "develop procedures for classroom and school drills, determine ways of evacuating the building, and practice the drills to determine their effectiveness."[18] More than a few complied, believing that it would prepare staff and students alike to anticipate their actions should the unthinkable—and improbable—occur.

The training drills implemented in many school districts around the country are intended to be as realistic as possible, down to the pretend dead bodies and the fake blood. One high school in West Virginia, for example, conducted a "Columbine drill" in which two students (of the many who volunteered for the role) acted as the shooters, roaming the halls carrying toy guns. Other students volunteered to lie as still as corpses, while still more practiced hiding out and avoiding the gunmen. The event was designed by members of the police SWAT team, who also played themselves in the charade.

Emergency drills are nothing new to public schools, of course. Simulated exercises to prepare pupils for fire and other natural catastrophes are commonplace. Yet the aggressive nature of shooting drills makes them qualitatively different and exceptionally more traumatizing to children of all ages. The psychological harm that may come from these simulations is not warranted in light of the low probability that such an event will occur. It is one thing to prepare the faculty and staff for what to do and how to instruct the students in the case of a violent episode; it is quite another to involve impressionable children whose innocence need not be compromised. Furthermore, many, if not most, children would not recall what they had learned during occasional shooting drills, especially in an atmosphere of panic that typically surrounds the real thing.

Without necessarily calling them "Virginia Tech drills," many colleges and universities have responded to the apparent rise of campus bloodshed by instituting their own tactical training exercises. Some have been staged successfully, particularly those conveniently and wisely performed during a school vacation week when the campus resembled a ghost town. Other attempts were not so smooth.

In February 2008, for example, a man carrying a fake assault weapon burst into an American foreign policy class at Elizabeth City State University in North Carolina. The seven unsuspecting students, along with a stunned professor who later remarked that he was "prepared to die at that moment," were held hostage for 10 minutes. During that time, the gunman said he would kill at least one of them. The class survived because the gunman was a volunteer, part of an exercise intended to test the university's system for responding to a possible campus attack. The university had alerted its students and faculty with e-mail and text messages, but not everyone had received or read them. Fortunately, no one was hurt in the simulation—at least not physically.

School shootings are not the only rare yet horrific events for which emergency training and preparedness can be critical for saving lives. School officials—for higher education or lower—could learn an important lesson of moderation and restraint from other venues that grapple with improbable yet deadly hazards, be they of natural or intentional origin. For instance, commercial airlines train their flight crews to handle disaster situations—such as the unlikely "water landing"—but passengers are only asked to watch a brief demonstration of grabbing hold of oxygen masks, without having actually to practice this maneuver. Cruise ships require that their guests adorn life jackets and learn the location of their evacuation stations, but no one has to step foot inside a life boat or suffer the experience of being lowered into the water. In case of a catastrophe in the air or at sea, the passengers will be told what to do.

This same reasonable posture should apply for schools: Prepare the staff but spare the students. As with the usual pre-flight or pre-cruise rituals, a few simple instructions on escape strategy may be sensible. However, over-preparing students needlessly risks intensifying their fears and anxiety.

Still, there are those security-minded professionals who insist that one can never be too well-prepared, even for a rare event like a campus shooting. Even so, there is an additional and critically important difference between preparing passengers for the unlikely crash and readying students for an improbable shooting. Airlines don't inspire dangerous ideas by reciting crash drills. By contrast, there are a few students for whom the notion of wreaking havoc on their schoolmates may seem like an exhilarating idea. Obsessing over the unlikely possibility of a campus shooting can unfortunately serve to inspire potential copycats and inadvertently increase the chance of tragedy.

ZERO TOLERANCE

Patterned after a controversial policing strategy that emerged in the 1990s for dealing with issues of public disorder, the zero tolerance response to school disciplinary matters became the rule of law in countless school districts across the country in response to heightened concerns over schoolyard terrorism. Hoping to send a stern message, school administrators alerted students that infractions involving weapons or the threat of serious harm would result in suspension or expulsion, no matter what the mitigating circumstances.

This unbending and absolutist posture was born out of the Gun-Free School Act passed by Congress in 1994. Although the focus was initially limited to firearms, the notion of zero tolerance was eventually expanded at the local level to encompass less critical behaviors as school personnel grew increasingly concerned about other types of weapons and threats, especially after the widely publicized school massacres in the late 1990s. Other forms of rule violation, even those unrelated to violence, were also added to the list of transgressions warranting a zero tolerance response.

As shown in Table 6.1, by as early as the 1996/1997 school year, the vast majority of schools maintained a policy of mandatory sanctions—zero tolerance—for a variety of transgressions, ranging from violence to possession of contraband. Although the differences are not large owing to a ceiling effect, reliance on zero tolerance discipline was greater among schools that had large enrollments, that were more urban in locale, and that had proportionately large minority student populations. There were minor differences among school types with respect to the practice of zero tolerance, with the sole exception of tobacco, where, understandably, tolerance increases with advancing grade levels.

Table 6.1
Percentage of schools with zero tolerance policies, 1996–97

School characteristic	Offense Type					
	Violence	Firearms	Other weapons	Alcohol	Drugs	Tobacco
All schools	79%	94%	91%	87%	88%	79%
Type						
Elementary school	79%	93%	91%	87%	88%	82%
Middle school	75%	95%	90%	86%	90%	77%
High school	80%	96%	92%	86%	89%	72%
Enrollment						
Under 300	76%	93%	89%	84%	84%	76%
300–999	79%	94%	91%	88%	89%	82%
1,000 and up	86%	98%	93%	85%	92%	72%
Location						
City	87%	97%	95%	89%	91%	83%
Urban fringe	82%	95%	90%	88%	90%	80%
Town	71%	90%	86%	82%	83%	77%
Rural	76%	94%	92%	88%	89%	78%
Region						
Northeast	78%	89%	90%	83%	84%	79%
Southeast	83%	95%	89%	90%	92%	80%
Central	72%	93%	88%	82%	83%	75%
West	83%	97%	95%	91%	93%	83%
Minority enrollment						
Under 5 percent	71%	92%	88%	82%	83%	75%
5–19 percent	79%	94%	92%	89%	90%	80%
20–49 percent	83%	95%	90%	87%	89%	79%
50 percent and up	85%	97%	94%	90%	92%	83%

Source: National Center for Education Statistics, *Violence and Discipline Problems in U.S. Public Schools: 1996–97*, Table 19.

The zero tolerance approach is designed, ostensibly, to achieve several objectives.[19] Most fundamentally, mandatory sanctions—regardless of the behavioral focus or context—are often assumed to achieve the greatest deterrent effect, as punishment certainty (rather than severity) tends to carry the greatest weight in the calculus of decision-making. At the same time, it is believed that removing from the school all serious violators of the student code of conduct, no matter what their intent or exact purpose, would create a calmer school climate, ensuring the safety and well-being of the overwhelming majority of the student population.

In addition to the stated objectives, school administrators embraced the zero tolerance approach because it eliminated any second-guessing that could potentially follow from discretionary use of sanctions. Similarly, it was also widely assumed to alleviate professional responsibility and civil liability should an under-response in disciplining a troublemaker lead, subsequently, to serious acts of aggression.

Without any particular evidence that zero tolerance would achieve its objectives and therefore reduce the risk of harm, school administrators blindly accepted this rigid approach, resulting in countless examples of absurd over-response to relatively innocent behaviors. In Tyrone, Georgia, for example, two second graders were suspended for making a hit list of potential victims, which included Barney the Purple Dinosaur and the Spice Girls pop group. A fourth-grade boy in Maryland was suspended for having fashioned a construction-paper gun when instructed by his art teacher to express creatively his reaction to recent publicity concerning a major school shooting.

At the other end of the age spectrum, an honors student at a Texas high school was transferred to an alternative school designated for troublemakers after a small knife was found in the back of his pickup truck while it was parked in the student lot. Apparently, the "weapon" had fallen from a box of kitchenware that he was transporting the night before as a favor to his grandmother. Despite several appeals for reason and sensibility, it took months before he was returned to his school and cleared of any wrongdoing.

The list of questionable responses goes on and on. A Colorado girl, who mistakenly grabbed her mother's lunch bag from the kitchen counter while rushing off to school, was punished after she learned of her error and volunteered the small paring knife that her mother had packed for slicing an apple. Ignorance was no excuse.

Notwithstanding these absurdities, the zero tolerance approach might still be defensible were there evidence that it had an appreciable deterrent effect on the likelihood of violent or threatening behavior, or a measurable incapacitation effect by keeping dangerous youth separate from their peers. However, no such evidence exists.[20] The lack of support for zero tolerance is either because the approach is fundamentally flawed or because our ability to measure such effects is limited. It is hardly practical to construct experimental or controlled studies of zero tolerance in a school-based setting. Moreover, even nonexperimental examinations of the association between the type of discipline and level of violence in schools cannot easily or adequately overcome the methodological constraints of confounding variables. That is, it becomes rather complex to disentangle disciplinary temperament and style from a host of other variables related to the student population and school context.

Of even greater concern than the silly and unnecessary application of overly rigid rules is when the level of tolerance is zero only for certain students, particularly minority children.[21] An inner-city 7-year-old youngster who had participated in a Massachusetts program that bussed underprivileged students to the suburbs—ostensibly to take advantage of the better education offered in more affluent towns—was summarily dropped from the program and the suburban school after being found in possession of a bullet. The child was without a gun, but also without a good explanation. An obvious question is whether the punishment would have been the same if boy had been a local resident—and had white skin.

Several investigators have examined how disciplinary measures are applied and the extent to which they discriminate against minority or underprivileged students. Most empirical studies have indeed found rates of suspension and expulsion to be higher for students of color. However, this could be a reflection of higher rates of misconduct among minority students, rather than of biased disciplinary measures. Ultimately, then, the question remains whether differences in rates of suspension and expulsion can be accounted for by the amount or types of infractions or other variables associated with the race-discipline correlation.

In a careful examination of the school disciplinary records of just over 11,000 middle school students in a large Midwestern city, Skiba and colleagues confirmed that race played a key role in the disciplinary outcome, even after considering differences in the pattern of misbehavior for which the students had been referred to school officials.[22] In particular, while 56 percent of the students in the study were black—two-thirds of the referrals—nearly 70 percent of the suspensions and over 80 percent of the expulsions involved black children. Thus, even though the prevalence of rule-breaking may have been greater for the minority students, as evidenced by the disproportionate distribution among referrals, the discrepancy in sanctioning (suspension and especially expulsion) was even more pronounced.

Taken together, these flaws in the application of zero tolerance discipline have prompted the American Bar Association, as well as a national network of outraged parents, to condemn the practice. Overall, the zero tolerance approach makes zero sense. It lacks the essential element of common reason and discretion. Fortunately, some degree of rational thinking prevailed at a Massachusetts high school when a 16-year-old student was ordered to remove a jersey that his aunt had given him, but was not punished. The jersey itself, a souvenir from the television series, *The Sopranos*, did not violate the dress code in any way. However, the Sopranos logo, with a gun shape used to form the letter "r," was deemed by school officials to be menacing.

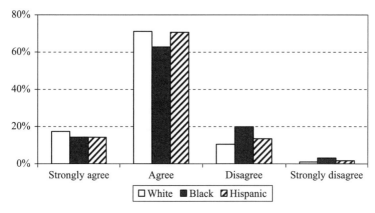

Figure 6.3 Perceived fairness of school discipline by race/ethnicity
Source: Based on the Bureau of Justice Statistics, National Crime Victimization Survey, School Supplement, 2005.

Although the rigid zero tolerance approach lacks merit, rule infractions and various forms of student misconduct still require a disciplinary response. As discussed in later chapters, the type and severity of the disciplinary action should be consistent: proportionate to the gravity of the transgression, but also considerate of relevant aggravating and mitigating factors. In order to achieve and maintain a positive school climate, the disciplinary process must avoid arbitrariness to appear respectful of student rights.

A sense of how students perceive school discipline is available from the 2005 school supplement of the National Crime Victimization Survey, which asked students about various school crime issues, including discipline. As shown in Figure 6.3, although most students believed school rules to be fair, black students were less apt to view them in a positive light. Whereas 87 percent of students overall agreed or strongly agreed that school rules were fair, the figure for Hispanic students was somewhat lower (85 percent), but that for black students was considerably lower (77 percent). Kupchik and Ellis, through an elaborate multivariate statistical analysis of these same survey data, reported similar results: Black students perceived less fairness and consistency of rules and their enforcement by school officials than did white students, while the differences between whites and Hispanics were small and not statistically significant.[23]

Notwithstanding the worthy objectives, zero tolerance discipline has been a failure. There is no evidence that the approach has made schools any safer. Rather than achieving uniformity in discipline, zero tolerance has been applied unevenly based on school and student characteristics. In addition, its reliance on expulsion as the recommended sanction has been shown to result in higher drop-out rates, ultimately a much larger concern in terms of life trajectory. Overall, school climate has been harmed, not helped, by this popular, yet excessively rigid and punitive, approach to school safety.

SECURITY IN ELEMENTARY SCHOOLS

For the most part, the available data and existing research on school violence have focused heavily on middle school and high school students. For example, the Health Behavior in School-Aged Children surveys, part of a multi-national research effort coordinated by the World Health Organization, cover only students in grades 6 through 10. The Centers for Disease Control and Prevention-sponsored Youth Risk Behavior Surveillance surveys, conducted biannually since 1993, focus exclusively on adolescents enrolled in public and private high schools. In addition, the National Crime Victimization Survey, and the school supplement in particular, captures respondents aged 12 to 18. The only regular data collection series to reach down to the elementary grades is the periodic School Survey on Crime and Safety (SSOCS), fielded by the National Center for Education Statistics; however, it polls school administrators rather than students.

To some extent, this relative lack of research focus on children in the primary grades may surround the practical and ethical hurdles associated with administering surveys of any type or length to young children. Furthermore, prescriptions pertaining to informed consent would generally require parental involvement. Of course, these issues are not prohibitive, as elementary-school-age children are, from time to time, studied by social and behavioral scientists. Likely, the decision not to survey young children is based partly on the belief that the levels of violence—especially serious violence—are just too low in most elementary school settings to merit any systematic empirical attention.

It would be a mistake, however, to conclude that campus security issues are exclusive to secondary and post-secondary venues and that the primary grades are essentially invulnerable. However, elementary schools do tend to have fewer problems related to fighting, violence, and disorder than do schools that enroll teenagers. Responses from school administrators based on the School Survey on Crime and Safety Survey sponsored by the U.S. Department of

Education bear this out. As shown in Table 7.1, far fewer elementary school officials indicate having had problems with violence during the 2005/2006 school year, as compared to those from other education levels. At the extreme, only 6.2 percent of elementary schools had any incidents of violence serious enough to warrant alerting the police, compared to 19.7 percent for middle schools and 29.5 percent for high schools. In terms of experiencing the wider array of discipline problems, elementary schools are far better off than schools at higher grade levels.

Table 7.1 also shows that elementary schools are less reliant on various security measures, most likely because their violence and disciplinary problems are relatively limited. A significant exception surrounds the extent to which schools control access to their building and grounds during school hours. Elementary schools are more guarded in terms of perimeter security, presumably in light of their students' greater vulnerability to assaults or even abductions by intruders.

Although all schools, from preschool to college, struggle with a variety of security risks, the concerns confronting elementary school administrators are in some respects unique. Violent crime—especially homicide—is comparatively rare at the elementary grade level; yet, younger students are more vulnerable to other kinds of threats, which demand more direct oversight from both faculty and staff. Although technology can contribute to a safe learning environment, school personnel are absolutely central in any successful effort to promote security. Therefore, the cooperation of faculty and staff, in particular, must be enlisted in the fight to prevent crime or other types of loss. Combining technology and human effort, day-to-day security and safety in the primary grades is largely determined by the operations, policies, and practices related to transportation, buildings and grounds, and management and supervision of young students.

TRANSPORTATION SECURITY

In an earlier era more than a half-century ago, shuttling children to and from school was a parental responsibility and, therefore, the school was essentially uninvolved with transportation issues. Schools were primarily populated by students who resided in the neighborhood, most within walking distance; those living too far from school to walk relied on bicycles or their parents to drive them.

School transportation needs changed, however, with the emergence and expansion of the suburbs and with the desegregation of public schools. Suburban sprawl increased the distances from homes to schools to the point where significant numbers of students were no longer able to walk or to ride their bicycle. Parents could still drive their children to school, but increasingly depended on the transportation provided by the local school system. In

Table 7.1
Violence, discipline problems, and security measures by school level, 2005–06

Violence, Discipline or Security Characteristic	Elementary schools	Middle schools	High schools	All schools
Violent incidents during the school year				
Percentage of schools having any:				
violent incidents	67.3%	94.4%	95.2%	77.7%
serious violent incidents	11.0%	25.2%	31.8%	17.1%
violent incidents reported to police	18.7%	63.1%	77.3%	37.7%
serious violent incidents repoted to police	6.2%	19.7%	29.5%	12.6%
Discipline problems during the school year				
Percentage of schools having problems with:				
student bullying	20.6%	43.0%	22.3%	24.5%
sexual harrassment among students	1.6%	8.6%	6.2%	3.5%
undesirable gang activity	7.6%	31.5%	38.7%	16.8%
undesirable cult/extremist group activity	1.1%	5.0%	11.0%	3.6%
Use of various security measures				
Percentage of schools with:				
controlled access to buildings	87.9%	84.4%	76.6%	84.9%
controlled access to grounds	44.5%	35.1%	36.4%	41.1%
random metal detector checks	2.3%	9.0%	10.8%	4.9%
random sweeps for contraband	2.3%	22.3%	29.8%	13.1%
cameras to monitor school	31.4%	52.5%	69.7%	42.8%

Source: U.S. Department of Education, National Center for Educational Statistics, 2005–06 School Survey on Crime and Safety.

addition, urban school districts that had previously been segregated along racial lines also came to depend heavily on school-provided transportation, as the neighborhood school concept was abandoned in the interest of racial desegregation. Because inner-city children were often assigned to schools that were not within walking distance of their homes, city school districts—like their suburban counterparts—were called on to provide transportation.

Table 7.2 summarizes the typical patterns of school transportation in terms of student-trips and student-miles (for children in primary and secondary schools combined) for the year 1995. While a majority of the trips and miles still involved travel by private vehicle (mainly cars, but sometimes bicycles), school buses accounted for one-quarter of the trips and a slightly larger share of the total mileage. Even though the modal form of transportation has remained rides from parents or other friends/relatives, schools have taken on a significant share of the transportation burden along with the associated responsibilities and liabilities.

Safe Vehicles and Drivers

As needs changed over time, school systems had several options with regard to how transportation was to be provided. They could purchase buses and hire drivers, which would have a considerable impact on school budgets. Alternatively, they could contract with a private company for both buses and drivers. Still another option was to lease buses and negotiate separate agreements with bus operators. From a cost-benefit perspective, the latter two choices usually made the most sense.

Regardless of the details, it would now be the school system's responsibility to ensure that students were transported in vehicles that were safe, and which

Table 7.2
Modes of transportation to and from school

	Trips		Miles	
Mode of travel	Number (in 100 mil)	Percent	Number (in 100 mil)	Percent
School bus	58	25%	313	28%
Other bus	5	2%	38	3%
Passenger vehicle (adult driver)	105	45%	580	51%
Passenger vehicle (teen driver)	34	14%	184	16%
Bicycle	5	2%	4	<1%
Walking	28	12%	15	1%
Total	235	100%	1,134	100%

Source: Committee on School Transportation Safety, *The Relative Risks of School Travel: A National Perspective and Guidance for Local Community Risk Assessment* (Washington, DC: National Research Council, 2002), p. 4., http://onlinepubs.trb.org/Onlinepubs/sr/sr269.pdf.

were operated by drivers who could be trusted with the welfare of their young riders. Moreover, school systems were unable to avoid this responsibility by contractually shifting it to the transportation providers. Because the ultimate responsibility for safety always lies with the school, bus transportation contracts should precisely outline the school department's requirements regarding both vehicles and drivers. For example, agreements should include random safety inspections over and above those required by state law, and these inspections should be conducted by qualified mechanics chosen by the school department.

There has been a continuing debate regarding whether seat belts should be required in all school buses. One side argues that requiring anything less of school buses than of private vehicles makes little sense and places millions of children in harm's way. In fact, although the federal government has failed to make a move in this direction, in 1987, New York became the first state to mandate two-point seat belts in all new school buses, with New Jersey and Florida subsequently taking similar action. Opponents, however, point to the substantial costs associated with requiring seat belts in school buses, and contend that many students would fail to wear them even if available. Moreover, they reference a 2002 report to Congress from the National Highway Traffic Safety Administration concluding that lap belts in school buses could even increase the risk of injury to children.

The requirements for bus operators must be carefully crafted to prevent harm to students resulting from driver misconduct. Regrettably, some districts, perhaps out of concern for privacy laws, are unwilling to conduct sufficiently thorough background checks, thereby increasing the chance of hiring drivers whose history of traffic violations, irresponsibility, or worse still, pedophilia, renders them unfit to operate school buses.

There is a wide range of hazards that can come from employing unqualified drivers. Careless drivers have been known to drop young children off at the wrong location or, in some cases, not to drop them off at all, leaving them alone on an unattended bus for hours until frantic parents call the school. Even worse, children are sometimes entrusted to the care of bus operators with criminal records. In 2000, for example, the Connecticut Department of Motor Vehicles investigated the criminal histories of some 6,000 school bus drivers, discovering that dozens had been convicted of offenses such as narcotics possession, assault, endangering a minor and illegal weapons possession. These drivers had been hired by private bus companies that were not required to conduct background checks.[1]

Whether bus operators are employed directly by school districts or by private contractors, steps must be taken to determine their honesty, reliability, and suitability for working with grade-school children. A thorough pre-employment screening should be conducted to verify the operator's status (i.e., citizenship or other legal authority to work), education, work history, business and personal references, credit record, and criminal history. All operators should then be required to undergo and pass a training program before they are permitted to transport students. Training should include not only the requisite skills to operate buses under a variety of weather or road conditions specific to the area, but also first aid and CPR procedures. This training is critical, considering that in many or most cases, drivers are the only adults accompanying children on their way to and from school, and are therefore the only adults available to respond in a medical emergency during those times.[2]

Besides the issues of driver honesty and competency, the chief concern surrounds road safety. Between 1996 and 2006, 273 children were killed in accidents involving school buses—114 as riders and 159 as pedestrians. Moreover, half of the pedestrian fatalities were of children ages 5 to 7 years old.[3] Table 7.3 displays data on fatalities as well as estimated injuries resulting from school bus accidents over a nine-year time span from 1991 to 1999. Over 200 children were killed and thousands more were injured while riding on school buses and as pedestrians involved in mishaps. Clearly, the safety of children in relation to school bus maintenance and operation is a significant matter for schools, regardless of the direct or contractual relationship with the transportation provider.

Without careful oversight, the human and financial toll can be significant. On April 27, 2001, four students from the Oak Hill Middle School in Newton, Massachusetts, tragically lost their lives in a school transportation accident. The school had contracted with Crystal Transport to take members of the school band to a concert 700 miles away in Halifax, Nova Scotia. However, just days before the scheduled trip, Crystal subcontracted the job to Kristine Travel & Tours. Most of the passengers were asleep, in the early morning hours, as the motor-coach traveled along the Trans-Canada Highway. Not far from the destination, the driver failed to maneuver a sharp hairpin exit ramp, causing the bus to flip, killing four youngsters and injuring many others. Three years later, victims' families reached a $15 million settlement with the bus manufacturer, bus companies, and bus drivers, averting what would have been many painful days in court.

Collisions and other mishaps related to operation are not the only perils involved in school bus travel. Although less frequent than roadway accidents, intentional acts by strangers can exploit the vulnerability of a busload of

Table 7.3
Fatalities and injuries involving school bus accidents, 1991–99

Victim	Fatalities	Estimated injuries
Passenger	55	60,883
Pedestrian	160	5,001
Total	215	65,884

Source: Committee on School Transportation Safety, *The Relative Risks of School Travel: A National Perspective and Guidance for Local Community Risk Assessment* (Washington, DC: National Research Council, 2002), p. 4., http://onlinepubs.trb.org/Onlinepubs/sr/sr269.pdf.

children with limited adult presence. In an extreme episode from Chowchilla, California, 26 children and the driver were kidnapped from a school bus on July 15, 1976, and held for ransom in the back of a moving van buried inside a quarry. Fortunately, the victims managed to escape some 16 hours later, and the 3 kidnappers were then captured, convicted, and sentenced to life imprisonment.

BUILDINGS AND GROUNDS SECURITY

Once students have been safely delivered to their classrooms, schools are responsible for not only the security and safety of students, but also that of faculty, staff, school grounds, buildings, and building contents. As a result, security concerns are bifurcated into physical security (e.g., building design, hardware, and technology) and safety policies and procedures (e.g., supervision and discipline).

The physical protection of school facilities spans a variety of security dimensions, including building design and layout, playground enclosures, locks, outdoor lighting, faculty and staff parking, and technology (see Appendix E). As a practical matter, as well as from a cost/benefit perspective, design and layout are most significant and effective in the planning stages of a new school's construction. Making changes on plans and specifications to ensure the incorporation of security and safety measures is far less expensive than retrofitting once construction is complete. In fact, the cost of retrofitting is often prohibitive, meaning that corrective action will be minimal or nonexistent.

Crime prevention through environmental design (CPTED), a concept first introduced by criminologist C. Ray Jeffery and architect Oscar Newman in the early 1970s, emphasizes the planning and utilization of built environment so as to limit opportunities for crime, violence, and disorder.[4] As applied to school settings, CPTED includes such tactics as:

- Structuring physical space, in terms of walls, windows, and doors, to maximize sight lines for routine monitoring of activity
- Using open layouts and lighting to minimize the number of dark, secluded areas
- Landscaping school grounds to restrict access to places that are not routinely supervised
- Decorating classrooms and hallways to promote a sense of comfort and orderliness
- Maintaining a clean environment, free of graffiti and other signs of chaos and disarray

Simple but effective strategies such as these, combined with technology and the involvement of individuals in the security effort, can and should be considered to enhance the safety of the school environment, both indoors and outdoors. Whatever measures are taken to provide a secure setting should not detract from the core mission of schools—to maintain an environment that is conducive to learning.

PLAYGROUND SECURITY AND SAFETY

In determining the most appropriate physical security measures, school officials should begin at the outermost edge of the property line, which is often defined by an adjacent playground. To enhance security, playgrounds should be enclosed, if feasible. Although enclosing a school playground for security reasons does not ordinarily pose a problem, choosing the type of enclosure to use can prove more difficult. Schools should consider the cost of installation and maintenance, and, since there exists a variety of material choices, aesthetics need not be ignored. A six- or seven-foot-high chain link fence is relatively inexpensive, easy to maintain, and not aesthetically offensive, making it a common feature of elementary school playgrounds. Alternatively, a brick or stone wall of similar height is also easy to maintain. The school's surroundings are, naturally, the most important factors in this decision, but it is nonetheless important to avoid the appearance of a penal colony.

Enclosures are intended to keep unwanted people outside the playground and students safely within, so prescriptions related to school access control depend on the intended use of the playground. If the playground is for the exclusive use of the school's students, a full enclosure with access through the school building's entrance is preferred. Because this type of enclosure denies access to the playground directly from the street, the students are better protected against contact with sexual predators, drug dealers, and kidnappers. In addition, the full enclosure helps prevent students from wandering off by themselves and creating a "lost child" crisis. However, the enclosure must have a secured gate that can be opened by a faculty or staff member in the event of an emergency within the building that necessitates evacuating the playground.

Because third parties are not the only cause of security and safety problems, merely monitoring access to the playground is not enough to protect the children. Indeed, students themselves are the most common source of security and safety issues. As a result, they should be supervised by faculty or staff when at play. In addition, their well-being can be enhanced by using closed circuit television (CCTV) to monitor playground activity.

While playgrounds may be accessible through the school building, it is critical that there be additional points of access in the event of a fire or other emergency. In addition, it may be necessary to provide a means for community utilization of the playground facility when school is not in session. As a consequence, however, access from the street will be possible at any time, including periods when students are present, and this increases student exposure to harm. Although it is unrealistic to expect that all unauthorized access can be prevented, risks can be mitigated by having only one additional opening in the enclosure coupled with the use of a turnstile. Even so, during school hours, access to the playground should be restricted to students, faculty, and staff.

Where there are playgrounds, there are usually swings, slides, and jungle-gyms, exposing students to a substantial risk of injury. Adult supervision of playground activities can certainly increase student safety. However, this does not absolve the school or school district of its duty to ensure that all playground equipment and installations meet the highest safety standards both at time of purchase and with regard to their continued maintenance.

BUILDING SECURITY

Building security primarily involves safeguarding the students, faculty, staff, their personal property, and the school's assets within the school structure. Thanks to modern building codes and the standards required to conform to the Occupational Safety and Health Act (OSHA), some safety features must be incorporated in a school's construction. For example, a combination of building codes and OSHA requirements ensure that smoke detectors and sprinklers or other fire suppression systems are installed, and that there is a proper number of emergency exits based on structure size. The use of fire retardant materials in construction may also be mandated by code.

But there are other important loss prevention mechanisms that concern the school building. One source of loss may result from having to replace broken windows caused by acts of vandalism or by playground accidents, and repeated incidents can prove a considerable drain on the school's resources. Using an unbreakable or shatterproof substitute for traditional glass can prove to be more cost-effective in the long run.

School buildings can have hundreds of doors—whether to classrooms, offices, storage, or other spaces—that require locking. Standard key-operated locks have inherent weaknesses, including key loss or duplication. It is important, therefore, to prevent the unauthorized duplication of keys and to replace locks whose keys are lost. In addition, schools can employ patented key systems, for which manufacturers selectively limit the distribution of key blanks, cylinders, and locksets only to certain locksmiths based on reputation and location, thereby reducing the risk of unauthorized duplication. Another related concern is that keys can be passed on to other faculty or staff members without informing the "keymaster" for record-keeping purposes. Keys should only be issued to those faculty or staff members who have a genuine need for them; status alone is not sufficient justification.

Be it for an existing building or new construction, alternative solutions can overcome the shortcomings of traditional locks and keys. The best and, incidentally, the most cost-effective overall protection would be to install an integrated building management system that incorporates a computerized card reader access control system, CCTV, safety and intrusion alarms, and heating, ventilating, and air conditioning controls.

Despite the ultimate savings to be realized from such an installation, some boards of education may feel that the cost and possible disruption associated with retrofitting an existing facility is more than they want to incur. In this case, a computerized card reader access control system should be installed in lieu of the "whole package." Cards issued to faculty and staff could contain photo identification and be worn at all times throughout the work day, and this, in turn, would facilitate detecting the presence of unauthorized persons on a playground or in the building.

Although they provide less protection than card reader systems, combination locks (with a key override in case of emergency) on all doors to protected areas, including the school's entrances, are more effective than a simple key-operated system. To maintain the highest level of security in this case, personnel who are given combinations must be warned against giving the codes to others, and combinations should be changed routinely and as needed.

The design and layout of elementary school buildings can either contribute to or detract from security, and cannot be divorced from certain access control considerations. However, this poses another challenge for school security: How can the school provide reasonable protection for students, faculty, staff, and assets and yet avoid the appearance of a correctional institution? Emphasis should be on the word "reasonable," since a balance must be struck between security interests on one hand and the need for a suitable learning environment on the other.

From a design perspective, the relationship of security and access control is mediated by two factors: the number of ways in which the building can be entered and the school's office location. The former has significant bearing on the latter. Although both state/local building codes and OSHA standards specify a minimum number of emergency exits for all buildings, architects must go beyond the minimum with respect to the number of exits from a school. These exits should be located to ensure a speedy and orderly evacuation. Moreover, building codes and OSHA standards do not require emergency exits to be means of ingress, and, indeed, the school building should have only one entrance. Incorrect interpretations of the codes and standards may result in multiple entrances, which could be detrimental to school security.

So-called "panic hardware" or "crash bars" tend to be the type of lock found on most school emergency doors; pushing the bar immediately opens the door. Because these doors allow people to leave the building unnoticed and enable students, faculty, and staff to let others into the building without authorization, it is recommended that all emergency exits be secured with alarmed fire locks that have OSHA or local fire department approval. These locks prevent unauthorized access and departure without interfering with a rapid evacuation in an emergency. Security can be further improved by installing one or more strategically placed CCTV pan-and-tilt cameras in all-weather housings on the rooftop, enabling office or other school personnel to monitor the building's entrances.

Schools are best served when all access to the building is through a single entry point located near the school's main office. Clear and prominently displayed signs should direct all visitors (parents included) to check in at the main office. To help enforce this requirement, glass panels instead of opaque walls should be installed around the office to facilitate easy observation of the entry door.

Whether additional security is needed depends on the nature and prevalence of the school's past security problems. If access cannot be controlled solely by the school office, a combination of hardware and technology is the most practical solution. One possible combination calls for the installation of a CCTV camera outside the building's entrance to view approaching visitors, a telephone to enable them to be connected directly (and only) to the office, and an automated lock on the outermost door that can be deactivated from within the office when access is granted.

Regardless of the access control measures, no visitors—including parents—should be allowed to roam the halls or enter classrooms when school is in session. If they have come for a parent-teacher conference, the teacher should meet them at the main office and escort them to an office or classroom; when the meeting is over, visitors should be escorted back to the main office. In all other instances, visitors should be restricted to the school's main office. All visitors should be signed in on arrival with their name, the date, the time, and the reason for their visit, and they should be signed out on departure.

Clear procedures should exist for taking a child out of school while classes are in session. It must be a basic and firm rule that the child is not allowed to leave the building with an adult unless that person can prove to the principal or school authority that he or she is either that child's parent or legal guardian or is acting on their behalf. Regardless of reason, schools should not release a child to a noncustodial parent, grandparent, sibling, neighbors, or anyone other than a custodial parent/guardian of record unless a parent or legal guardian has been called to obtain authorization. When approved, the dismissal should be fully documented, including the names of the child and his or her escort, as well as the date, time, and reason.

CHILD ABDUCTION

Special dismissal protocols are particularly critical for preschools and elementary schools in light of the vulnerability of young children to abduction by strangers or noncustodial parents. Elementary schools may also need to implement procedures to prevent children from being driven away in the wrong vehicle during the after-school pick-up process. Even though the likelihood of child abduction from a school is relatively low, the potential consequences can be major. Finkelhor, Hammer, and Sedlak estimated that only about 5 percent of the nearly 60,000 nonfamily child abductions reported in the United States during 1999—abductions for at least one hour by either acquaintances or strangers—involved a victim being kidnapped from school or day-care.[5] The same research team estimated that roughly 7 percent of the approximately 200,000 children abducted in 1999 by unauthorized family members—most often noncustodial fathers—were taken from schools, preschools, or day-care facilities.[6]

Despite the safety of schools compared to sidewalks, yards, playgrounds, and parking lots, there apparently still are several thousand abductions from schools each year—some by strangers, more by acquaintances, and most by family members. Fortunately, the overwhelming majority of children—as high as 99 percent—are recovered alive. Still, the high rate of recovery hardly alleviates the anxiety that many parents feel as they drop their youngsters off at the bus stop or school door.

PROTECTION OF RECORDS AND ASSETS

Although the protection of students, faculty, and staff is undoubtedly the school's top security priority, the fact remains that with school budgets notoriously underfunded, no school district can afford to leave its personal and real assets unsecured. The building is protected primarily on the basis of its construction and its compliance with state and local codes and OSHA standards. However, security goes beyond protecting real estate. Failure to safeguard records, as well as a school's personal property—including both expendable and nonexpendable assets—can lead to embarrassment and an avoidable loss.

Records Protection

Record keeping, on one medium or another, is a critical school function, as schools must maintain personnel and student files, as well as records pertaining to school assets. Statutory or other legal requirements may dictate the length of time for which certain kinds of records must be retained and kept safe. Moreover, personnel with record access must be trained in matters of privacy and confidentiality.

Although the particular type of record storage is dictated by the medium used, there should always be off-site backup of all records. If hard copies are maintained, these backups should be kept in steel file cabinets; whether they should be stored in an insulated container depends on the degree of importance. If the backups are in electronic form, protection against heat, humidity, and magnetic fields may be needed.

Proper protection of records necessitates a policy that designates those specific individuals with access authority and establishes measures of accountability. For instance, it should not be presumed that all faculty members are automatically entitled to access records. Permission should be based on a legitimate "need to know," rather than a person's status. To ensure compliance with the policy, the principal or head of the school should entrust a minimum number of office personnel to make records available to others.

Whenever records are released, they should be replaced with an insert in the storage receptacle indicating the borrower's name and the date. With few exceptions, released records should not be retained overnight, and, to this end, file cabinets or other storage containers should be checked for inserts before the end of the school day.

Protecting Other Assets

Cost-benefit considerations dictate that expendable assets should be treated differently than nonexpendable property. Whereas imposing a system of controls over expendable assets is acceptable in a corporate environment, such a system might be onerous and not particularly cost-effective for schools. This is especially true in the primary grades, where expendables include such things as paper, pens, pencils, chalk, and erasers. Still, asset controls should not be ignored altogether just because the primary grades are involved; instead, a certain degree of compromise with standard management practice may be appropriate.

The inventory of expendables should be kept in a locked space. As with the authorized release of records, only one or two members of the staff should be allowed to issue expendables to teachers or their aides when needed. Moreover, requisitions for supplies should be reviewed monthly to avoid shortages as well as to identify any consistent but suspicious patterns that would suggest possible abuse of the requisition system.

Protecting nonexpendable items—such as furniture, computers, copying machines, and other office equipment—is somewhat more difficult, because inventory is typically handled at the school district level through a central purchasing office. Immediately on receipt at the central supply, nonexpendable property should be affixed with bar-coded asset tags, and each item, its serial number (if applicable), and its tag identifier should be recorded.

Apart from the specific allocation designated by the school district, nonexpendable assets should be distributed to schools only in response to prenumbered requisitions. Delivery should be made using pre-numbered bills of lading that include all of the asset's identifying data. Furthermore, signed receipts acknowledging arrival of property at the school should be obtained. The recipient school, in turn, should retain its copy of the delivery ticket and note in which classrooms, laboratories, or offices the nonexpendable assets can be found. If any of these assets are disposed of or otherwise displaced, the changes should be recorded.

Using this information, and in accordance with its security policies, each school should take an inventory of its nonexpendable assets at least semi-annually. Doing so will ensure that the assets are both accounted for and where they should be.

FIELD TRIPS

Though an important part of the grade school learning experience, field trips have the potential to create a wide range of safety problems if not carefully and thoughtfully planned. To minimize risk, school administrators, teachers, and aides must understand that, beyond destination and means of transportation, field trip security is crucially affected by other variables such as age group and class size, length of trip in terms of time and distance, and student exposure to strangers.

Certain basic factors should be considered in planning and carrying out field trips, including the length of time needed to travel to and from the destination, and the form and provider of the transportation. The number of teachers and aides (and possibly parent chaperones) necessary to protect the children adequately depends on the age group, class size, and risk of exposure to strangers or other potential threats. For example, more oversight or supervision may be appropriate for children in the lower grades visiting an open-air site, such as a zoo, than for older students going to a museum.

Transportation

Once the field trip's destination has been chosen, parental consent has been attained, any necessary permits have been acquired, and, where appropriate, arrangements for authoritative guides have been made, transportation needs must be addressed. These decisions can be quite complex. Each mode of transportation (e.g., walking, public transportation, school or charter buses) is associated with its own unique security considerations. Whatever the means of travel, school officials must ensure that there will be an adequate number of adults accompanying the group. There is no alternative for responsible adult supervision when it comes to providing for student security and safety. What constitutes an appropriate number of adults must be decided on a case by case basis, taking into account the number of participating students, their ages, and what their teachers and aides know about their individual needs or personalities.

Some might assume that lower-grade students require more adult chaperones due to their immaturity and need for assistance and supervision. But to expect that older students are more responsible can be dangerously naïve. Fifth- or sixth-grade students may be more adventurous and apt to wander off on their own. Regardless of age group, school officials must consider whether there are any students in need of special attention based on known behavioral issues or other circumstances.

Excursions to destinations within walking distance of the school are deceptively difficult to plan. Beyond the usual considerations (e.g., child age, size of group, etc.), the logistics must account for the number of blocks to be traveled and streets to be crossed, the time of day, and whether vehicular traffic is expected to be light or heavy.

Public transportation is generally the least desirable means of travel, although there are situations in which this may be the only available option. The concerns associated with walking trips might still apply, if the children must travel to and from the bus or subway stop on foot. However, no matter the number of adults available for the trip, the risks of public transportation can be insurmountable, and the ability to control a group of children can be unavoidably compromised. Students could become distracted and intentionally or unintentionally get separated from the group. Participating students must therefore be instructed—if not quizzed—on what to do in this situation, including where to go and whom to approach for assistance.

Notwithstanding the cautions noted earlier, school buses are, by far, the preferred means of transporting students on field trips. A trusting relationship with a bus driver does not, however, absolve or mitigate the need for an adequate number of adult chaperones. In fact, when students feel especially comfortable with drivers and chaperones, they may be more inclined to misbehave. Whatever mode of travel is chosen—walking, public transportation, or school bus—the importance of accounting for all participants at all times during a field trip cannot be overemphasized. Supervising faculty should rely on both a student buddy system and frequent head counts throughout the course of the excursion.

Distant and Overnight Trips

Distant travel may make it advisable, or even necessary, to obtain both the vehicle and driver through a charter bus company. When doing so, it is not sufficient to rely on the charter company's reputation alone. That the company is properly registered with and licensed to do business by the appropriate authorities—whether state, federal, or both—must be verified. The company must be fully, rather than minimally, insured and a valid certificate of coverage should be obtained from its insurance agent or provider before any agreement is signed. It is equally important to verify the charter's safety record and make sure that the company is financially sound.

Overnight excursions carry increased security risks, and therefore demand extra effort in planning. In addition to transportation and oversight responsibilities, overnight trips must consider food and housing needs for students and chaperones. Reservations for accommodations must be made well in advance to ensure the availability of a contiguous block of rooms, so that adult staff can maintain proper control at all times. Under-supervised children who show no regard for other guests or for the hotel's property will diminish the school's reputation and may significantly add to the trip's cost should property be damaged.

Finally, overnight or extended field trips involve additional safety concerns related to health. The school must obtain from parents any relevant medical information about their children, including food and environmental allergies. The trip leaders should control custody of all medications and be provided with specific instructions for their use, as well as physician and emergency contact numbers.

LOST CHILDREN

A lost or missing child is a nightmare for both a child's family and the school personnel who are responsible for that youngster's well-being. Although at greatest risk when away on field trips, students can go missing at any time and in a variety of ways, including situations in which students disappear from a playground during recess or are unaccounted for when they should be in class.

Given the special vulnerability of playgrounds, it is not enough to depend on limited access and CCTV monitoring. Teachers or other staff members must be physically present to oversee the children's activities and reduce the risk of students being lost or injured. Schools should not rely solely on CCTV monitoring because it does not allow for an immediate response to an emergency situation observed on camera. Response time is particularly critical if there is direct access between the playground and the street.

When it appears that a child is lost, both the parents and the police must be notified immediately. Parents should be asked for details regarding the youngster's clothing when he or she left for school. In addition to a full physical description, information about any special needs in the way of medication, allergies, or illness should also be obtained. If there is reason to believe that the child left in the company of a third party, the police should be provided with any available descriptive information about that individual and, if applicable, his or her vehicle. Ideally, the police should be provided with a recent photograph of the child.

DISRUPTIVE CHILDREN

Disruptive children not only annoy their classmates and divert the time and attention of their teachers, but they can potentially present a security problem as well. A determination of what issues or events prompted a particular student to misbehave can often lead to a logical and direct solution. Misconduct can be the result of boredom—the absence of a challenge or intellectual stimulation, lack of interest in subject matter, or too much time with too little to do. Misbehavior can also reflect a weak emotional attachment to school, suggesting that teachers and other staff members might use extra attention and praise to increase the child's connection to the school environment.[7]

When assessing the precipitants of misbehavior, it is important to consider not only the personal characteristics and background of the disruptive youngster, but also the total classroom environment, taking into account other students and faculty members alike. Although disruptions are often created by an individual student, classroom chaos can also reflect group behavior. Considering the source of trouble—individual or group—will help determine the best response to each case.

In some instances, a student's disruptive behavior may be linked to a learning disability or to some other medical or emotional condition. The school may have some role in handling these issues, but the responsibility is primarily that of the child's parents and outside health care providers. Although parents are often crucial in dealing with health-related issues, it is possible that the child's behavior stems from physical or emotional abuse at home. If this is suspected, state laws require school personnel to report their concerns to the proper authorities.

Attempts by teachers and administrators to change the pattern of misconduct of chronically disruptive children are often to no avail. Children who remain a potential threat to the security and safety of others must be disciplined appropriately. The range of possible sanctions is quite broad, from having the child sit apart from the class to sending him or her to the principal's office, and from depriving the student of certain privileges to suspension or expulsion. The degree of punishment should be proportionate to the severity of the misconduct in order that the child is not alienated and the behavior not exacerbated by excessively harsh sanctioning. Whatever the approach, fairness and uniformity are essential: The same punishment must be given for the same offense, regardless of the student, although sanctions can appropriately be enhanced in light of the child's previous history of misconduct or reduced if mitigating circumstances exist.

There are moral, if not legal, limits to the manner in which teachers should respond to disruptive behavior by a student. Although the sorry days of corporal punishment are largely and thankfully gone, episodes still occur from time to time in which teachers take control much too forcefully. A 2009 report from the U.S. Government Accountability Office (GAO) found hundreds of cases since 1990 alleging physical abuse and even death related to over-aggressive school discipline involving the use of restraints or seclusion.[8] The more egregious incidents uncovered by the GAO study included a 5-year-old who suffered a broken arm after reportedly being tied to a chair with cords and duct tape by a teacher and, worse still, a 7-year-old who died apparently after being held face down by a school staff member for several hours.

Unfortunately, there currently exists no federal law prohibiting the use of restraints on students, even though school personnel have been prosecuted for injurious outcomes. However, in the wake of the GAO findings, several advocacy groups, such as Florida Families Against Restraint and Seclusion, are hoping for Congressional action to prevent such abuses in the future.

FIGHTING

Exceptionally disruptive and chronic misbehavior often results in fighting among students; this most often takes place on the playground, but a significant share of incidents can occur within the classroom or elsewhere in the school building. In addition, the time period just after the school day ends—when many children are unsupervised and restless from having been cooped up in class-rooms—is particularly problematic. In fact, according to police statistics, nearly half of violent incidents involving school-age children occur during the few hours after school, a consistent pattern that has been called the "prime time for juvenile crime."[9] Even when fighting occurs after school lets out, the source of conflict often stems from issues that arose during school. School officials, therefore, have a responsibility to confront and resolve disputes among students, even if the combatants settle matters elsewhere. Indeed, the potential for injury or death inherent in fighting exists at all grade levels, whether the fight is between two individual students or between two rival gangs.

The extent to which fights can be prevented or their effects mitigated depends on whether a school's administration is attuned to what transpires between and among students. The administration's powers of observation provide it with a form of intelligence collection that can help in controlling the escalation of conflict, if not in actually preventing fights. In addition, efforts to prevent and control fighting depend on the degree to which playgrounds and other high-incident locations (e.g., bathrooms, cafeteria, etc.) are supervised. Through observations as well as conversations with involved students, teachers and administrators can try to prevent fighting and attempt to find a peaceful resolution.

The most critical question for school administrators is whether weapons are likely to be used in a fight. The "weapon" of choice is typically just words—name-calling or "trash talk"—or even fists. Although shouting and shoving matches remain commonplace, the escalation to knives or firearms is a source of concern for all school administrators.

Although it may be impossible to eradicate the problem of student fighting completely, much can be done to reduce its frequency and effects. The strategy should emphasize the importance of faculty and staff getting to know the students well enough to recognize the subtle warning signs that a fight might be brewing. Observant faculty and staff should also try to identify who the likely targets are and, with the administration's help, should make every effort to keep belligerent and targeted students separated both in class and during activities periods.

If, despite the best efforts of the administration, a fight does take place, the combatants must first be separated, and then bystanders must be dispersed, for their very presence can encourage the fighting to continue or escalate. Administrators should determine precisely what caused the fight and who initiated it, so that discipline is meted out in proportion to each child's actions. If possible, school authorities should determine whether the fight was provoked or unprovoked. If the fight caused significant injury or involved the use of weapons other than fists, the punishment should be severe and swift. Appropriate disciplinary actions can consist of a stern lecture, denial of privileges, suspension for a period of time, expulsion, or, in rare cases, turning the child over to law enforcement authorities. As appropriate, parents should be informed about the incident and involved in the effort to prevent a recurrence.

PREHABILITATION AND LIFE SKILLS

Despite the emphasis in recent years on safety and security, many schools remain chaotic places where some undisciplined students enjoy free rein. Though trying their best to respond, teachers and administrators often feel overwhelmed. Three-quarters of educators surveyed in 2004 by Public Agenda, a New York opinion research organization, said they would be more effective in teaching if they did not have to spend so much time dealing with misbehavior and disruption.[10] Overall, they felt ill-prepared and unwilling to be a "cop with chalk." In addition, almost 40 percent of elementary school faculty members indicated that student misbehavior interferes with their ability to teach the curriculum, according to survey data from the National Center for Education Statistics.[11]

As early as preschool and the elementary grades, students need to be taught the skills needed for survival and success in real life, skills that many have not acquired. Teaching social skills must be a priority for public education, arguably as important as grades and test scores. The challenge is that many teachers are not trained in how to coach these social skills. Many do not see how important the connection is between teaching such skills and teaching academics. In many school districts, the emphasis for professional teacher development is on helping them to elevate their students' academic abilities. Teachers cannot teach if the children aren't prepared to learn. Children must be taught fundamental life skills in the same sequential and straightforward way they are taught the alphabet and the number line.

Based on the Response to Intervention (RTI) model, elementary school education increasingly looks to blend academic and social development through a multi-tiered approach. Broad-based interventions are designed to reach all students, layered on which are more targeted interventions for needier students and intensive, individualized interventions for those with greatest need.[12] When the RTI approach is used in the teaching of academics, the goal is to reduce the number of children referred to special education. When the focus is on social and emotional skills, RTI aims to reduce the number of incidents of disorder as well as suspensions and expulsions.

Although the rate of violence—especially acts of serious violence—in the elementary grades is considerably lower than that for the secondary school level, lowers grades are hardly invulnerable. In fact, as many as 13 percent of the students expelled during the 2003/2004 academic year for bringing a gun to school were in elementary school.[13] Moreover, according to a Yale University study, pre-kindergarten students are expelled at a much higher rate than their older counterparts in grades K–12, although the criteria for exclusion may be very different for pre-kindergarten given that enrollment is not mandatory.[14]

Clearly, violence prevention and intervention are an essential component to the early education curriculum—"prehabilitation" early on is preferable to rehabilitation down the line. However, these programs must be developmentally appropriate in design. For example, asking first graders repeatedly to use self-control will accomplish nothing if they don't comprehend the concept. Thus, the language of skills development must begin with helping children to understand and make tangible such tools as cooperation, self-control, self-confidence, problem solving, and responsibility.

These important social/developmental skills are integrated in the Lesson One's ABCs for Life curriculum through the principle that young children learn more from actual experience than from verbal explanation.[15] Accordingly, the curriculum offers students a variety of challenges, through activity, to help them internalize social skills. For example, one exercise has the teacher blow bubbles in front of young children, telling them to use their self-control to resist the temptation to break them. A simple activity like this can generalize into not touching a gun, alcohol, cigarettes, and avoiding a confrontation with a bully. It also gives children a point of reference for what it feels like to use the skill of self-control. In this way, they can develop an alternative response to frustration, besides disruption or worse—violence. Also, teachers, as role models, lead by sharing their own experiences with their students and encourage them to do the same, thereby promoting a sense of community within the classroom.

All adults, both teachers and parents, can teach skills such as self-control, responsibility, and cooperation to children through defining, discussing, and helping them experience the skills. Similar in emphasis to the Lesson One program, Gilbert Botvin of Cornell University has developed a drug and violence prevention curriculum centered on teaching elementary and middle school children various life skills, such as stress management, communication, friendship development, and assertiveness.[16]

Regardless of the specific program elements, the most critical feature of the Lesson One and Botvin curricula is their relevance to elementary school age children—prevention that highlights the prefix "pre." While it would be ill-advised to give up on a seemingly recalcitrant adolescent, the greatest opportunity for positive change comes with a focus on children in grade school—those who are young and impressionable and will be impressed with what a teacher or some other authority figure has to say. It is well-known that early prevention—during grade school, if not earlier—can carry the greatest and most lasting impact, before a youngster is seduced by gangs, drugs, and crime.

Blending life skills with academics can benefit all children. Of special concern are those youngsters whose blank expressions mask years of pain—those who have been bullied, physically abused, or mentally scarred to the point that they are indeed a danger to themselves and others. These are the children who, without warning, might someday grab a gun and start shooting or otherwise erupt in unforeseen rage. Emphasizing violence reduction in the elementary grades does much more than enhance the school climate for young children. Just as importantly, it serves a carry-over effect, mitigating the levels of violence and disorder once these same children reach middle and high school.

8

SECURITY IN SECONDARY SCHOOLS

In some respects, the safety and security challenges for secondary schools—middle schools and high schools—are comparable to those that primary schools confront. For example, many students in middle school and even high school still commute by school bus, and so the same transportation security criteria established for the primary grades would apply. In addition, designing physical structures and spaces so as to limit vulnerabilities to crime and enhance routine supervision remains a wise approach for secondary school security.

Notwithstanding the seamless extension of certain school security principles and practices, not all measures applicable to elementary schools can be modified and adopted for middle schools and high schools given some fundamental differences between the school environments and populations. Elementary schools almost invariably consist of one building, and the size of the student body tends to be relatively small. As a consequence, access to the building is, or can be, limited to a single entry point. Moreover, playgrounds controlled by elementary schools tend to adjoin the building. Junior and senior high schools, by their very nature, have much larger student bodies. Consequently, larger buildings, if not multiple buildings, are needed to accommodate the student body size, and this typically necessitates more than a single school entrance to expedite the flow of pedestrian traffic. Junior and senior high schools may share a unified campus, or each may each have its own. Instead of playgrounds, many middle schools and especially high schools have athletic fields of various sizes that are often adjacent to the school and thus part of the campus.

The expanded variety of courses taught in the upper grades requires greater investment in the school's personal property. Much more is involved than protecting laptops or other computers, furniture, gym equipment and erasers from being stolen. Upper-level schools must also protect various kinds of laboratory equipment, and supplies, some of which may be hazardous or even toxic.

Extracurricular activities are also more varied in the upper grades, especially in high schools. This usually means that school-owned and school-provided goods such as musical instruments, athletic equipment, and uniforms need protection against loss. If a school's personal assets are not adequately protected, replacement costs can prove to be a major unanticipated expense, impacting negatively on other areas of the school budget.

Because most elementary schools are typically small and located in residential neighborhoods, they do not generally require much parking space. To accommodate faculty and staff who drive to school, a parking lot secured by closed circuit television (CCTV) can usually be established at minimal cost. At the junior and senior high school levels, however, providing secured parking can be more of a challenge. High school campuses are often most easily accessible by automobile, and so larger staff and student populations—combined with the increasing numbers of students who drive to school in today's society—necessitate much more campus parking and increased focus on traffic safety.

Although it is an advantage that students in upper grades are older and able to assume greater personal responsibility, they are in some respects more vulnerable to temptation and at greater risk. For example, alcohol consumption and drug use are more likely to be serious issues at middle schools and high schools than at lower-level schools. Despite laws and law enforcement efforts, drug dealers may see middle schools and high schools as fertile ground for expanding their market shares. Furthermore, bullying, weapons, and gang activity are far more likely to emerge as problems in middle schools and high schools than in grade schools. And as students grow older, and in some cases bolder, discipline may be harder to enforce.

EXPANDED SECURITY ISSUES

Between mid-August and the end of the following June, it is a rare day when the news media does not report on a school security-related incident of one sort or another. For example, in February 2008, while most Americans and media outlets were focused on the hotly contested Presidential-nomination races, two school shootings brought attention back to the all-too-familiar problem of high school violence: One student critically wounded another during an argument in gym class at Mitchell High School in Memphis, Tennessee;[1] in Oxnard, California, a 14-year-old junior high school student shot and killed a 15-year-old classmate.[2] Then, months later, in August 2008, a student shot and killed a 15-year-old classmate at Knoxville, Tennessee's Central High School.[3]

Of course, fatal and nonfatal shootings are hardly the only manifestations of school security problems. Also in February 2008, an apparent hate crime was under investigation at the prestigious St. Paul's School in Concord, New Hampshire, after threatening letters were received by most of the school's black students.[4] In May 2008, a campus-wide brawl at Locke High School in Los Angeles, involving an estimated 600 students, forced the school officials to shut down the building and keep students in their classrooms until the police managed to seize control of the situation.[5]

Middle school and high school administrators around the country have employed a wide range of strategic initiatives—both technology and supervision—to help address existing security problems. Survey data gathered from students in middle and high schools nationwide demonstrate the pervasiveness of security and the extent to which their daily lives and movements while at school are monitored and controlled. Table 8.1 summarizes responses solicited from students ages 12 to 18 concerning the use of different security measures, estimated from the bi-annual school supplement of the National Crime Victimization Survey (NCVS). Several approaches are quite commonplace in America's secondary schools, including visitor sign-in requirements, codes of conduct, and hallway monitoring by staff, all of which are indicated by at least 90 percent of respondents. Locked entrances/exits, security cameras, security guards or police presence, and locker checks are all confirmed by a majority of students in the survey. By contrast, neither metal detectors nor student photo IDs/badges are as prevalent as other security strategies, although both appear with some regularity.

As a cautionary note, the NCVS is designed to be representative of the nation's student population—rather than the nation's schools. Schools with large student enrollments would tend to be reflected more in the statistical results. Thus, to the extent that school security may vary by school size, the findings would be distorted. Notwithstanding this methodological caveat, schools across America have clearly responded aggressively to the perceived need for security.

The pattern over time in the increased utilization of these various measures indicates very clearly that the concern for school security is hardly temporary or transitory. Even though years have passed since the Columbine massacre and other similar school shootings, the extensiveness of security in junior and senior high schools has not diminished. To the contrary, certain measures have only become more widespread. In all likelihood, security will remain a fundamental part of school life, with the emphasis on assessing the effectiveness and sufficiency of various strategies.

Although the Columbine massacre prompted greater use of such security measures as surveillance cameras and police patrols, it is noteworthy and ironic that Columbine High School had both a camera system and a School Resource Officer (SRO) at the time of the shooting spree. In fact, the cameras were able to capture graphic images of the gunmen stalking their victims in the school cafeteria, but did nothing to avert the tragedy. In addition, the armed officer on duty was hardly able to be at all places at all times in the sprawling high school populated by some 1,900 students. While these and other security measures may enhance the overall safety and well-being of the students and staff, they should never be viewed as an infallible safeguard against criminal activity. In fact, the presence of various safety measures can occasionally challenge a disgruntled student to prove he or she can outmaneuver the administration by breaching security. A fiercely determined student wishing to wreak havoc can usually find a way to do so, despite the best efforts of school administrators to discourage violence. For example, 16-year-old Jeffrey Weise shot and killed a security guard who was monitoring the metal detector at the entrance to his school in Red Lake, Minnesota, and then easily passed through the device and murdered five students and a teacher inside the building. In Jonesboro, Arkansas, 13-year-old Mitchell Johnson and 11-year-old Andrew Golden set off the fire alarm at their middle school and then waited with loaded guns in the nearby woods and ambushed their classmates and faculty as they fled the building.

ACCESS CONTROL AND MONITORING

The principle articulated previously with regard to elementary schools—that physical security and access control begin at the property line—holds true for junior and senior high schools, notwithstanding the differences in building design and layout. Nevertheless, every school is unique, and therefore must

Table 8.1
Percentage of students ages 12–18 reporting various school security measures

Security measure	2001	2003	2005	2007
Metal detectors	8.7%	10.1%	10.7%	10.1%
Locker checks	53.5%	53.0%	52.9%	53.6%
Security cameras to monitor the school	38.5%	47.9%	57.6%	66.0%
Security guards and/or assigned police officers	63.6%	69.6%	67.9%	68.8%
Other staff/adult supervision in the hallway	88.3%	90.6%	89.8%	90.0%
Students required to wear badges or picture ID	21.2%	22.5%	24.7%	24.3%
A code of student conduct	95.1%	95.3%	95.1%	95.9%
Locked entrance or exit doors during the day	48.8%	52.8%	54.2%	60.9%
A requirement that visitors sign in	90.2%	91.7%	92.7%	94.3%

Source: Bureau of Justice Statistics, National Crime Victimization Survey, School Crime Supplement, 2001–2007.

evaluate its own needs and vulnerabilities before appropriate steps to enhance security and safety can be identified.

Thus, the first stage in implementing an effective school security program is to establish means for controlling and monitoring access. Access control is a vital part of every security or loss prevention program, and it can benefit from the appropriate use of technology and hardware. However, unless the control system is itself subject to some system of monitoring, it will provide little more than a false sense of security.

School Grounds

As a general rule, the preferred approach for controlling access to school grounds is to enclose the property, limit the number of entry points, and employ gates or turnstiles. Cost considerations aside, however, these measures may not be feasible and, more importantly, they ignore the importance of campus surveillance and monitoring. In practice, appropriate strategies for grounds security depend on whether and how the school property is utilized when school is not in session (i.e., during evening hours, weekends, or vacation periods).

A cost-effective approach to after-hours security can generally be achieved through a combination of high-resolution cameras in all-weather housings, high-density lighting, and recording equipment held in a secure office. A regular review of the recordings will reveal any suspicious activities or security vulnerabilities. If concerns arise, copies of the recorded images can then be provided to police or other agencies for the identification of possible trespassers and the determination of an appropriate response.

When the grounds are being used by students or other authorized groups, cameras and recording equipment must be supplemented by on-campus security personnel. If the grounds are enclosed, staff members are best deployed at the points of entry; otherwise, patrolling may be necessary. The number and type of staff members needed are largely determined by the nature of the after-school activities taking place. For example, faculty and staff, assisted by students, often suffice to control and monitor athletic events that tend to draw small crowds of spectators. However, when larger turnouts are expected, as might be the case with a football game against an archrival school, it may be advisable to enlist police presence.

School Buildings

In general, decisions regarding access must balance security and convenience while sacrificing neither. When protecting middle school and high school buildings, the large size of both the student population and the structures themselves typically make it impractical or impossible to limit access to just one entry point. Based on these size factors, the absolute minimum number of entrances should be determined. By contrast, the multiple exit points required by building codes and OSHA standards can routinely be kept locked, except for during emergency evacuations.

Although cameras and recording equipment can be useful in controlling and monitoring access to buildings, they are insufficient for protecting both people and property within the walls of the school. Therefore, after determining the number of entrance points needed, the school should assess other means of access control to supplement monitoring with cameras. Many schools have chosen to require coded photo identification badges for all faculty, staff, and students; other schools have gone so far as to install electronic card readers at building entrances. The imbedded codes in identification cards (which can be changed as needed) can be programmed to control the days and hours that cardholders have access to specific buildings, particular offices, rooms, and other secure areas on campus. When cards are reported lost or stolen or become obsolete, they can be deleted from the database to maintain the integrity of the security system.

Whether card-insert or proximity-type card readers are used, they can provide valuable monitoring data, especially if there is evidence of unauthorized attempts to access buildings or spaces within them. From a cost-benefit perspective, installing card readers is a one-time capital outlay that is far less expensive than employing personnel to control and monitor access. To accommodate occasional visits from parents or other individuals, the entryway camera and direct telephone system recommended earlier for elementary schools can serve the same purpose for secondary schools.

All exterior entrances (and most interior doors as well) should be equipped with suitable locks. On a routine basis, these devices protect people as well as assets, especially after normal school hours, and provide the means to "lock down" the building in certain emergency situations. Doors at critical locations should be outfitted with advanced locking devices, such as electronic card-readers. By contrast, deadbolt locks operated by key may be adequate for doors leading to less secure spaces, including classrooms needing to be left unlocked during class hours. Consequently, determining the appropriate type of lock to be installed on a particular door should be based on the hours of use and the value of the contents of the room or area.

In addition to locks and card-readers, schools also require alarm systems for protecting certain doors and spaces. A school's location—urban, suburban, or rural—determines, to some extent, the nature and complexity of the appropriate alarm system. In some situations, alarms that connect directly to the nearest police station or sheriff's office are a wise investment. However, relatively small spaces may be adequately protected with local alarms that have high-decibel levels, an automatic shutoff, and a reset mechanism.

BUILDING DESIGN AND LAYOUT

Access control is only part of an overall strategy for protecting assets and people. Therefore, the design and layout of junior and senior high school buildings, such as the location of the main office and other rooms containing sensitive information or expensive items, can be tailored to maximize security. For example, when a school has multiple entrances, a central location for the main office is preferable for both security and school operations. In addition, the school's more valuable assets should be stored conveniently near the main administrative office, making it easier to issue these items on request while maintaining appropriate control over their allocation and inventory.

Local building codes and the OSHA standards will dictate the required minimum number of emergency exits for a school, as they do for all buildings, but these regulations do not specify their locations. While it is important to have a sufficient number of exits, schools must also locate exits in such a way as to facilitate the most expeditious evacuation from the premises in case of an emergency.

Finally, the placement of gymnasiums and auditoriums should allow direct access to these facilities. This will permit their use during nonschool hours for various school and community activities while, at the same time, limiting visitor access to other parts of the school property.

BULLYING

Up to this point, the focus has largely been on physical security matters and associated personnel considerations. However, bullying and the other forms of fighting and aggression that confront junior and senior high schools are created and can only be mitigated by human actions. Schools must therefore examine the factors that motivate bullies and expose their victims to harassment, as well as the role of faculty, staff, and other students who are affected by such troublesome behavior. All too often, third-party witnesses to fighting and bullying choose not to intervene, and school administrators ignore the problem or respond inappropriately. At the extreme, school administrators at a high school in Dallas, Texas, reportedly encouraged students to fight it out inside a metal cage while others looked on for amusement.[6]

As discussed in the opening chapter, bullying has long been a significant and perplexing problem in middle schools and high schools. In many respects, adolescent bullying is an extension of the disruptive behavior displayed by some grade school children, but with the potential for far more serious consequences. Unlike disruptive children whose conduct tends to impact an entire class, bullies often direct their aggression at specific targets. As middle or high school students, they are physically bigger and stronger and willing to use their size and strength to intimidate and control others.

Intervention and Prevention Strategies

Unfortunately, there is no practical way for a school to eliminate the problem of bullying entirely; there are only strategies that can reduce its likelihood and impact (see Appendix C). Furthermore, schools cannot afford to wait until incidents occur to take action. As discussed earlier, the consequences of bullying can be as extreme as retaliatory mass murder. If schools are merely reactive to their bullying problem, they may miss the opportunity to avert tragedy before it strikes. They should instead be proactive, which involves gathering "intelligence" about conditions that encourage bullying behavior and those students most likely to be involved, either as perpetrators or victims. For example, junior and senior high school students will have already amassed a record of their conduct and behavior from grade school on. To the extent permissible by privacy laws, teachers, counselors and administrators at the secondary school level should have some indication in advance of which students have shown tendencies toward bullying and aggression.

Because behavior can change over time with growth and development, it would be unwise to rely solely on a student's past conduct record. Some students may engage in bullying during junior or senior high school despite having shown no earlier signs of such aggressive behavior in the lower grades. Thus, the intelligence gathering process must also rely on the ongoing observations by faculty, staff, and students—observations that include conduct in class, on the athletic fields, on the school bus, and in the cafeteria.

Ultimately, all observations should be relayed to the principal and guidance staff for interpretation and assessment. All conclusions and remedial actions should then be communicated to those members of the faculty and staff who have regular contact with the individual student so that everyone concerned is aware of the problem and the recommended intervention.

Another aspect of prevention involves seeking to create a school climate that inhibits acts of bullying, harassment, and intimidation. To establish a culture that is intolerant of bullying, school officials should solicit the help of concerned students, which can be done during orientation and periodically throughout the school year. School officials should promote awareness among the entire student population about what constitutes bullying, and they should make it clear that such conduct will not be tolerated.

Students can be an important part of the prevention effort. With appropriate protections for anonymity and confidentiality, they should be encouraged to provide information regarding problem behavior. No student wants to be considered a "snitch" or an "informant," especially by their peers. Consequently, students must be continually reminded that their help is essential for identifying bullies or victims and that coming forward is in everyone's best interest. The emphasis on students as information sources does not suggest that schools and SROs should recruit a cadre of young confidential informants (CIs). Rather, it is important for schools to maintain a climate that fosters trusting relationships between students and faculty/staff through which information sharing becomes a normative process.

The information that students provide may enable administrators, faculty, and staff to be aware of potential problems and, when incidents occur, to minimize their effects. At the first indication of bullying, problem students should be confronted. As with any disciplinary matter, the first approach should be to treat the situation as a learning opportunity. Rather than immediately threatening suspension or expulsion, the discussion should revolve around the impact of their behavior on their victims as well as themselves in terms of future educational and career opportunities.

Of course, if this approach does not improve the students' behavior, further action, consistent with the severity of the transgression, should be taken. This may include consulting with the students' parents and psychological counseling, as well as more punitive steps, from detention to suspension or expulsion.

Any anti-bullying intervention strategy must also consider the role of the victim. The reactions and retaliations of bullying victims can sometimes pose an even greater threat to safety and security than the bullying itself. Therefore, information should be gathered about both aggressors and victims. Here, too, the cooperation of concerned students can be of immeasurable help. Whereas bullies can be identified by their aggressive behavior, assessing whether victims are likely to pose security risks depends on insight into their out-of-school interests. Evidence that a victim is interested in or has access to weapons of any kind would call for immediate intervention, beginning with a meeting with the student and his or her parents.

Because bullying victims may already feel threatened and ostracized by their peers, whatever intervention steps are taken should do nothing to intensify their feelings of insecurity and persecution. The focus should be on reassuring them of the school's plan to improve the situation and helping to improve their self-esteem and confidence. If victims are unreceptive or unresponsive to these efforts and there is reason to believe that they may pose a threat to themselves or others, they must be referred for counseling in an effort to prevent a potentially hazardous situation.

For too many years, schools often responded to reports of bullying by placing the blame on the shoulders of victims, implicitly assuming that they were somehow responsible for their victimization, if only because they did not stand up for themselves. In cases where a student had to be transferred from one class or homeroom to another to prevent bullying, it was often the victim and not the bully who was displaced. In the past couple of decades, however, school administrators have come to take—or have been compelled to take—a more enlightened view of the causes of and solutions to bullying. Rather than focusing just on the victims and offenders, schools have had far greater success by addressing the broader school climate. Indeed, to reduce the incidence of bullying requires an investment by all impacted parties—administrators, teachers, and students.

The most widely known and longest standing approach to combating bullying is the Olweus Bullying Prevention Program, first implemented in the 1980s by Norwegian schools and later adopted by countless schools in the United States. The Olweus program includes a variety of strategies that are organized by whether they act at the school, classroom, or student level:

School-level components
- Formation of a Bullying Prevention Coordinating Committee
- Distribution of an anonymous student questionnaire assessing the nature and prevalence of bullying
- Training of committee members and staff
- Development of a coordinated system of supervision
- Adoption of school-wide rules against bullying
- Development of appropriate positive and negative consequences for students' behavior
- Staff discussion groups related to the program
- Involvement of parents

Classroom-level components
- Reinforcement of school-wide rules against bullying
- Regular classroom meetings with students to increase knowledge and empathy
- Informational meetings with parents

Individual-level components
- Interventions with children who bully
- Interventions with children who are bullied
- Discussions with parents of involved students

For any anti-bullying program to be effective, it must focus on the entire school environment and its social networks rather than just on the individual victims and victimizers. Moreover, as prescribed by the Olweus program, school officials need to reach out to parents for support. Often times the roots of bullying behavior are located in the home, where aggression can be learned through the process of imitation and reinforcement.

The Olweus program has been empirically tested in a variety of countries and contexts. The earliest evidence of positive impact came from a large evaluation involving some 2,500 Norwegian children enrolled in 42 elementary and middle schools. Overall, student self-reports indicated that the program substantially reduced bullying, fighting, vandalism, and other problem behaviors.[7] The program's implementation in American schools has been marked by two large-scale assessments, one involving 18 middle schools in South Carolina and the other with 12 elementary schools in Philadelphia. Both of these American assessments found significant reductions in self-reported bullying and victimization.[8] Another evaluation of the Olweus approach implemented in 10 middle schools found bullying victimization decreased significantly among white students, but not among minorities.[9]

Notwithstanding the widespread adoption of the Olweus program and several other school-based curricula, the empirical evidence with regard to their preventive effect is actually rather mixed. Merrill and colleagues produced a meta-analysis of 16 empirical evaluations of several anti-bullying interventions conducted over a 25-year time period from 1980 to 2004, limiting their focus to only those assessments that met certain criteria for methodological sound-ness.[10] Overall, the effectiveness of bullying prevention programs was modest at best, and mostly impacted knowledge and attitudes rather than actual bully-ing behavior. Regardless of approach, the social and tangible benefits that some youngsters derive from harassing weaker and more vulnerable classmates can sometimes be too gratifying to be so easily discouraged.

A more recent and more exhaustive analysis of 59 controlled evaluations of 30 anti-bullying programs implemented worldwide reached a more optimistic conclusion. Pooling across those assessments that passed methodological mus-ter, Ttofi and Farrington estimated the overall reduction in bullying for exper-imental schools over control schools to be just above 20 percent, with those programs patterned after the Olweus model fairing better than other curric-ula.[11] Although no program can be considered anything close to a panacea, when it comes to combating school bullying, something is absolutely better than nothing.

PEER MEDIATION AND MENTORING

In discussions of youth and school violence, the influence of peers is typi-cally cast in a decidedly negative light: Adolescents, it is often said, are encour-aged to do the wrong thing by peer pressure, and this force can be so intense that it tends to trump the positive influences of teachers and parents. How-ever, peer pressure can be harnessed and redirected to encourage positive behavior. Indeed, many schools have successfully implemented peer mediation programs that enlist third-party students to help resolve conflicts that arise within the school setting. Peer mediation can be informal (e.g., one student intervenes to help settle a classroom dispute) or formal (e.g., two students set-tle their conflicts through a prescribed mediation process).

Although having third parties assist in conflict resolution is not a new idea, it is important that students receive adequate training in conflict negotiation, because untrained mediators will often intensify the level of conflict. There is some empirical support for the effectiveness of programs that train students in negotiation and mediation. Not only do these programs tend to decrease the number and severity of student conflicts, but they also reduce the number of suspensions, indicating that conflicts are being efficiently resolved by and among students themselves.[12]

Despite the apparent potential for nonviolent resolution, peer mediation programs can sometimes do more damage than good. For example, bullying behavior often stems from a power imbalance between victim and tormentor. Without adequate controls, this power differential can easily carry over into peer-based resolution processes and further intimidate a vulnerable student.[13]

The influence that peers can have in assisting conflict resolution comple-ments the critical role that teachers, guidance counselors, coaches, and other

school personnel can play as mentors. With an increasing number of children
growing up without a supportive and positive parental presence, the various
adults associated with a student's school can fill the void. The empirical evidence concerning the effectiveness of mentoring programs is, on balance, fairly
favorable. Based on a meta-analysis of 39 rigorous evaluations, Tolan and his
colleagues concluded that youth mentoring programs, in general, tend to have
a modest positive effect on aggression, drug use, delinquency, and academic
achievement.[14]

Unfortunately, the potential value of mentoring relationships provided by
teachers and other school staff members is sometimes unappreciated. Several
years ago, for example, a Utah school district decided that a group of 33 students would benefit from a teacher-supervised fishing trip, and spent $1,000
of federal funds from the Safe, Disciplined and Drug-Free School initiative for
rods, tackle boxes, and bait. Sadly, a *Los Angeles Times* investigative reporter,
unable to see the tremendous mentoring potential, criticized and mocked the
notion of fishing as a violence and drug prevention initiative.[15] The reporter
failed to recognize that violence prevention programs do not have to be
explicitly concerned with violence to be credible and successful.

GANGS, WEAPONS, AND DRUGS

No matter how successfully a school might implement a bullying prevention
and intervention strategy, other security options remain if members of the
school's population are at significant risk. Some schools have considered it pru-
dent or necessary to increase safety on campus by installing metal detectors
(walk-through or hand-held wands), conducting random or targeted searches
of students or their lockers, or using SROs to monitor and respond to various
types of student misconduct, from drug or weapons possession to violence.

Whether a school employs detectors, drug sweeps, or SROs is a judgment call
to be made by individual school districts or administrators. These decisions
should be based on an objective security assessment; no school should be
unfairly stigmatized on the basis of its locale or its student demographics alone.

If metal detectors are to be used, they must be placed at building entrances
and should be monitored at the beginning of the school day. In addition, if
students are permitted to come and go during the day or if others have reason
to enter the campus, it will be necessary to have security screeners at each
checkpoint during all hours of school operation. Despite the additional personnel costs, these screeners must be in place to reduce the risk of unauthorized access and weapons on campus.

GANGS

The strength of gangs lies in their numbers. Unlike the individual bully
who might victimize one or a few students, gangs are willing to terrorize an

entire school. Gangs and gang activity on campus greatly increase the likelihood of weapons on school grounds. Also, if members of two or more gangs
attend the same school, the risk of violence over turf and territory escalates.

Problems related to gang affiliation and inter-gang conflict within the perimeter of a middle or high school largely reflect a spillover from the street
corner. Thus, the extent and severity of gang violence at school tends to
parallel trends in the surrounding communities. Based on data from the
NCVS school supplement, as shown in Figure 8.1, the extent to which students perceive the presence of gangs in their schools has increased in recent
years, after having declined during the late 1990s. Moreover, the surge has
been particularly pronounced in urban areas. For the most part, these
patterns are consistent with data on street gang activity showing a retrenchment and subsequent reemergence of gang violence.[16] The student perceptions of expanding gang presence are fairly consistent with the views of
SROs, based on a 2008 survey of nearly 800 officers assigned to schools
around the country. Notwithstanding a potential bias based on self-interest
in justifying their role, 27 percent of the officers indicated that gang activity
was increasing in their schools, compared to only 8 percent who said that
gang presence was subsiding; another 32 percent reported that gang activity
was unchanged, and 33 percent believed that gangs were simply not an
issue in their schools.[17]

Howell and Lynch, also using the NCVS school supplement data, correlated
student perceptions of the gang presence in their schools with an index of the
number of security measures (e.g., guards or other hall monitors, metal detectors, visitor sign-in requirements, locker checks).[18] Overall, the perceptions of

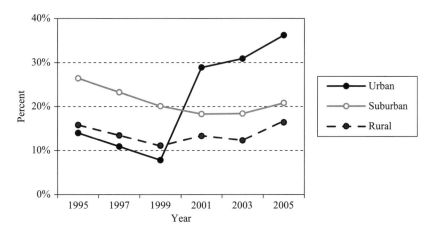

Figure 8.1 Percentage of students ages 12–18 reporting gang presence at school
Source: Bureau of Justice Statistics, National Crime Victimization Survey, School Supplement, various
years.

gangs increased with higher security levels. Of course, rather than suggesting the total ineffectiveness of security, it is far more plausible that schools implement enhanced security in response to gang involvement, or that security levels and gang presence are both functions of school setting.

School-based gang suppression efforts cannot depend solely on physical security measures and the threat of suspension or arrest. Any successful strategy for confronting the gang problem must recognize the special attraction of gang membership and the many positive benefits that recruits derive from joining a neighborhood gang. Notwithstanding all the downsides, gangs offer young recruits many desirable advantages—status, excitement, power, praise, profit, protection, mentoring, and the opportunity for advancement—healthy goals fulfilled in unhealthy ways. Society's challenge, therefore, is to identify and promote healthier means for children and adolescents to achieve the same need fulfillment—constructive ways to feel good about themselves and their prospects for the future.

Most at risk are those students who have a weak sense of attachment to school and who fail to achieve much success through academics or extracurricular activities.[19] Under these conditions, adolescents may respond to the praise and status-attainment offered by gangs, particularly if their connectedness to family is limited.

Implemented in countless schools nationwide, the Gang Resistance Education and Training (G.R.E.A.T.) program is a school curriculum taught by police officers that focuses on life skills. G.R.E.A.T. is designed to discourage children, especially at the middle school level, from joining gangs and engaging in delinquent activity. Early results from a national assessment suggested that students participating in the G.R.E.A.T. program had more pro-social attitudes than those who failed to complete the curriculum or who did not participate at all.[20] However, a subsequent, more comprehensive evaluation of the program's gang reduction effects yielded somewhat mixed results. According to the assessment team:[21]

> As a review of risk factors reveals, a significant reduction in gang activity may be too much to expect from any program if the more fundamental causes and attractions of gangs (i.e., social, structural, community, and family conditions) are not simultaneously addressed.

Although G.R.E.A.T. may be the best-known school-based approach for gang prevention and suppression, a number of other programs and strategies have proven to be somewhat more successful in combating the gang problem. For example, the Comprehensive Gang Model is a broad-based approach to gang reduction that involves various community organizations and representatives, including schools, in the effort.[22] In fact, what may advantage the Comprehensive Gang Model and other community-wide initiatives is that they move beyond the school setting to confront and combat the profoundly difficult and deeply entrenched problem of neighborhood gangs, particularly in urban environments.

Whatever the value of G.R.E.A.T. or other curricula in dissuading children from pursuing gang affiliation, administrators struggling with significant gang presence in their schools must find strategies for keeping peace and managing the gang impact. Before gangs can be controlled, however, they must be identified and the nature of their activities understood. Generally, gangs are distinguished by the specific colors or tattoos that they wear, the graffiti or hand signs that they use, and their coded language.[23] Gangs, like all organizations, have a hierarchy of authority. Successful gang suppression efforts, therefore, should focus heavily on those members with the most power and control over affiliates. It can also be helpful to learn about the gang's operations, whether they include drug selling, illegal gun trafficking, or other activity.

On occasion, obtaining this kind of intelligence about a gang, its leadership, and its activities can pave the way for a dialogue between school officials and gang members. Such negotiations might also involve law enforcement officials, social workers, school psychologists, or former gang members who have abandoned the street life. Regardless, school officials should make clear their awareness of gang presence at school and indicate that illegal gang-related activity will not be ignored.

Weapons

Many instruments qualify as weapons, including some that are not intended primarily for the purpose of injuring or killing someone. For example, baseball bats or hockey sticks are meant for recreational use, but can be used in a dangerous fashion. Even hands can be weapons, especially if they belong to a trained fighter. For schools, however, the primary concern surrounds guns, knives, and explosives, all of which are primarily designed to cause damage, injury, or death.

An effective approach to confronting the problem of weapons at school should start with an unambiguous weapons policy that is communicated to the entire school population and enforced fairly and evenly. Crafting a policy requires some care, because the terminology used must be rather broad in some regards yet specific in others. A school might define a weapon generally as any instrument that can be used to cause injury to others or to destroy property, thereby preventing a student from arguing that some dangerous instrument is not prohibited simply because it falls outside a specific list of prohibited weapons. By contrast, the policy should specifically state what penalties will be imposed on those who violate the rule. Students should also know in advance that all weapons will be permanently confiscated, and that law enforcement will be alerted when appropriate. All students, faculty, and staff should be required to acknowledge with their signature that they have read and understand the weapons policy.

It is undeniable that today's campus reality necessitates strong weapons policies, but enforcing such policies is much harder than crafting them. Schools must demonstrate a commitment to enforcement by providing and maintaining the personnel and financial resources needed to ensure compliance. In addition, as discussed in Chapter 6, policies should never be so rigid as to punish students regardless of reason or mitigation.

Drug-Free and Gun-Free Schools

Although school safety is critical at all age levels, junior and senior high school students are particularly at risk because experimentation with drugs and guns is especially widespread at this age. Nearly two decades ago, the U.S. Congress responded with legislation that defined certain drug- and gun-free buffer zones (see Appendix B).

The drug-free zone is an area within a certain distance, most commonly 1,000 feet, of the nearest school, park, or other public area identified with appropriate anti-drug signage. Due to the extensive size of these zones, enforcement is a police responsibility rather than a school matter. The police are authorized to keep school zones drug-free by employing a variety of established practices, such as uniformed patrols, undercover officers, surveillance, and the use of informants to identify drug sellers.

Keeping school zones free of guns has also been a challenge for school administrators and law enforcement. In recent years, efforts to enact gun control legislation have typically met with political resistance, and court decisions have made enforcement of existing laws difficult or impossible. For example, despite the more than 200 people killed in Philadelphia in 2008, the Commonwealth Court invalidated five City Council measures that were passed the year before to strengthen gun restrictions.[24] Also in 2008, the U.S. Supreme Court upheld a decision by a federal appellate court to remove a handgun ban that had existed in the District of Columbia for 31 years.[25]

Meanwhile, the U.S. Congress appeared to take a "hands-off" approach in terms of controlling gun markets. In 2004, Congress passed the Tiahrt Amendment, which drastically limits the utilization of ATF gun-tracing information, thereby shielding rogue dealers from scrutiny.[26] Then, in 2005, federal lawmakers enacted the Protection of Lawful Commerce in Arms Act, which immunizes gun manufacturers and sellers from civil litigation arising from injury and death associated with gun offenses.

Of course, there was a time when leadership on Capitol Hill took a very different position on gun control. Focusing specifically on the problem of guns in schools, Congress passed the Gun-Free School Zones (GFSZ) Act of 1990 as part of the Crime Control Act of 1990.[27] In 1995, the Supreme Court, addressing the case of a 12th-grade student who brought a handgun to school, held that Congress lacked authority to restrict the carrying of handguns. Therefore, the Court declared the GFSZ Act unconstitutional because it violated the rights of individuals protected under the Second Amendment.[28] This position was then reaffirmed in 2000.[29] In response, Congress revised and limited the GFSZ Act so that it applied only if a gun had been involved in interstate commerce, an area over which Congress has authority provided under the Constitution.

The tactics described earlier to combat drugs in or around schools cannot be readily adapted to confront the problem of guns. And although well-meaning, federal legislation intended to keep guns away from schools has not worked. Aside from loopholes in existing federal and state gun control laws, possession of guns—unlike possession of illicit drugs—is lawful. For the most part, as noted in Chapter 3, guns used in school shootings typically were purchased by the shooters' parents and kept in their homes. Therefore, preventing guns from being brought to campus is difficult. The problem, however, can be mitigated through the use of access controls, metal detectors, SROs, and other security measures.

School authorities cannot meet this challenge alone. Reducing the risk of students bringing guns to school requires a cooperative and concerted effort on the part of administrators, law enforcement, parents, and especially students, who are often aware of or hear rumors about weapons in their schools. The critical role of students in averting tragic acts of violence has been particularly emphasized during the post-Columbine era. In recent years, students have repeatedly been encouraged to come forward, often anonymously through a special tip line, to report knowledge or suspicion regarding threats by classmates against individual students or the entire school. Indeed, according to an FBI analysis of school rampages, a majority of assailants had previously told others about their violent intentions.[30] Accordingly, many of these episodes may have been prevented had students alerted school officials.

To some extent, the message has been heard. Aware of the potentially deadly consequences of remaining silent, students have in many cases helped to thwart an impending act of violence by informing parents, teachers, or other adults in authority. Daniels and his colleagues uncovered 30 such episodes over a three-year time span—from October 2001 to October 2004—in a content analysis of the common features of averted school rampages.[31] In one widely publicized "success story," a mass murder plot by three high school students in New Bedford, Massachusetts, was stopped when another student, who had overheard talk of the plan to bomb the school, informed her teacher. When police followed up on the lead by searching the suspects' homes, they found shotgun shells, knives, a notebook containing bomb-making instructions, and photographs of the boys holding what appeared to be handguns.

Notwithstanding these peaceful outcomes, many students remain reluctant to inform on their classmates. Although based on a relatively small study of 100 students, Brinkley and Saarnio reported that one-quarter of students who had information about possible violence were unwilling to come forward, especially those who had a relatively negative view of their school.[32]

Finally, because the firearms brought to campus most often come from students' homes, it is imperative that parents become involved in confronting the gun problem at school. Parental responsibility is not absolved just because the guns are legally purchased or properly licensed. Parents must fully secure their weapons and be able to account for them at all times.

SEARCHING FOR CONTRABAND

In the spirit of school safety, student civil and privacy rights have been tested. As early as 1985, the U.S. Supreme Court ruled that the need to keep schools free of drugs and weapons trumps the usual Fourth Amendment protection against unreasonable searches and seizures (see Appendix F). Even though the case involved the search of a student's purse for cigarettes rather than illicit drugs or weaponry, Justice White, speaking for the majority, expressed a generalized concern for contraband: [33]

> Against the child's interest in privacy must be set the substantial interest of teachers and administrators in maintaining discipline in the classroom and on school grounds. Maintaining order in the classroom has never been easy, but in recent years, school disorder has often taken particularly ugly forms: drug use and violent crime in the schools have become major social problems. How, then, should we strike the balance between the schoolchild's legitimate expectations of privacy and the school's equally legitimate need to maintain an environment in which learning can take place? It is evident that the school setting requires some easing of the restrictions to which searches by public authorities are ordinarily subject.

With the Court's endorsement for placing safety over privacy, school officials frequently conduct searches of students and their property. As shown in Figure 8.2, based on the 2005–2006 School Survey on Crime and Safety, as many as 30 percent of high schools and 22 percent of middle or junior high schools reported having performed random sweeps for contraband. In terms of searching for drugs on school premises, over 60 percent of high schools and over 40 percent of middle and junior high schools have employed drug-sniffing dogs.

Whatever the data may say regarding the extent to which schools conduct random or routine searches for contraband, numerous abuses have been alleged. At the extreme stands a November 5, 2003, police raid at the Stratford High School in Goose Creek, South Carolina, a residential community some 15 miles north of Charleston. Following an anonymous tip that drugs were being sold in the school, the principal ordered the raid, but may not have anticipated the excessive tactics used by the authorities in conducting the surprise search. In an ugly scene captured on the school's video surveillance system, students were ordered to lie face down on the floor and were threatened with guns pointed at their heads, while police dogs sniffed for illegal drugs.

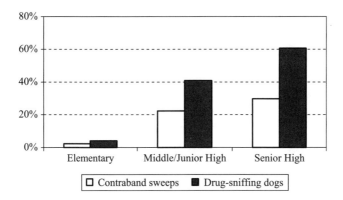

Figure 8.2 Contraband search procedures by school level
Source: U.S. Department of Education, National Center for Education Statistics, 2005–06 School Survey on Crime and Safety.

Making the whole ordeal all the more outrageous, no drugs were discovered and no arrests were made.

Another controversial case that was battled all the way up to the U.S. Supreme Court involved a 13-year-old girl at the Safford Middle School in Arizona. The lawsuit stemmed from a 2003 episode in which the girl was strip-searched by school personnel following a tip alleging that she had been distributing ibuprofen pills to her classmates. According to court documents, the girl's backpack and outer clothing were first examined, after which she was ordered to remove her slacks, show the inside waist band of her underpants, lift her shirt and expose part of her brassiere. No drugs were found. At the end of the long appellate road, the Supreme Court held, by a narrow 5-4 margin, that the strip search was inappropriate—that given the relatively innocuous nature of the contraband in question and the small likelihood the student was indeed concealing it inside her clothing, the school lacked sufficient justification to carry out such an intrusive search.[34]

STUDENT DISCIPLINE

Whether the issue involves guns, drugs, or other rule violations, it is inevitable that some student behavior will call for disciplinary action, and school administrators must decide on the nature of this response and by whom it will be administered. Although there is an inclination to associate discipline with punishment, the objective of discipline is to maintain order and ensure orderly activity. Punishment may not be the most effective way to achieve this goal. Indeed, although punishment is one approach to discipline, the other side of discipline is the opportunity for learning.

After the highly controlled and supervised structure of elementary school, middle and high school students enjoy a comparative sense of freedom, which, coupled with peer influences, makes them more susceptible to acting in inappropriate ways. Regardless of the underlying reasons, school administrators cannot tolerate misconduct if educational goals are to be met.

Aside from the most egregious of offenses, administrators and teachers should first opt for a pedagogical approach. As Skiba and his colleagues argue, "an instructional approach (i.e., one based in educational and learning principles) to school discipline will be more effective than a punishment approach in teaching students the skills they need to get along in school and society."[35] As with bullying, a nonthreatening discussion of the student's behavior to explain its impact may be enough to prevent recurrences. However, some students are chronic offenders who continue to act out despite attempts to reason with them. In these situations, school officials may be forced to take punitive action following appropriate due process respectful of students' rights. On occasion, disciplinary action may also call for direct parental intervention.[36] More egregious cases, such as those involving a threat of serious injury to classmates or faculty, may need to be referred to law enforcement authorities.

Regardless of approach, discipline must be evenhanded. Although it is reasonable to take into consideration any prior history of student code violations, all else being equal, one student cannot be treated more harshly than another who has committed a similar offense. Disparate punishment will only serve to make a mockery of the process and undo its intended benefits.

School officials are fairly quick to use suspension or expulsion for a wide variety of transgressions. In addition, transfer to an alternative school—initially intended to serve those students with a high likelihood of academic failure—has increasingly been used for placement of children who pose disciplinary problems. Table 8.2 details, for the 2005/2006 school year, the extent to which these disciplinary measures are used by school administrators for several common types of student misconduct. As shown, suspension for at least five days tends to be the typical response, except for drug-related offenses, which tend to result in transfer to an alternative school. This may reflect a perception of drug use as a relatively habitual behavior requiring a different school placement, as opposed to a more episodic form of misconduct that may be deterred by some term of punitive separation from school.

Unfortunately, for some students, out-of-school suspension may be seen as a reward instead of a punishment, providing them with a brief vacation from classes. In addition, sending students who have committed acts or threats of violence out onto the street during school hours may place the community at a greater degree of risk. However, from the perspective of school administrators and teachers, this may simply be far less a concern. Ultimately, the long-term consequences of school exclusion (suspension or expulsion) can be quite negative, as these sanctions tend to encourage some students to leave school permanently without ever finishing their high school education.[37] Dropping

Table 8.2
Serious disciplinary actions by schools, 2005–06

Type of violation	Schools disciplining		Disciplinary actions		Type of action			
	Number	Percent	Number	Percent	Suspend 5+ days	Expel for school year	Alternative school	Total
Firearms/ explosives	3,700	4.5%	14,300	1.7%	67.8%	10.9%	21.2%	100%
Other weapons	15,900	19.3%	46,600	5.6%	60.0%	10.8%	29.2%	100%
Fighting	26,000	31.5%	323,900	39.0%	80.8%	4.1%	15.1%	100%
Insubordination	17,500	21.2%	309,000	37.2%	75.9%	4.1%	20.0%	100%
Illegal drugs	17,200	20.8%	106,800	12.9%	55.6%	10.2%	34.2%	100%
Alcohol	8,400	10.2%	30,100	3.6%	77.0%	4.5%	18.5%	100%
Total	39,600	48%	830,700	100%				

Source: National Center for Education Statistics, School Survey on Crime and Safety, 2006.

out of school, in turn, is a frequent precursor to embracing a career in crime and lawlessness.[38]

Given the range of negative repercussions that derive from a decidedly punitive disciplinary approach, many schools have opted for a restorative justice framework to handling school-based infractions. Rather than focusing so much on the person who is responsible, the restorative justice model emphasizes the person(s) who have been impacted or harmed. Instead of seeking measures to deter and punish wrongdoing, it features strategies to repair the harm that was created.[39] Several evaluations of the effects of adopting a restorative justice approach have been quite promising.[40] Most important, this philosophy on discipline fosters a positive school climate based on connectedness and trust, rather than a negative climate based on suspicion and disrespect. In the long run, the positive approach leads to healthy, safer school environments in which both intellectual growth and social development are immovably center-stage.

SCHOOL RESOURCE OFFICERS

Besides the upgrades in physical security that were implemented in response to the 1990s surge in major school shootings—from metal detectors and surveillance cameras to protocols for access control—schools across the nation became fortified with an expanded police presence. Law enforcement support for controlling school crime and disorder involved either the deployment of regular police officers to school details (through contractual arrangements between those police or sheriff departments and school authorities) or specially trained law enforcement personnel under the rubric of School Resource Officers.

Some school districts operate their own police departments, a practice that has existed for decades. The Los Angeles Unified School District, for example, has maintained its own police force since 1948, currently employing several hundred sworn officers to serve a population of nearly one million students and staff members spread across over 1,000 schools. Miami, Houston, Baltimore, and other major school departments also established their own police and security forces long before the Columbine shooters were even born.

Even so, the apparent increase in the level of violence in schools forced many school administrators and civic leaders to rethink the outdated notion of truant officers, as concern for guns and gangs in schools extended well beyond enforcing attendance and the student code. The penetration of law enforcement into the educational sphere was fully consistent with the community policing paradigm that emerged in the 1990s. Rather than passively awaiting calls for service, the community policing approach focused on deploying cops in community settings—especially high-crime contexts—to be in a position to avert trouble before it spiraled out of control. With this in mind, many community leaders saw middle and high schools as a logical place to station police personnel.

The major push for promoting the use of SROs came from President Bill Clinton, who had established community policing as a centerpiece to his administration from the very start. Clinton responded to the late 1990s classroom carnage, which included a mass shooting at a middle school in his home state of Arkansas, by advocating the placement of more police officers in school halls. In 1999, with strong encouragement from the Clinton White House, the U.S. Department of Justice created the "COPS in Schools" program, as part of the Office of Community Oriented Policing Services (COPS). Overall, $68 million in grant funds was allocated for hiring up to 600 SROs for hundreds of communities nationwide. In view of the specialized skill set expected of SROs—from counselor and mentor to investigator and enforcer—Congress provided $8 million over a two-year period to provide training for the specialized role of police/school liaison. Over the next few years, federal appropriations for SROs continued to grow, reaching $180 million annually. In August 2005, the COPS Office reported that more than $753 million had been awarded to some 3,000 law enforcement agencies to fund over 6,500 SROs through the "COPS in Schools" initiative.[41]

Because the federal COPS grant program has not been the only funding source for SROs, there is no direct measure of the exact extent to which schools employ police and security officers. However, besides the student surveys noted earlier, in which two-thirds of respondents reported the presence of police or security guards, periodic surveys of local police agencies conducted by the Bureau of Justice Statistics provide national estimates of law enforcement staffing and utilization. In 1997, 38 percent of local police agencies nationwide used full-time resource officers. Collectively, these departments employed an estimated 9,400 police officers in these school-based assignments. By 2003, 43 percent of departments had at least one full-time SRO, with an estimated total of 14,300 officers. Thus, while the spread of departments using SROs was modest, the number of officers assigned to SRO duties increased by as much as 50 percent.

The range of tasks performed by SROs is exceptionally broad—from instructing students, staff, or parent groups on safety-related issues to enforcing various policies pertaining to student conduct. A 2001 survey of over 700 SROs—drawn from a pool of affiliate members of the National Association of School Resource Officers (NASRO)—provides a glimpse at the daily activities of officers associated with their school assignments. As shown in Table 8.3, the activities performed by most SROs extend well beyond the usual duties of law enforcement personnel, and often involve some sort of assistance to students rather than the use of their police powers and authority. It is worth noting, however, that these results indicate the percentages of SROs who say that the various tasks have been some part of their job, but not necessarily a common component of their daily activity. In addition, some respondents may have been inclined to highlight those activities that are consistent with an image of SRO duties that sets it apart from typical law enforcement, whether or not it is accurate.

Table 8.3
Tasks performed by School Resource Officers

Tasks performed	Percent of SROs
One-on-one consulting with students	93%
Calls for service to classrooms	88%
Classroom instruction	87%
Crisis preparedness planning	83%
Security audits/assessments of school campuses	82%
Special safety programs/presentations	78%
Faculty/staff in-service presentations	75%
Truancy intervention	70%
Group counseling with students	69%
Supervising/coordinating extracurricular activities	60%
Field trip chaperone	57%
Parent organization presentations	57%
Coaching athletic programs	30%

Source: Kenneth S. Trump, 2001 NASRO School Resource Officer Survey. National School Safety and Security Services, 2001, p. 4, http://kentrump.org/resources/2001NASROsurvey%20NSSSS.pdf.

A somewhat different perspective of SRO functions comes from a federally sponsored national survey of 322 police agencies that provide resource officers to school systems. Based on these data, Finn and McDevitt found that "SROs programs spend an average of 20 hours per week on law enforcement activities, 10 on advising or mentoring, 5 on teaching, and 6 to 7 on other activities combined."[42] Thus, despite the expanded range of duties, the majority of time is still devoted to enforcement activities.

The assignment of police details in schools and the employment of SROs are premised on the notion that these officers have training and expertise far beyond that of most school administrators in confronting various issues of crime and disorder. That said, if they are to make a significant contribution to security and safety, the effort must be a collaborative one among officers and school administrators, faculty, and staff. A successful working relationship depends to a large extent on the interpersonal and communications skills of the officers and the training that they are provided.

Since prevention is the cornerstone of all effective security programs, SROs must act proactively. In other words, they must do more than monitor metal detectors or patrol hallways and school grounds. In order for their contribution to security to be meaningful, they must establish good working relationships with students, faculty, and staff.

Most parents teach their preschool and grade school children that police officers are their allies. The junior and senior high school experience needs to promote rather than degrade that notion. To that end, SROs must have personality traits and skills that will enable them to cultivate relationships with members of the student body. It is critical that they be able to enlist student assistance and support in confronting the wide range of security issues impacting schools. For this to happen, students, as well as faculty and staff, must be treated with respect, encouraging them to feel comfortable enough to seek help and advice from SROs. This is not a matter of SROs recruiting CIs, but of minimizing or preventing problems by being aware of ongoing activity at school.

SROs must bring to their job more than just positive personal characteristics and enthusiasm for their work. The usual academy curriculum may serve them well in dealing with gangs and gang members. However, their training must also cover the many crucial differences between the situations found on school campuses and those encountered on the streets.

The issue of whether SROs should be armed at school is a contentious one. Of course, if they are sworn police personnel with full police powers, they will be armed. They may also carry Mace or pepper spray. However, if they are not sworn officers and have limited powers of arrest, school officials may be confronted with difficult decisions regarding whether and with what weapons to arm their SROs—decisions that are likely to be second-guessed by local residents.

In a crowded school environment, the risks associated with handguns—even in the possession of trained officers—are substantial. Arming SROs with either Mace or pepper spray is the least risky alternative since they neither kill nor permanently injure. However, to be effective, SROs must still be properly trained regarding when and how to use these nonlethal weapons.

Aside from the violence-prevention goal that motivated the expansion of the SRO program, the increased presence of police officers in schools may have some unintended consequences, not all of them positive. Many scholars and civil libertarians have expressed concern that police involvement in routine school activities may have caused a shift from informal school-based sanctions for student misbehavior to formal prosecution. Kupchik and Monahan argue that the expanded use of SROs will ultimately lead to the outsourcing of school discipline to other state agencies.[43]

With the presence of police officers instead of (or in addition to) hall monitors, school security guards, and assistant principals—all individuals who traditionally have handled discipline and who are paid by schools and report to the school principal—it is more likely now than in years past that students will be formally prosecuted rather than simply punished in house.

Beyond the matter of discipline, the closer alliance between school officials and police officials may put a strain on parent-school relations, especially if school administrators become viewed more as adversaries aligned with law enforcement than as advocates for their children. However, even while some parents are concerned that police officers in school will threaten rather than protect their child, the vast majority of parents and school administrators report being satisfied with the role and involvement of SROs. Students are somewhat less sanguine, although a majority remains favorably disposed to having officers routinely involved in school life. As part of a national assessment of the SRO initiative, McDevitt and Panniello surveyed some 900 students across several secondary schools concerning their reactions to having police officers regularly assigned to their schools.[44] While 9 out of 10 middle school students were satisfied with the SRO program, only 64 percent of high school students viewed the SRO initiative in a positive light. At the extreme, positive responses were obtained from only 43 percent of the 210 respondents at one high school (the largest sample from any of the schools surveyed).

Unfortunately, there is little solid empirical evidence either to support or to contest the effectiveness of SRO programs. Commenting on the paucity of rigorous research, Mayer noted:[45]

> Although most study authors have suggested that SROs help reduce violence and disorder in schools, the scientific evidence in support of these conclusions is quite limited. Of fifteen studies of SROs over the past 14 years that were reviewed, almost all relied on opinion surveys and study designs that could not provide solid evidence of the impact that SROs have on schools.

At least for the time being, the utility and value of SRO programs may just have to be taken somewhat on faith. Despite the somewhat hyperbolic concerns of turning schools into police states, many school administrators have remained quite willing to accept a "free security service," paid for by federal or state funds. As one school official from a particularly quiet and safe suburban community remarked, "It's like having a social worker in the school," begging the question of whether the students would be better served by a fully licensed social worker/counselor rather than a police officer.

In the long run, the size and scope of SRO programs may come down to finances. By the 2008/2009 school year—a full decade after the dreadful shooting at Columbine—the nation struggled with a deeply recessional economy. As the U.S. Congress looked to reduce spending, the federal gravy train for SROs left the station. At the local level, schools have been forced to cut their budgets. The SRO initiative began to resemble not so much an important violence-prevention strategy, but a luxury that most schools could no longer afford. For countless school administrators, the "COPS in Schools" program was apparently a great idea, as long as someone else footed the bill. Time will tell whether this retrenchment proves tragic.

9

SECURITY IN COLLEGES AND UNIVERSITIES

For parents, one of the hardest things about seeing their children going off to college is the helpless feeling of losing control over their safety and security. Worried parents won't know how late their daughter returns to the dorm at night or, for that matter, whether she returns at all. They won't know what their son is doing when he ventures off campus, or with whom. Although the need for some assurance is understandable, anxious mothers and fathers sometimes expect or demand campus security measures that may, in fact, be impractical.

For instance, there are parents who, out of concern for the well-being of their college-bound children, think that installing metal detectors all around campus, as has been done at thousands of middle and high schools nationwide, would make colleges safer. In a national telephone survey of 1,007 adults conducted a week following the April 2007 Virginia Tech shooting, as many as 61 percent of respondents agreed that it would be reasonable to install metal detectors at the entrances to all public buildings on college campuses.[1] Except for the relatively few single-building colleges, this hardly makes sense. Screening students and their book bags at the doorways of classroom buildings would create lengthy queues during the few minutes between class periods. By the time students are all seated in the lecture hall, it would be time to dismiss them. Beyond the logistical hurdles, such an approach is incompatible with the fundamental openness of most college campus environments.

The public perception of what constitutes effective security is often at variance with reality; truly effective programs are predicated on the principle that, to the extent *possible* and *reasonable*, protecting and conserving an organization's assets, including its human resources, is of paramount importance. This principle is as essential to the security of academic institutions as it is to that of any business or industry.

Two inextricably connected ideas follow from this premise. First, the emphasis on preventing losses to the greatest extent possible implies that some losses are inevitable. The goal, of course, is to keep losses—in terms of dollars and human suffering—as limited as can reasonably be expected. Second, security should be viewed as a business function, closely integrated with all aspects of the organization's operations. Whether in a corporate or academic context, the design and implementation of a security program must be balanced with other goals and interests. As important as security is, it cannot be allowed to override an institution's primary mission by inhibiting normal routine. Maintaining both convenience and security is an ever-moving target of conflicting needs and goals.

Many of the safety and security issues confronting school administrators are shared across all educational grade levels, but are magnified with each upward step on the education ladder, from preschool to college. The size of college and university campuses, their facilities, and their financial worth are far greater than those of elementary and secondary schools. In fact, it is not uncommon for universities to extend their activities, academic or otherwise, to more than one city or state. In addition, colleges and universities must accommodate and protect a significantly larger number of students, faculty, and staff.

Whether situated within designated communities or outside of municipal limits, many colleges and universities are virtually self-contained cities, consisting of multiple academic buildings, sports venues, and research facilities. They provide housing, food, parking, banking, and health services. The school bookstore, whether owned and managed by the school or by an outside vendor, may sell anything from a limited stock of textbooks and supplies to a full-scale retail line of trade books, music, gifts, and clothing. Some campuses feature public museums, and universities with medical and dental programs may operate their own full-service hospitals and dental clinics. Most colleges also maintain their own police departments. Consequently, security programming in these large, city-like environments must take into account a wide array of constituents and assets.

With prevention as the cornerstone, a careful and thorough risk-assessment of existing and potential problems should be completed (and updated periodically) before designing and implementing a security program. Moreover, the conditions that have previously permitted recurrent losses must be identified. Unfortunately, these important security steps are not always incorporated sufficiently into college and university administrative operations.

A RANGE OF SECURITY CONCERNS

Despite the apparent care-free atmosphere that characterizes most campuses, college administrators and concerned parents have long been aware, at least to some extent, of most potential dangers and safety hazards. However, until recently, little was known about the actual levels of risk. Prior to 1990, there was no coordinated or required compilation of campus crime data. The collection and publication of any statistical information were completely at a school's discretion. Nevertheless, various isolated incidents of campus crime and victimization came to light from news media reporting or through civil litigation.

In 1983, for example, word surfaced about a Massachusetts woman who successfully sued Pine Manor College through a claim of inadequate security after having been raped while a student at the school six years earlier.[2] Even though the Pine Manor case became the bellwether for campus law enforcement administrators and premises liability professionals, it did not catch the attention of the media until the finding of legal responsibility. However, it was the rape and murder of a student in her Lehigh University dormitory room in 1986 that would lead, years later, to a significant change in campus record-keeping by motivating the passage of the Jeanne Clery Disclosure of Campus Security Policy and Campus Crime Statistics Act.[3]

As discussed in Chapter 2, the Clery Act, which became effective in August 1991, requires two-year and four-year institutions that participate in federal student aid programs to prepare, publish, and distribute annual reports of campus crime statistics and security policies "to all current students and employees, and to any applicant for enrollment or employment upon request." The statistics are based on criminal offenses known to campus security or local police agencies, including murder, manslaughter, forcible and nonforcible sex offenses, robbery, aggravated assault, burglary, motor vehicle theft, and arson. Furthermore, the mandated statistics include "arrests or persons referred for campus disciplinary action for liquor law violations, drug-related violations, and weapons possession," as well as hate crimes—crimes in which the victim is "intentionally selected because of the actual or perceived race, gender, religion, sexual orientation, ethnicity, or disability of the victim."[4]

Notwithstanding all the reliability and validity issues outlined earlier in Chapter 2, the distribution of campus crime data is designed to inform students, parents, faculty, and staff about the level of risk on campus. However, despite the online availability of crime and arrest counts for thousands of two- and four-year colleges around the country, the general public continues to learn about and judge campus security solely from news media coverage, especially when the news concerns serious acts of violence involving an active shooter or student riots following a major sporting event.

Each story of this sort tends to generate probing questions about the sufficiency of campus security. Allegations that inadequate security resulted in two former Duquesne University students being shot and injured at an on-campus dance prompted the victims to file suit against the school in June 2008.[5] And long after 32 people were killed at Virginia Tech by a disgruntled and deeply troubled undergraduate, families of the deceased still have questions about the school's security response to the unfolding shooting spree and its legal culpability.[6]

Regardless of the actual frequency, the frightening specter of homicides and mass shootings on campus can give college officials sleepless nights. But homicide is hardly the only security issue facing higher education. Other forms of student misconduct—from public drunkenness to vandalism—can result in injuries, damage to property, a tarnished school reputation, and impaired relations with a school's surrounding community.

One poignant example in early 2008—at the Amherst campus of the University of Massachusetts—involved a three-week period of aggressive, rowdy behavior by students. The student misconduct—allegedly due to binge drinking—was a source of great distress to the school officials, the campus police, and the local police department. Partygoers were attacked in late-night dormitory confrontations, leaving two students to face charges of attempted rape and murder.[7]

In light of the prominent role that alcohol plays in countless episodes of campus mayhem, a debate surfaced in July 2008 about the possible advantages of lowering the legal drinking age, with particular attention focused on college and university students. The discussion engaged Mothers Against Drunk Driving (MADD), safety experts, politicians, and school and transportation officials, yet no consensus was reached. Known as "The Amethyst Initiative," a petition was generated and signed by the presidents and chancellors of 135 colleges and universities in which they contended that not only was the drinking age of 21 not working, but it was fostering a "culture of clandestine binge drinking and that students' use of fake identification has eroded their respect for the law."[8]

Whatever the effectiveness of alcohol prohibitions or parietal regulations in residence halls, it is obvious that students must be made aware of rules. Moreover, the rules should be both enforceable and enforced; and all violators should be disciplined fairly and with due process. Without proof that violators were sufficiently alerted to the rules, disciplinary action in any form can only result in resentment, and this would make all enforcement much more difficult.

An administrator's recognition of the need for security is one thing; choosing the appropriate type and level of response is another. To advocate a completely closed campus contradicts the purpose and spirit of a higher education, which is to learn to live and succeed in an open society. On the other hand, it is the very openness of an open campus that elevates the risk of a wide range of security problems.

No one questions the importance of safeguarding students, faculty, and staff. However, it is also necessary for a school's security program to protect against the loss of assets. This lesson was learned the expensive and embarrassing way by Wellesley College when, in an extreme case of campus asset loss, a highly valued piece called "Woman and Child" by the French painter Fernand Leger went missing. The oil painting was gifted to the college's Davis Museum in 1954, where it was displayed until early 2006. At that time, Davis was undergoing renovations, so the painting—along with other works of art—was loaned to the Oklahoma City Museum of Art. In early 2007, the collection was returned to Davis but the artworks were kept in their shipping crates since the renovations were not complete. It was not until November that the painting was discovered missing and presumed to have been inadvertently left in a crate that was sent for destruction.[9] The insurance claim was paid, but this hardly made up for the loss, which ultimately forced the resignation of the museum's director. It also raised serious questions about the way in which the museum was being managed.[10] Not only was the episode unfortunate in terms of the loss and embarrassment to the college, but it could have a more long-lasting effect on the museum's ability to attract other valuable contributions from potential donors due to concerns over security.

SECURING THE CAMPUS

Appropriate types and levels of security vary considerably from campus to campus, depending on school size, location, and available resources. What remains constant, however, is the need to incorporate physical security measures and the human element in any comprehensive security initiative.

Buildings and Grounds

Consistent with the notion that campuses are like self-contained cities, security activities must protect both a variety of assets and the various people who use them. Unlike the buildings and grounds of elementary and secondary schools—which are usually shut down at the end of the school day—buildings on a typical college or university campus may be used at virtually all hours of the day and on all days of the week. Thus, the protection of assets cannot be divorced from the protection of those entitled to use the facilities.

Building security must address the unique circumstances and risks associated with classrooms, offices, research laboratories, museums, utility plants, indoor sports venues, and housing. Grounds security must take into account the protection of outdoor sporting facilities and other open spaces on campus, including roadways, walk paths, and greens.

Administrative, academic, and research buildings and the assets within them are protected to a degree by applicable OSHA standards, state and local building codes, and possibly insurance requirements. Further, institutions that conduct federally funded research may have additional security requirements depending on the type of project. The large size and significant asset value found at institutions of higher education tend to magnify the risk of loss.

Chapters 7 and 8 noted that physical security consists of more than locks, metal detectors, closed circuit television (CCTV), and alarm systems. The design and layout of both buildings and grounds are also factors, and the strategies for building security recommended earlier apply to colleges and universities, but, of course, on a much larger scale. The hardware and technology employed must be accompanied by a commitment from the campus community to respect the equipment and maintain its integrity. Added to this is security's role as a business function: accountability for and control over the school's personal assets. When these elements truly complement each other, significant security benefits can be realized.

Grounds security and landscaping play a particularly critical role at the college level, with added importance on safety without sacrificing aesthetics. Consistent with the principles of crime prevention through environmental design (CPTED) discussed in Chapter 7, landscaping features that offer places of concealment for either people or stolen property should be avoided. Moreover, blue-light emergency telephones, which provide a direct connection to the campus security/safety department, should be visibly placed throughout the campus, regardless of how they may detract from the appearance.

Adequate lighting and use of CCTV cameras can contribute significantly to campus security. Lighting design and type (e.g., low- and high-pressure sodium vapor) must be appropriate for the area to be illuminated while being mindful of limiting light pollution and affecting neighbors. Cameras used for exterior applications should be enclosed in all-weather housing and interior cameras in vandal-resistant enclosures. Pan-and-tilt features, either controlled manually or motion activated, enhance the operation and coverage of CCTV over fixed cameras although they tend to be more expensive. The decision to employ personnel to monitor the cameras continuously or to combine monitoring with another function—say, that of a dispatcher—is dependent on the needs of the institution, the number of cameras, and the funding available. While one person can easily observe 8 to10 cameras, that cost must be multiplied by the hours monitored and increased when additional cameras are added. This approach is often used successfully to supplement foot or vehicle patrols.

Video surveillance technology has expanded rapidly since the first CCTV units were introduced for monitoring campus activity. Videotape formats and analog data systems have been supplanted with digital recording, offering increasingly fine resolution, color imaging, and the ability to search and archive images quickly with a few key strokes. Communications bandwidths have advanced to allow speed and detail in image transmission and mesh networks have allowed for better, more reliable wireless transmission. Most importantly, video analytic systems allow "smart" camera movement programmed to respond to various suspicious objects, sounds, and actions/movements.

Despite the common interest in enjoying a safe environment, it is not unusual for segments of the campus community to question the appropriateness of cameras and to bristle at the idea of installing high-tech surveillance equipment. The prevailing culture at many schools typically embraces the sanctity of individual privacy. However, the argument that cameras constitute an invasion of that privacy ignores the fact that an expectation of privacy is not realistic in open and public spaces. Still, the concern for overreach in monitoring is fairly commonplace, and should not be ignored. At one major research university, for example, the faculty forced the administration to adopt an explicit prohibition against monitoring the comings and goings of employees before agreeing to a proposal to equip the campus with video surveillance.

Whatever the form and function, technology must be reasonably user-friendly to be effective. Security equipment is of little value if those who are being protected by the devices are unable (or unwilling) to use them properly. Furthermore, if students, faculty, and staff feel unduly burdened by protective measures, they will find ways to avoid or circumvent the security systems, thus compromising their integrity. Therefore, it is best to keep things simple.

Each college and university must decide what kinds of security hardware and technology will best protect both its campus community and its assets. The parameters that vary across schools are far too many to enable a "one size fits all" solution. Those in charge of security must be knowledgeable about product and system availability and have the authority to choose whichever hardware and technology will best serve their particular school environment.

DESIGN FOR SECURITY

Security planning includes choices about windows, locks, alarms, cameras, and environmental design features. Using glass enhances appearance, but it also exposes the contents of the enclosed space, whether it is a building, office, laboratory, or room in which valuable property or sensitive data are kept. Those employees working within interior spaces are also exposed. Shatter-resistant windows offer more protection than standard plate glass, and they do not detract from aesthetics.

Buildings, offices, classrooms, laboratories, libraries, museums, and store-rooms have various types of doors, all of which need to be secured. The choice of locking devices must accommodate the odd hours worked by members of the academic community. Some students, especially those in graduate or professional schools or in the arts, want access to laboratories, studios, or other facilitates after class periods, at night, or on weekends, just as faculty may need access to their offices at all hours. As an alternative to deadbolts, spring-locks, or combination locks, electronic locking systems can be easily controlled remotely, but at a cost. Proper security is a matter of making the right choice in relation to the degree of security required and the resources available.

For the most highly sensitive areas, biometric systems that match retina, hand, or fingerprint scans might be best. For other spaces that need tight access controls, computerized locks and card readers offer a high degree of protection and many advantages. Every card used for access can be pro-grammed to restrict admittance to specific spaces, times of the day, and days of the week. Photo identification cards with embedded codes (e.g., bar codes, magnetic stripes, or microchips) are used with card swipe or proximity readers for access control purposes and can provide better and more convenient security for less money in the long run than keys and standard locksets.

Enclosed areas that house assets or data of significant value or that must operate uninterruptedly (e.g., a boiler plant or a file server room) require the installation of alarm systems to supplement other forms of access control. Over and above the standard burglar/intrusion alarms, additional options include motion, heat, and water detection systems, as well as local and central station alarms.

For relatively small spaces containing assets that are not especially valuable yet still need protection, alarms that sound locally with a high decibel-level and automatic shutoff/reset can be effective. However, the most sensitive spaces are best protected by a monitored central station system. Monitoring can either be outsourced to a third-party central-station provider or handled through a fully proprietary system. Schools that use CCTV or have their own police or public safety departments may find a proprietary central-station alarm system to be a wise investment.

The presence of cameras can occasionally be a deterrent to violent crime, theft, and vandalism. More readily, CCTV can help identify and lead to the apprehension of assailants, thieves, vandals, intruders, or trespassers. Besides their use for monitoring campus grounds and parking lots, CCTV can also serve as a supplementary component of building security. These systems can function as adjuncts to access controls and can be employed to monitor activity in highly sensitive areas during times when pedestrian traffic is minimal. In September 2009, for example, 24-year-old graduate student Annie Le vanished from Yale University medical research laboratory—her body was found days later stuffed inside the wall of the building. Surveillance video and swipe-card record data proved instrumental in identifying her movements within the building leading up to her disappearance as well as those of a male lab technician who was subsequently arrested for suspicion of murder.

RESIDENCE HALLS

So far the focus has been on protecting those buildings that are dedicated to the academic, research, administrative, and operational functions on campus, as well as their occupants and contents. But suitable physical security measures must also be provided for residence halls and other school-provided housing facilities. In residential settings, the usual objective of providing adequate security with minimal inconvenience is especially important.

The same measures proposed for the general protection of buildings and grounds can, with appropriate modifications, be applied to protect residential facilities. For example, landscaping should avoid blind spots near or around housing that could be used to conceal trespassers or stolen property.

Computerized card-reader access control systems for the buildings, supplemented by CCTV cameras, can contribute to the protection of residents, personal property, and school property. Residential security can be further enhanced by extending the access control systems to individual living quarters and rooms. Use of card access or punch code combination room locks can be complemented by doors and lock hardware that close and secure automatically when the door is closed so unattended rooms are less vulnerable to would-be thieves.

Beyond these considerations, however, residential security differs from other elements of security programs in that it must accommodate residential visitors. This may necessitate the combination of a CCTV camera outside the building's entrance (or just inside, if the building has a vestibule), with an intercommunications system connected to individual rooms or suites to announce visitors. Release mechanisms that can remotely free the lock on the secured door are not recommended in residence halls as they increase the likelihood that unauthorized individuals will gain access to the building. Some schools also rely on reception attendants or building proctors.

Figure 9.1 illustrates some of the housing security measures adopted by both public and private colleges and universities around the country, based on the responses to a 2008 survey sponsored by *Reader's Digest*. As shown, the range of security approaches includes surveillance, access control, and locking devices. To avoid the costs associated with 24-hour monitoring by security staff or other attendants, some schools have explored the use of electronic card-swiping devices. Unfortunately, this approach is easily compromised by the common practice of "piggy-backing," whereby one or more visitors—authorized or not—gain access in tandem with one access card holder. Sometimes, the traditional approach—of monitoring and controlling access by use of a responsible receptionist to serve as the gatekeeper—works best.

PARKING

The planning and design of campus parking, particularly at urban campuses where real estate is limited, must take into account lot security, parking authorization, and space requirements. Reasonable measures for protecting vehicles and their owners include strategically installing blue-light telephones and high-pressure sodium vapor lighting, and supplementing these fixtures with periodic patrol.

At many schools, parking problems are compounded when more students, faculty, and staff desire to park their cars than there are available spaces on campus. Having students and faculty wait in holding queues at parking lots is both inefficient and a potential source of conflict. When parking demand outpaces supply, the immediate question is how to control and manage access to the available parking spaces. Gates (or arms) with card readers that restrict drivers to specific parking areas are helpful; however, space utilization may

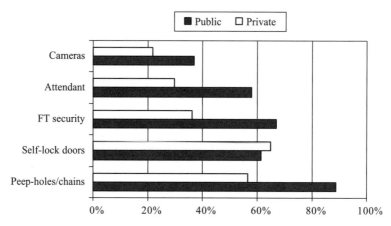

Figure 9.1 Percentage of students with various security measures in dorms
Source: Based on *Reader's Digest,* College Safety Survey, February 2008.

not be optimized if permits are distributed on a "one space, one permit" ba-sis. Issues of authorization and adequacy of space are not easily resolved.

Permit-to-space ratio recommendations should be made based not only on the population to be served, but their perceived needs. For example, resident students need to have access to parking 24 hours a day, while continuing edu-cation students or part-time faculty may require parking only during limited day or evening hours. Carpoolers may be given a hangtag that can be rotated among the group members, rather than individual tags for each member of the group. Campuses may wish to consider hiring a parking consultant to determine the applications that will optimize space for their needs.

PROTECTING ASSETS

Colleges and universities make sizable investments in purchasing and main-taining assets other than real estate. These assets include tangible property, such as laboratory equipment, computers, furniture, and paper documents, as well as intangible items, such as electronic files and data. Accountability and asset control are critically important at the college and university level.

The initial step in asset protection is creating a physical inventory of all tan-gible assets. Although this process is time-consuming and burdensome, prop-erty cannot be controlled and tracked without accurate cataloguing. As part of this inventory process, all tangibles should be affixed with identifying tags, and each tag should display the school's name, the property identification number, and an electronic bar code. This facilitates the task of periodically updating inventory, which should indicate precisely where each listed item can be found. Whenever an asset is discarded or relocated, the record for that item should be adjusted accordingly. This process can be difficult when departments make purchases independent of the institution's purchasing guidelines, so it is imperative that policies supporting this principle are developed, disseminated, and enforced.

The proliferation of highly portable equipment, such as laptop computers and LCD projectors, and student expectations that faculty will be more accessible electronically, have increased the practice of permitting off-campus use of certain college-owned equipment. Whether for maintenance purposes or for use off-campus, these assets should be documented, tracked, and periodically inventoried. Many institutions have also installed tracking software (similar to *Lojack* or *OnStar* for vehicles) on laptops so they can be located if stolen.

As a general rule, few compelling justifications exist for anyone to remove electronic or physical records—a particularly sensitive asset class—from the campus. However, there obviously will be times when authorized staff or faculty—those with a "need to know"—may require access to records other than their own personal documents. Dated charge-out slips should be inserted as place-holders in the file cabinets or other storage facilities from which the documents are being removed, indicating the item(s), borrower, and projected return date. Individuals permitted access to college records electronically from off campus must be authorized by the appropriate administrator to do so and must have a virtual private network (VPN) installed to safeguard the information from hackers. Despite the paperwork involved in property tracking, these procedures provide efficient control over and accountability for assets. In all cases, it is important to perform regular and periodic follow-ups to ensure that items have, in fact, been returned.

Documents and files should be categorized on the basis of sensitivity, purpose, and reproducibility if lost. Particularly sensitive materials should be stored in insulated, fire-rated safe-type file cabinets with combination locks; less sensitive documents can be kept in metal file cabinets protected by security bars and combination padlocks. Computerized data should regularly be backed up and archived onto a shared remote network server.

CAMPUS LAW ENFORCEMENT

In response to their increased complexity, most colleges and universities have established their own campus police or public safety departments, be they sworn or unsworn, armed or unarmed, and contract or proprietary. This move raises important questions pertaining to the authority, training, duties, and responsibilities of personnel, relations with local law enforcement and the surrounding community, and the use of lethal and nonlethal weapons.

In earlier times, especially during the tumultuous Vietnam War era when student demonstrations and sit-ins were commonplace, college campuses were not particularly welcoming to a police presence, whether of municipal or campus departments. Of course, much has changed in the last 40 years in terms of campus politics and attitudes. Still, it is of paramount importance that a campus law enforcement agency cultivates and maintains good relations with students, faculty, and staff. Without their cooperation and assistance, no campus police department can hope to succeed in its mission. Awareness and appreciation of the unique roles and expectations of students, faculty, and staff will go far in fostering mutually respectful interactions with the various segments of the college community.

STAFFING LEVELS

No firm standards have been established for campus police staffing levels, but the national averages displayed in Figure 9.2, drawn from the 2004–2005 Bureau of Justice Statistics (BJS) survey of 749 campus law enforcement agencies (606 four-year colleges/universities and 143 two-year colleges), provide some rough guidelines based on campus size and type.[11] With usual staffing levels ranging from about 2.0 to 5.0 per 1,000 student enrollment, private schools tend to maintain higher rates. In addition, schools that employ sworn officers—whose pay grades tend to be substantially higher than their non-sworn counterparts—typically have lower staffing levels than schools that do not use sworn personnel.

Comparing staffing resources in 2004 to 2005 to those from 1994 to 1995 indicates that colleges and universities had been boosting their levels of police protection even before the recent and widely publicized campus shootings at Virginia Tech and Northern Illinois University. Specifically, campus law enforcement agencies for four-year institutions averaged 3.8 full-time employees per 1,000 students in 2004 to 2005, up from 3.3 employees per 1,000 students a decade earlier. Among the three-quarters of institutions that utilize officers

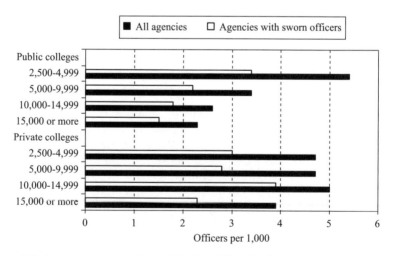

Figure 9.2 Average campus police staffing levels by school size and type
Source: Bureau of Justice Statistics, Survey of Campus Law Enforcement, 2004–05.

with arrest powers, the number of full-time sworn officers per 1,000 students rose from 2.1 to 2.3 over the 10-year time span.[12]

Apart from campus size, local crime levels and the availability of municipal, county, or state law enforcement resources are key variables in determining staffing needs. Once these needs have been assessed, a school must choose whether to rely on campus police officers, proprietary security staff, contract security staff, or mutual aid agreements with local law enforcement agencies. In addition, staffing levels and assignments should recognize the higher risk of violence during the late-night hours and weekends at residential campuses as well as coverage for special events such as rallies, concerts, and athletic events.

AUTHORITY AND TRAINING

Not more than a few decades ago, campus safety personnel were typically empowered to perform a limited range of duties, mostly relating to security and patrol. More recently, colleges have been tending toward granting full police powers to their departments to confront increasingly complex crime and safety concerns. Campus law enforcement officers derive the authority to protect college property and personnel from their institutions and their appointments as police officers (either special police officers or deputy sheriffs). In some cases, these appointments also allow campus police officers to be trained at the same police academies as local, county, or state police personnel. This has its advantages: Shared education among officers can help sustain close working relations between campus departments and surrounding law enforcement agencies.

Although there are no universal standards, some state legislatures have moved to establish minimum training requirements for nonsworn security officers. New York's Security Guard Act of 1992, for example, requires 24 hours of training (8 pre-assignment and 16 on-the-job) during the first 90 days of employment with an additional 8 hours of in-service training annually.[13]

COMMUNITY RELATIONSHIPS

It is imperative that campus law enforcement build and maintain positive relationships with the local residential community and, especially, the campus community. Consistent with this goal, campus police departments nationwide have incorporated the principles of community policing into their operations to an extent far greater than have municipal police agencies.

Authority and professional training are no substitute for interpersonal and communications skills, and these abilities should be an absolute prerequisite for appointment to an effective campus police force. According to the 2004–2005 BJS survey, campus law enforcement agencies place much greater emphasis on community-relations skills in their recruitment screening than do local police departments, including an assessment of analytic problem solving abilities (58 percent versus 37 percent), understanding of cultural diversity (57 percent versus 16 percent), and skills related to mediation and conflict management (42 percent versus 11 percent).[14]

A range of tools and strategies can assist campus police in maintaining positive relationships with students, faculty, and staff. Liaison officer programs assign law enforcement personnel to particular residence halls, academic departments, or student organizations to increase opportunities for positive interaction in nonenforcement situations. Officers on foot, bicycles, or Segways eliminate the steel confines of the traditional patrol vehicle and create additional possibilities for conversation. Some departments routinely survey their campus communities to obtain feedback about the delivery of services.

Apparent deficiencies in the police-community interactions became a significant matter for one of the nation's leading schools, Harvard University. Between 2004 and 2008, Harvard's image was tarnished by a series of embarrassing incidents in which black students and faculty alleged unfair treatment by white campus police officers, suggesting a general pattern of racial profiling. Harvard law professor Charles Ogletree, outspoken critic of racial injustice, remarked, "there's still this unfortunate assumption that equates the color of a person's skin with involvement in criminality."[15] An August 2008 incident in which a black student was confronted by campus police officers while trying to unlock his own bicycle, prompted Harvard's president to appoint an independent six-member committee to review officer recruitment, diversity training, and community outreach. Following its charge, the study team advanced a wide variety of recommendations for improving the level of fairness, openness, and accountability among campus police personnel.[16]

In addition to interpersonal skills, it is helpful for campus police personnel to possess the temperament and sensitivity needed to distinguish student pranks from malicious or destructive deeds. As an example, shortly after the campus police force was established at a major research university, it was tested by a group of students who managed to get a cow onto a dormitory roof. The campus police director chose not to respond in an enforcement capacity, believing that if the students were bright and inventive enough to lift the cow up onto the roof, then they would also be able to figure out a way to bring it down safely. When the matter was resolved, the uninjured cow was back on the ground and the campus police had won over the students' respect.

The efficient and effective way in which the cow-on-the-roof incident was handled came as no surprise to those familiar with the process used to recruit, train, and supervise the officers who serve this urban campus community. Also contributing significantly to the successful resolution were the skillful manner in which patrol officers performed their jobs, and the security director's position vis-à-vis student on-campus activities.

Whereas other campus police departments in the area relied on hiring former or retired sworn police personnel under the theory that they needed no training, this department instead sought out former or retired military personnel who had achieved top noncommissioned officer grades at time of discharge. Moreover, the pre-employment physical included an interview by one of the university's psychiatrists in an effort to weed out candidates whose main interest was in being able to wear a badge and carry a gun.

A featured qualification expected of recruits was experience in working with and helping develop young people. Important as well was that they took pride in their professional appearance in uniform. Additionally, the university provided them with formal classroom training specifically tailored for its campus population. Communication and interpersonal skills were emphasized. Toward that end, the new patrol officers, once activated, were chiefly deployed on foot rather than in cars, and encouraged to become well acquainted with faculty, staff, and students while making rounds.

With the establishment of the campus police force, student leaders wanted to know how the police presence might affect student activities. The director assured them that campus police officers would interfere with student activities only if (a) failure to do so could result in personal injury or death or in damage to property, (b) not acting might result in intervention by the city's police department, and (c) members of the university's administration or student leaders asked them to intervene.

ARMING CAMPUS POLICE

The question of whether campus police should carry firearms remains a matter of much debate. At one extreme, the University of Texas at Austin, which was the site of Charles Whitman's historic campus shooting in 1966, maintains a fleet of squad cars fully equipped with high-tech and high-powered gear to respond to any type of emergency situation. Other colleges and universities prefer not to arm their campus police with anything more deadly than a flashlight or baton.

According to the BJS surveys of colleges and universities, about 40 percent of private schools and about 80 percent of public schools employ armed campus police officers. As illustrated in Figure 9.3, the trend between the mid-1990s and the mid-2000s is for an increasing number of campuses to maintain an armed police force. Moreover, the most recent survey was completed prior to the Virginia Tech shooting, and it is likely that the growth rate has since accelerated, particularly given the recent recommendation from the International Association of Campus Law Enforcement Administrators (IACLEA) that all college campuses arm their police forces:[17]

> If the institution employs a full-service, sworn law enforcement agency, then the officers should have access to a range of use of force options including lethal (firearms) and less-than-lethal (impact tools, chemical and electronic control devices). In short, sworn officers should be armed.

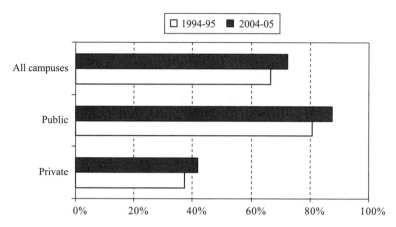

Figure 9.3 Trends in armed campus police officers in the United States
Source: Bureau of Justice Statistics, Survey of Campus Law Enforcement, 1994–05 and 2004–05.

Given the widely established "best practice" that encourages first responders to neutralize an active shooter, there is considerable merit to the IACLEA position. Because campus shooters often use sophisticated weapons, campus police officers must have access to appropriate armament to respond effectively. In addition, since most of the force is dressed in uniform and essentially indistinguishable in appearance from other uniformed law enforcement personnel, campus police may be targeted by armed felons who have committed crimes on campus or are fleeing from local law enforcement officers through campus grounds. Because campus police may be targeted by armed criminals with little hesitation about shooting anyone with arrest powers, they should be equipped to respond.

Finally, there may be times when campus police are confronted with a life-threatening situation and are called on to protect others or themselves. If unarmed, they can offer little in the way of protection, thereby diminishing their value to the school and the campus community. If armed, however, they can respond as needed. In some circumstances, shooting an assailant, albeit as a last resort, may well be their only option. Though likelihood of such an encounter may be small, this does not negate the justification for arming campus police. However, a college may choose to use various types of less-than-lethal weapons or ammunition as a less drastic means of overtaking an offender.

Of course, none of these policy prescriptions and situational advantages makes the decision concerning weapons any easier for college administrators. Following the shooting sprees at Virginia Tech and Northern Illinois University, the case for arming campus police may have become more compelling, but is by no means convincing or self-evident. While many campuses have recently decided to arm their public safety departments, others remain reluctant to move in this direction, either because of campus resistance or a belief that the security risks simply do not justify it.

Political consequences aside, the decision to arm campus police raises concerns about the ensuing cost and exposure to liability. The first expense is the initial outlay for weapons and supplies of ammunition. Then schools must pay for the training of personnel in the proper use of firearms, including wages and fringe benefits associated with time spent away at training or practicing on the firing range. Additionally, insurance premiums may increase because of the added risk of someone being injured or killed as a result of a gun's discharge, accidental or otherwise. And, of course, should a questionable shooting indeed occur, the legal expenses and potential settlement costs stemming from a lawsuit against the institution promise to be considerable. Finally, there is the cost to the school's reputation and image once the news media begins to focus on the dangers of campus cops with guns.

THE SCHOOL PUBLIC SAFETY ADMINISTRATOR

An effective security program must have the full support and cooperation of the faculty and staff. To that end, the administration must clearly delineate the school's security concerns, tailor the security program to the given academic community, and convince the campus community that the implementation is in everyone's best interest. High-level administrative support for security, as a central feature of campus operations, is absolutely imperative, as key personnel must lead by example rather than by fiat.

The administration's most critical consideration is determining the right individual to implement, administer, and promote the security program within the academic community. Certainly, a person with law enforcement or public safety experience would be best qualified to develop and oversee a college security program, especially if a campus police force exists. However, crime is only one of a wide array of security issues confronting an institution. Therefore, public safety experience alone is not sufficient. The chief security administrator must have the interpersonal and communication skills needed to gain the trust of the many campus constituencies. An authoritarian attitude in dealing with students, faculty, or staff will do the program far more harm than good.

THE HUMAN ELEMENT

The role of people—students, faculty, and staff—has been the common thread throughout the discussion of physical security, behavioral concerns, asset control and accountability. The overwhelming majority of security problems results from some type of human behavior, whether deliberate or accidental. Fortunately, people can have a major role to play in preventing problems and the consequent losses.

No matter what resources a college dedicates to safety and loss prevention or the steps it takes to fortify the campus infrastructure, the key to its security program's success or failure rests with the members of the academic community. Faculty, staff, and students have shared responsibility for staying safe and protecting property, be it their own or that of the school. This responsibility holds regardless of the physical security provided and the existence and size of a campus police force.

Despite their mutual interests, the relationship between students and administrators can sometimes be adversarial. New arrivals on campus, the vast majority of whom are but a few short months out of high school, are often inclined to consider themselves as free to do what they want, when they want, and where they want. At the same time, colleges and universities have learned (sometimes the hard way) that although students are entitled to privacy and a good deal of freedom, there must be some restraints on student behavior. Unless these conflicting perspectives can be reconciled with mutual respect for each side's position, the safety and security of both people and property will ultimately suffer.

COMMUNITY PARTICIPATION

Virtually all members of the academic community participate (knowingly or not) in the security program. Although substantial investments may have been made in various kinds of hardware and technology to enhance security and safety, if these physical security measures are used thoughtlessly or carelessly by any member of the campus community, the entire school stands to suffer.

For example, suppose a school issues all administrators, faculty, staff, and students embedded photo identification cards or keys for controlling access to designated offices, rooms, laboratories, residence halls, or other secured spaces. The objective, of course, is to protect both people and property. However, one or more members of the community might lend their cards or keys to friends who do not have the authorized access to the same locations. Others, thinking it only courteous, might hold open the door to a secured space to allow another person to enter.

Thoughtless or deliberate violations of security procedures can have far-reaching consequences, from property theft to an assault by a campus intruder who just happens to look like a student. To avoid these consequences, faculty, staff, and students must realize the potentially grave risks of assisting either friend or stranger in gaining access to protected areas. Physical security measures are effective only when users respect their integrity.

Cultivating trusting relationships among members of the student body and school personnel is critical. Students sometimes become aware of suspicious activities or of troubled classmates/roommates long before others do, and their timely input can lead to successful early intervention. However, this type of referral will likely happen only if students feel comfortable in communicating their concerns to someone in authority. Likewise, faculty and staff members must also be alert to students or colleagues who may be dangerous to themselves or others. Having an open channel of communication may well be the difference between responding to an incident and preventing one.

The proactive strategy of threat assessment/management, the elements of which were discussed in Chapter 4, was derived from a model initially crafted in 1990 by the Los Angeles Police Department.[18] Since then, many other law enforcement agencies have followed suit. If there is reason to believe that certain persons or activities may pose a threat, agencies gather data and intelligence to determine the nature of the threat, its immediacy, and the likelihood that it will be carried out. Once the assessment has been accomplished, a determination is reached regarding what further action, if any, is warranted.

In response to the 2007 tragedy at Virginia Tech, countless universities have used this basic model to develop threat assessment teams and protocols. As outlined by Deisinger and colleagues, threat assessment and management teams should ideally operate and convene on a regular basis and be prepared to respond quickly to emerging concerns forwarded to it.[19] When assessing a combative student, a belligerent staff or faculty member, or a troublesome outsider, the team should use its broad-based and collective wisdom, along with all available and pertinent data, to determine if a threat exists and what the appropriate response should be. Team members should be at a fairly senior level so that they have the authority to act as needed. They should be mindful of privacy regulations. However, if the assessment team believes that a subject poses a substantial threat, their duty to ensure public safety takes precedent over the subject's privacy.[20]

STUDENT PRIVACY

The issue of student privacy is a frequent cause of concern for academic administrators across the nation. Because they are no longer minors, college students are protected by a host of thorny privacy regulations prescribed by the Health Insurance Portability and Accountability Act (HIPAA) and the Family Educational Rights and Privacy Act (FERPA). Campus officials need to be clear on the allowances and limits of federal and state privacy laws. Underutilizing available information on students carries the potential for significant human and fiscal costs. Over-reaching, however, can adversely affect the level of trust on campus, as well as create the potential for costly and time-consuming litigation.

There is much confusion about what information can be shared between schools and between entities within the same school.[21] Oftentimes, it is assumed that HIPAA and FERPA prohibit all information sharing about students when, in fact, they both provide broad exceptions for health and safety concerns (see Appendix G). For example, "[i]n an emergency, FERPA permits school officials to disclose without student consent education records, including personally identifiable information from those records, to protect the health or safety of students or other individuals."[22] Any confusion should be addressed and clarified, so that information necessary to assess properly the risks and to safeguard campuses may be obtained.

By contrast to the privacy exceptions pertaining to specific at-risk individuals, some lawmakers have sought a wide-net approach. A couple of state legislatures have attempted, perhaps misguidedly, to dismantle the privacy shield by mandating mental heath privacy waivers from all incoming college students. Generally, however, the risk of campus violence does not trump sacred rights to privacy.

COUNSELING

As discussed in Chapter 6, the hype and hysteria that followed high-profile campus rampages prompted a range of overly reactive, counterproductive, and impractical measures to fortify school security. At the same time, concerns that "Virginia Tech could happen here" motivated certain important and long-overdue changes that could have wide-ranging impacts. In particular, images of a deranged student ambushing a packed classroom of students renewed a much-needed focus on mental health services. Schools were lacking in these resources even though—in contrast to the limited threat of random shootings—the risk for suicide and death linked to substance abuse continued to be relatively high.[23]

According to an annual survey taken by the Association of University and College Counseling Center Directors, one-third of campus counseling centers added at least one new staff member and 15 percent had their budgets enhanced in the year following the extraordinarily devastating event at Virginia Tech.[24] Additionally, the percentage of campus facilities with psychiatrists on staff (in addition to counselors) increased from 57 percent to 62 percent. There is still much room for improvement: Whereas the International Association of Counseling Services prescribes that colleges maintain a student-counselor ratio of 1,500 to 1, 2007 figures suggest that the national average is nearly 2,000 to 1.[25]

The role of counseling services extends beyond the routine assistance offered to students who are having trouble making the transition to campus life or are struggling with various interpersonal conflicts. Many students arrive with or develop drug or alcohol addictions, clinical depression, eating disorders, and other illnesses that require counseling and possibly pharmaceutical intervention. To respond adequately in mental health emergencies, colleges and universities may need to call on outside resources, including community mental health providers. Indeed, the availability of counseling services to supplement those offered on campus may be critical in preventing violence and other problematic behaviors. Therefore, colleges are wise to establish formal or informal relationships with outside agencies and private vendors, so that they can be called on quickly and efficiently when needed. Clearly, progress in this area carries wide-ranging benefits beyond the exceptional case of a random shooting.

An emerging challenge for campus counseling departments surrounds the recent influx of students who have served the country in the armed services and are taking advantage of veterans' benefits to complete their educations. Those men and women who served in areas of conflict often require additional levels of counseling support to deal with post-traumatic stress issues related to their military experiences.

RESPONDING TO TRAGEDY

The Virginia Tech shooting prompted colleges and universities, large and small, to reexamine and prioritize issues of violence prevention and campus security. College officials needed assurance that they were well-prepared, not just for the remote but frightening possibility that some dispirited student might decide to replicate the Blacksburg massacre, but also for the reality that students and their parents would question the adequacy of safety procedures on their own campus. Fortunately, colleges and universities have responded by increasing their emergency readiness through enhanced strategic planning, communications protocols, and notification systems.

ALL-HAZARDS EMERGENCY RESPONSE PLAN

Colleges have been quick to adopt all-hazards Emergency Response Plans (ERPs) to be prepared both for campus shootings and for a variety of natural disasters or critical incidents that could threaten the safety and well-being of the campus community. As shown in Figure 9.4, the 2008 *Reader's Digest* survey of 135 colleges and universities throughout the country found that over 90 percent of schools had ERPs in place. The larger, yet older, BJS survey found similarly that 94 percent of four-year colleges had developed an ERP.[26]

However, as Figure 9.4 also reveals, a majority of schools moved beyond just crafting an ERP by developing lockdown plans as well. Rooted in correctional nomenclature, "campus lockdown" is a popular security catchphrase, often raised in parental inquiries about safety procedures. Leaving aside the impossibility of truly locking down a sprawling campus, most college shootings actually take place in just one building, if not just one classroom. It is also true, notwithstanding the unique lull in activity in the Virginia Tech murder spree, that campus shooting sprees typically begin and end so quickly that locking down students in residence halls and classrooms and turning away off-campus students and visitors does not necessarily help.[27] Furthermore, there is a significant downside to sealing off access to buildings during an active shooter episode: Although an armed assailant loose on campus grounds may not be able to enter classrooms and other buildings, potential victims

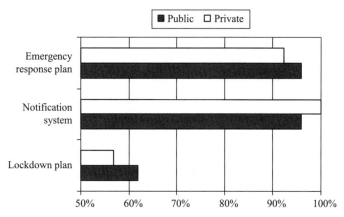

Figure 9.4 Campus-wide security responses of colleges and universities
Source: Based on *Reader's Digest*, School Safety Survey, February 2008.

seeking to enter these spaces would also be left stranded without refuge if stalked by the shooter.

It is hardly sufficient just to have an emergency response plan in place. Some form of practice exercise—either table-top scenarios or field drills—can be useful for working through potential implementation and coordination problems. According to the 2004–2005 BJS survey, whereas 94 percent of four-year colleges had crafted an ERP, only 73 percent engaged in preparedness exercises.[28] Finally, as discussed in Chapter 6, these training exercises can and should include various on-campus and off-campus agencies, but should avoid involving the student population in any way.

INTEROPERABLE COMMUNICATIONS SYSTEMS

If and when a violent incident or other type of emergency does occur on campus, police and other college officials may need to communicate with various noncampus agencies and emergency service providers. This outreach can be difficult and slow if the available communications technology is not compatible with radio systems used by local law enforcement, fire, and emergency medical responders. For this reason, colleges and universities have been eager to acquire interoperable communications systems.

The federal government has recognized the role of emergency responders, including campus law enforcement, in managing critical incidents. By virtue of a Homeland Security directive, all emergency responder agencies must be trained in the National Incident Management System (NIMS) and the Incident Command System (ICS).[29] Adopted by all governmental and nongovernmental agencies, NIMS is a standard tactical approach for responding to emergencies such as natural disasters and terrorist attacks.[30] This framework has several components, including incident command, resource management, and communications and information management. ICS, in turn, prescribes personnel roles and responsibilities during a crisis. By establishing an operational standard, ICS makes it possible for agencies that normally do not work together to achieve an efficient and coordinated response. Campus emergency personnel should be familiar with these protocols to minimize miscommunication and other problems that can arise during a crisis situation.

MASS NOTIFICATION SYSTEMS

It is vital that a college or university be able to communicate quickly and effectively with its entire community in the event of an emergency to ensure that everyone is notified about the situation and to relay critical information regarding the event. Fortunately, this has been one area of security that has been embraced and pursued almost universally by schools.

The overall effectiveness of any all-hazards mass notification system depends on several factors, some technical and others logistic. The devices range from low-tech alarms and sirens that signal an emergency of some unspecified kind, to high-tech electronic text alerts and digital message boards that can provide detailed information during an emerging crisis. Although it seems incontrovertibly wise to install such mass notification systems, the efficacy of these systems depends entirely on how they are implemented and the anticipation of foreseeable limitations.

The most important factor is the level of campus participation. Whether participation is required of everyone or optional via either opt-in or opt-out processes, it is critical that notifications can reach as many members of the campus population as possible. Unfortunately, at many campuses, students have been slow or reluctant to subscribe for emergency alerts.[31]

Colleges have many choices for communications modalities. An August 2008 survey of 342 colleges conducted by the National Campus Safety and Security Project (CSSP) reported significant variability among schools in the range of technology currently being used. As shown in Table 9.1, schools have adopted high-tech methods (such as e-mail, Web page announcements, or text messaging) almost universally, while relying less often on older, low-tech devices (such as public address systems, speakers, and sirens), and then only as backup.

Few students have land-lines and many do not regularly check their campus e-mail or their cell phone voicemail. As a result, many campuses have begun using alternative communication tools and technology—setting up pages on social networking sites such as *Facebook, MySpace,* and *Twitter,* or creating department Weblogs. At this point in time, text messaging is the quickest means of reaching students as they are rarely without their cell phones. This, in turn, creates challenges for crafting a sufficiently clear notification message that can be received on all students' text-message systems, most of which impose severe limitations on character length. When needed to alert the

Table 9.1
Use of mass notification systems at college campuses

Communications method	Percentage using
E-mail	95.3%
Web page	87.4%
Text messaging	76.9%
Land-line messaging	70.8%
Telephone tree	60.8%
Public address system	42.1%
Pole-mounted speakers/sirens	36.8%
Electronic message boards	35.4%

Source: National Campus Safety and Security Project, 2009, p. 23, http://www.nacubo.org/
Documents/Initiatives/CSSPSurveyResults.pdf.

campus about a violent crime, natural disaster, approaching storm, or out-
break of contagious disease, the initial messages should be provided in a
timely manner across multiple media and include brief instructions on actions
to be taken. Messages should be updated as additional information becomes
available and particularly when the threat has been sufficiently mitigated or
has passed. It is equally important not to transmit misinformation hastily;
spreading unfounded statements that might unnecessarily terrify the community should be avoided.

The right balance between timeliness and accuracy can sometimes be difficult
to achieve. In one recent incident, students at the University of Iowa frantically
ran for cover following a campus-wide text alert informing them about an active
shooter nearby. It turns out that "nearby" was actually many miles away on the
opposite side of town, posing very little threat to the campus. In another episode, public safety officials at St. Johns University in New York City notified all
its students and staff about a possible gunman spotted on campus wearing a
Fred Flintstone mask and toting a .50-caliber rifle. What they failed to mention
in the text alert was which of the school's three campus locations—Queens,
Staten Island, or Manhattan—was being threatened, thereby causing needless
panic at the unaffected locations.[32]

In addition, campus officials must be ready and able to communicate both
with the media and especially with concerned parents once word spreads of
an emergency situation. The CSSP survey of colleges found, not surprisingly,
far less emphasis on establishing means for reaching parents of students and
families of staff. In fact, over half of the schools rely on their Web site for
external notification, and this may not always be timely or effective.

Reacting to the shootings at Virginia Tech and Northern Illinois University,
the U.S. Congress, through the 2008 Higher Education Act (see Appendix H),
established funding for college campuses to develop and publicize their

emergency response plans.[33] Fortunately, a provision of the Act that did *not* pass was the requirement that colleges launch a notification within 30 minutes of word of an emergency. Given how fluid and unreliable such early information can be, critics were rightly concerned about the potential "Cry Wolf" effect.

Finally, mass notification systems are of limited effectiveness if students, faculty, and staff are not aware that they exist, are not registered in the system, or do not understand how they work. Student orientations and faculty and staff information sessions provide excellent opportunities to familiarize the campus community with these and other emergency response procedures.

In 2009, the U.S. Department of Education announced changes to the Jeanne Clery Disclosure of Campus Security Policy and Campus Crime Statistics that would take effect in Fall 2010. Included in the new regulations were enhanced requirements for mass notification as well as prescribed annual testing of emergency response plans. Time will tell whether the federal security mandates will indeed make college campuses safer.

Of course, no matter how diligent and responsible academic administrators, safety officials, and police are in improving violence prevention and security, there can be no absolute guarantees that a tragedy like Virginia Tech will not recur. If a prospective student—undergraduate or graduate—requires 100 percent assurance of safety at school, then the only recourse might just be an online degree.

THE SCHOOL WORKFORCE

As emphasized in the preceding chapters, security needs and solutions largely center on the behavior of people, regardless of the type of school or work setting. As Kenneth Trump of the National School Safety and Security Services has framed the challenge, "People will always be the weakest link in school security and emergency plans. The question is, how weak will we allow them to be?"[1]

Human behavior—whether it is due to malice or neglect—can create a wide array of security risks ranging from violence and theft to vandalism and waste. Moreover, the success or failure of any school security and safety program depends in large part on the support and participation of faculty and staff as well as students. Without sufficient cooperation and buy-in, even the best security policies and procedures can be rendered meaningless.

For the most part, schools have relatively limited control over the composition of the student body. Of course, the admissions process provides private schools and most colleges with some ability to screen applicants; however, the scope of available background data about prospective students is rather narrow, beyond the usual scholastic measures contained in completed school applications and records of serious infractions. By contrast, schools at all academic levels have much greater control over the makeup of their workforce, including administrators, faculty, coaches, staff, and maintenance crews. That control is manifested in terms of three interrelated yet distinct processes: pre-employment screening, training and supervision, and discipline and retention. Weakness in any of these three domains can have serious negative ramifications for the safety and security of the entire school community.

PRE-EMPLOYMENT SCREENING

The first, and arguably most critical, step in successful workforce development is pre-employment screening, the process of assessing whether a prospective employee appears trustworthy. Experience and skill provide no guarantee of an individual's character, and it is a serious mistake to confuse competency and integrity. If character is not a consideration during the hiring process, the results can be embarrassing and expensive. Consequently, pre-employment screening and selection must examine, to the extent permitted by state and federal law, both talent and temperament, regardless of the applicant's prospective position. In particular, schools and colleges should maintain a thorough screening process—including school, work, and criminal history—for every job candidate, from faculty and administrators to staff and support personnel.

The depth of background screening and the types of information that would render a candidate unsuitable for the job depend, of course, on the nature of the position. Coaches for high school athletics, for example, are necessarily vetted with a thorough criminal background investigation as are those who would be entrusted with financial responsibilities. Similarly, an employee being considered for work within a student dormitory would need to clear a more extensive background check than would, for example, a landscape worker.

The importance of pre-employment screening for contract support personnel, such as some bus drivers and food service employees, also depends on the extent to which they have frequent contact with students, particularly in elementary and secondary schools. Providers of contracted workers should be required, under the terms of the negotiated agreements, to screen all personnel who will be assigned to work at a school. Although this does not signify that any school or school system assumes full responsibility for these employees, it does mean that the suppliers of the services must comply with a contractual obligation in assigning personnel to a school district. This helps to ensure that the standard for quality employees is met even for contract personnel.

The employment process, including pre-screening, is ultimately a task for human resources, despite the legitimate interest of the security department. However, security professionals, who typically have experience in confronting post-employment problems that stem from inadequate or inconsistent pre-employment screening, can offer useful guidance in relation to application format, application completion, and data verification.

The Application for Employment

A standard application is a way to glean as much information as legally permissable from an applicant and should be mandatory for all positions, regardless of whether résumés or curricula vitae are additionally accepted. The application's format should be designed, with existing federal and state laws in mind, to elicit as much detailed information about the job candidate as possible. As an additional safeguard, applicants should be informed that employment offers are contingent on verification of background information and possible drug testing, and asked to provide written consent/agreement in advance of the process.

An employment application should, of course, begin logically with questions concerning the candidate's education, including all schools attended, dates of attendance, highest grade completed, and any degrees awarded. For positions where academic achievement is a significant factor in selection, applicants should be instructed to have official transcripts sent directly from the schools.

Transcripts provided directly by applicants should never be considered sufficient. In one scandalous episode, a ream of transcript forms was stolen from a college registrar's office. Investigation of the crime eventually revealed that the thief, a graduate student, had also managed to have the school's official seal copied and was in the business of selling "official" transcripts to other students. The price per transcript was based on the grades requested by the buyer.

The education portion of the application can be followed by a section related to previous employment, which should ask for information about jobs held over at least the preceding 10 years. In addition to the names of past employers, applicants should provide dates of employment, job titles and descriptions, names of immediate supervisors, and reasons for leaving. Additionally, applicants should supply the names and contact information for at least three references, with the mix of personal versus professional depending on the nature of the position sought. Ideally, these references should come from individuals, preferably supervisors, who have first-hand knowledge of the candidate's work habits and responsibility.

Despite a widespread belief that personal references never produce information of much value, there are occasions when hard truths are revealed directly or indirectly through reference checks. In one case, the friend of an applicant for a critical support position praised his effort and dedication in dealing with an addiction problem.

If a position requires any form of licensing, applicants should be requested to provide the nature of the license, place where issued, years for which the license is valid, and whether a license has ever been suspended or revoked. Moreover, official certification from the licensing organization/agency should be required.

Although applicants cannot be asked whether they have ever been arrested, they can be required to disclose any convictions for a felony or serious misdemeanor. Because the definition of "serious misdemeanor" varies from state to state, this second component of the criminal history is frequently excluded. A question about felony conviction is, nevertheless, always appropriate. The implications of a felony record, in terms of employability and necessary oversight, depend on the nature of the position as well as the type and recency of the criminal conduct.

APPLICATION COMPLETION

The human resources representative is responsible for ensuring that all application questions are answered appropriately and that all periods of time are accounted for in some way. Unexplained breaks in the applicant's professional history should raise concerns. In one extreme—but not uncommon—example of a failure to investigate an incomplete work history, a school employee failed to show up for work three days in a row and could not be reached. At the request of the supervisor, security investigated and learned that the absent employee was in police custody after having been arrested for armed robbery. An internal investigation determined that the human resources representative who initially interviewed the employee had ignored an unexplained three-year gap in the employment timeline, which coincided with his previous confinement in a correctional facility.

Further, it is important that human resources personnel compare the applicant's résumé or curriculum vitae to the completed application. Oftentimes, an inconsistency between the two reveals falsifications or exaggerations in one or both documents.

Once these responsibilities are met, the application and any attachments should be forwarded to the administrators most involved in making the hiring decision, such as managers, principals, department chairs, or college deans. Any other individuals involved in the hiring/search process (e.g., members of a search committee or panel of interviewers) should be solicited for their written input. If an applicant is considered to be a viable candidate, the human resources department should then be contacted to launch the verification process.

DATA VERIFICATION

Employment decision-making and background verification are distinct processes that can be handled by separate departments. However, the latter task should always be the responsibility of human resources personnel, who may utilize an outside agency that specializes in conducting background investigations/verifications. Authenticating the information in an application may take considerable time and effort, but it can prove to be rather cost-effective. Since most of the verification process can be accomplished by telephone, mail, or e-mail, the expense pales in comparison with that of hiring an unqualified person and subsequently having to replace him or her.

Educational information at the college and university level is easily verified by requesting transcripts from the relevant schools; this is particularly convenient because the contact is between two educational institutions. In addition, making contact with deans and select faculty members can help fill in any missing information with regard to an applicant's work habits, extracurricular activities, community service, and disciplinary problems. Prior to making these overtures, unit representatives should be briefed by human resources on the strategies and regulations for conducting reference calls.

In general, acquiring reference input from previous employers is neither easy nor straightforward. Previous employers are typically reluctant to do more than confirm dates of employment because they fear being sued if anything they reveal results in the applicant not being hired. Such caution often prevails even though no liability exists as long as any adverse information is both true and documented. It is often possible to overcome this hurdle by asking former supervisors to verify that the applicant's explanation for leaving a previous job is accurate, though there may still be some reticence to comment. A key question to ask all previous employers is whether they would be willing to rehire the applicant; any hesitation in responding to this query tends to signal a separation that was not under the best of circumstances.

THE HIRING PROCESS AND ORIENTATION

Once the applicant's background information has been verified, those empowered with the hiring decision will determine if the applicant should be invited for one or more interviews and, where appropriate, a faculty colloquium or class presentation. For most positions, the interview arrangements should be coordinated through human resources. However, college faculty recruitment interviews are best handled by the office of the dean or department chair due to the elaborate and often multi-day process typical of a faculty search. Hiring senior college administrators, on the other hand, is often best managed by an outside search firm.

Although most formal job offers should be made through the human resources department, offers for academic appointments at the college level are often processed by deans and department chairs; in such cases, support and guidance from human resources specialists can avoid unforeseen problems. Importantly, once hired, the successful recruit becomes an employee of the school, not of the academic unit that made the selection.

All employment offers should be extended in writing and require a signature of acceptance. Offer letters should include the job title, salary, starting date, name of the person to whom the new hire will report, and any other language required by law or school policy. If feasible, appointment letters should be accompanied by all relevant policy documents or handbooks outlining the position's expectations and responsibilities.

New hires normally spend their first day of work completing forms (e.g., payroll, tax, and insurance), learning about fringe benefits and parking, and obtaining a photo identification card. The institution/school orientation should include an introduction to the overall mission and goals, the short-term priorities and long-range plans, and the identities and roles of key leaders in the organizational hierarchy. Furthermore, new employees should be briefed on critical school policies and practices, on standards for accountability and advancement, on privacy rules related to students and colleagues alike, and on obligations with regard to handling health, security, and safety concerns that might arise.

In addition to the general institution-level introduction, a secondary position-specific orientation should be held to familiarize the new hire with his or her immediate surroundings. A well-qualified, newly hired employee may come from an environment where certain wasteful or questionable practices were tolerated (e.g., using work time or supplies for personal reasons), and, if not briefed on what is and what is not acceptable, there is a risk that the old habits will be retained in the new position. Should a reprimand eventually follow, the new hire will feel unjustly singled out without having been given adequate warning. Similarly, although new faculty members may already be familiar with syllabus content and procedures for testing and grading, they might not be sufficiently alerted to local expectations and standards.

TRAINING AND SUPERVISION

As is the case with initial orientation, training involves certain matters that are common to all school/campus employees and others that are germane to a particular department or job function. Regardless of position, virtually all employees may benefit from workshops related to sexual harassment, diversity, or other issues of ethical conduct. Many employees, faculty, and staff alike, may also gain from training related to certain computer skills, particularly given the fast-changing nature of technology. For the most part, however, employee training—individualized and group—surrounds the particular tasks expected for the role.

Not all employees require on-the-job training regarding their job functions. Faculty members will generally have all the necessary skills by the time they are appointed, whether because of prior teaching experience or as a result of their exposure to teaching as graduate assistants. However, all employees, regardless of job function or authority, should be adequately supervised and have their performance regularly evaluated with the primary emphasis on growth and development.

Training

Although job descriptions often include educational requirements, an employee's educational background does not replace the need for training, and the importance of this kind of preparation should not be dismissed on the theory that "we only hire experienced people." Whatever the employee's prior work experience, it may be at variance with the new employer's expectations. Ordinarily, the primary purpose of training is to enhance performance by familiarizing new employees with their work environment and local culture. A college faculty secretary, for example, may know how to take messages but not the new school's particular method of ordering books. Likewise, a newly hired maintenance engineer needs to know how to order supplies and from which approved vendor. Ideally, training should be given by the employee's supervisor or a senior employee with substantial knowledge of the job's responsibilities. Finally, given the tremendous security risks associated with information technology, training for most employees should emphasize school policies related to accessing databases, e-mail, and the Internet.

Supervision

Nearly all organizations have hierarchies of accountability involving some element of supervision at each level of employment. In the academic community, the form of supervision varies depending on the school level. Principals of elementary and secondary schools report to their boards of education and private school headmasters to their trustees. These chief administrative officers are, in turn, responsible for supervising all personnel assigned to their schools, and this supervision is often handled by intermediate administrators.

The manner in which college and university presidents are overseen depends on whether their institutions are private or part of a state system. Chief executives at private colleges typically work with governing boards of trustees comprised of alumni and other prominent members of the community. At state colleges and universities, presidents report to state departments or boards of education. College presidents are assisted by and provide supervision to vice presidents and provosts, who, in turn, oversee deans, academic department heads, and the managers of various administrative or business departments.

Faculty, especially college professors, hold a unique position in the academic hierarchy. Although they are overseen by department heads and their job performance must conform to the prescriptions of a faculty handbook, they enjoy the independence conferred by academic freedom. However, the protections of academic freedom apply to teaching and scholarship and should not be construed to mean that the faculty can function without constraint. No institution can succeed without accountability, and this means that faculty members must be held responsible for their actions through adequate supervision and performance evaluation.

Delicate issues pertaining to academic freedom can pose challenges for college and university administrators. Deans and department heads are responsible for the overall operation of their respective colleges and departments, so they must be prepared to differentiate between administrative and educational matters, and faculty members should be prepared to respect the distinction.

An important aspect of management and supervision is maintaining realistic controls over and accountability for assets to prevent material loss. Managerial and supervisory personnel must be neither too nonchalant nor overly imposing since either extreme tends to result in losses. If there is an appearance of laxity, subordinates may be inclined to take advantage of it, and the resulting losses can be the result of accident, waste, or carelessness rather than criminal activity. In contrast, if supervisors continually micromanage asset protection, employees may become inclined to relinquish all responsibility to their superiors and the resulting indifference can lead to increased losses.

Finally, the school should have a clear-cut policy with regard to outside activity and conflicts of interest. Faculty and staff alike should be required to report any potential conflicts and certify that their conduct and associations are within proper boundaries.

DISCIPLINE AND RETENTION

The relationship between supervision and discipline extends in both directions; the ways in which people are supervised and the responsibility of supervisors to their superiors may raise questions with regard to disciplinary rules and procedures. Conversely, the ways in which discipline is administered can have a bearing on a school or school district's ability to retain its employees and to avoid unnecessary conflict. When there are allegations or suspicions of employee misconduct—criminal or otherwise—disciplinary action must be preceded by an investigation to avoid potentially costly repercussions.

Disciplinary Policies and Practices

Just as it is sometimes necessary to discipline students, disciplinary concerns can arise with respect to faculty and staff when an employee has acted in a manner inconsistent with a school's policies, procedures, or operating practices. Moreover, the type of disciplinary action clearly depends on the frequency and severity of the behavior. For example, repeatedly failing to complete certain tasks in a timely manner will generally call for a more measured response than single acts of violence, theft, or fraud.

Except for the most egregious infractions, the first attempt at discipline should generally be nonpunitive, and should include a warning to an errant employee and clarification of the rules in question. With repeat offenders, depending again on the severity of the rule violations, the wisest course of action may be to terminate their employment. Before employees can be legitimately charged with violating rules, they must already be fully versed in school policies and procedures. With that in mind, it may be too risky to rely completely on verbally or even electronically transmitted guidelines, for these neither offer proof that employees received the information nor that they understood it. Moreover, transmitting important prescriptions verbally can sometimes lead to an employee feeling intimidated and hesitant to ask questions.

Often linked to a school's overall vision/mission statement, policies and procedures serve distinct, yet related, functions: Policies inform employees of essential rules, and procedures indicate how these policies are to be achieved. For example, a school policy might be not to discriminate while the corresponding procedure might prescribe how to hire, reward, or promote employees without discriminating. Whereas day-to-day operations at a school may change frequently and as needed, policies and procedures tend to be long-term and lasting position statements. To avoid misunderstanding or unfair disciplinary action in the event of confusion, policies and procedures should ideally be made available to employees in a hardcopy format, with online access to materials—updated regularly—serving as a backup. Employees should be required to confirm in writing that they have read and understand the policies and procedures.

Disciplinary Action

Academic administrators, wary of insulting their intelligent workforce, are sometimes reluctant to ask employees to acknowledge receipt and understanding of policies and procedures. But even with written affirmation, there is no guarantee of full compliance. Realistically, some policies and procedures will be ignored or possibly violated willfully, and this will require some form of disciplinary action.

To avoid allegations or the appearance of discrimination or unfairness, an objective investigation without preconceived ideas of guilt or innocence must precede taking any disciplinary action. This investigation must prove three things:

1. that the policy or procedure allegedly violated does in fact exist;
2. that the person charged with the violation knew of its existence; and
3. that there is documented evidence to support the allegation.

If the preliminary investigation uncovers sufficient evidence to support an allegation of significant wrongdoing, a formal hearing should then be convened, compliant with pre-established policies and practices regarding employee discipline. Any disciplinary measures ultimately imposed should, of course, be administered even-handedly; penalties must not vary from employee to employee for the same offense, except to the extent that any prior history of rule violation may increase the appropriate sanction or any mitigating circumstances may reduce it.

Although what constitutes discrimination or unfairness in disciplinary matters varies considerably, the adverse impact can be substantial. Morale, and with it productivity, suffer; normally content, nonunion employees may decide to unionize. Reputations may be damaged, making it harder to retain existing personnel and much more difficult to recruit new employees. Failure to be nondiscriminatory can do far more than undermine the concept of discipline; it can have a negative impact on an entire institution.

Retention

Employee turnover, although to some degree inevitable, can be rather expensive in light of the significant costs associated with recruiting a replacement. The extent of faculty and staff turnover depends not only on wages, fringe benefits, and working conditions, but also on the opportunities for advancement through employment elsewhere. For the most part, those who select careers in any segment of education do not base their choice on compensation. However, a wide differential in compensation available at other schools or through other types of employment can be hard to resist.

At elementary and secondary schools, administrators share responsibility for retaining employees. Salaries and fringe benefits need to keep up with reasonable increases and on-time contract renewals. Working conditions—including cleanliness, comfort, and the availability of teaching tools—should meet the highest standards, because work environment is an important part of teaching and learning, and students, employees, and the entire community are the beneficiaries when quality conditions are the norm. Communities as a whole must be committed to improving and maintaining high quality working conditions in their schools. Regrettably, school employees are not paid their worth in relation to their contributions to society. To remedy this, administrators must learn to do a better job of communicating their systems' needs to both parents and those who actually control resources.

Similar deficiencies in compensation are typical for college staff and support personnel. Though paid less than they might be at other jobs, college employees often remain in large part because of the benefits, chief among them the ability to take courses or pursue a degree for themselves or their children without charge. Generally speaking, staff retention for these positions poses few problems for administrators.

The bulk of university faculty is employed full-time, and although there may be some contractual teaching appointments, faculty members are, for the most part, either tenured or on a probationary tenure track. In addition to being compensated reasonably well in terms of salary and fringe benefits, faculty members, including those with contractual appointments, are usually allowed time for outside work, such as consulting or writing. These activities can supplement their earnings and enhance their professional stature. Moreover, the prestige associated with the position of college faculty can be significantly rewarding in itself.

A significant source of turnover at colleges and universities comes from tenure-track faculty who are recruited and hired yet later denied tenure and terminated. For these individuals, the experience can be expensive and traumatic, and it also negatively impacts their colleagues and students. Moreover, a high turnover rate among faculty because of tenure denial is exceptionally costly for a university, both in terms of its finances and its reputation. The detrimental effect on reputation can make future recruiting that much more difficult. To reduce the rate of turnover and the risk of embarrassment (for the institution as well as the employee), those responsible for hiring decisions should realistically assess current and future institutional needs before the search process is initiated.

Given the major significance of the tenure decision to the career trajectory of faculty, exceptional care is required to ensure that all procedures are closely followed, combined with sensitivity to the potential impact of a negative outcome. The faculty and administrators responsible for evaluating candidates for tenure are hardly infallible, and too often departmental politics taint the assessment of teaching and scholarship. The tenure candidate as well as the entire academic department can suffer as a consequence of a shoddy process. A thorough process of appeal is essential to avoid the potential for costly litigation or worse. At the extreme, the consequence can be catastrophic.

On August 24, 1992, the "publish or perish" adage was rendered tragically literal when Valery I. Fabrikant, a Russian-born professor of mechanical engineering who had been terminated months earlier by Montreal's Concordia University, returned to campus armed for revenge. He executed four of his former faculty colleagues whom he believed had treated him unfairly. Earlier that year, Fabrikant had sent e-mails to hundreds of faculty members at universities throughout Canada and the United States, accusing Concordia engineering professors of engaging in fraud. He suggested that his department sought to get rid of him before he was able to expose their unethical behavior.

Fabrikant was arrested at the scene of the shooting, and was later convicted and sentenced to prison for murder. Meanwhile, two independent investigations of the circumstances leading up to the murders were commissioned.[2] While condemning Fabrikant's horrific retaliation, the investigations found support for some of his claims about scholarly misconduct and lack of professional integrity. Moreover, the authors advanced several recommendations regarding the manner in which Fabrikant was treated, and this ultimately led to enhancements in the school's formal policies and procedures.

More recently, on February 12, 2010, Professor Amy Bishop, a 45-year-old biologist as the University of Alabama in Huntsville, who had been denied tenure despite a fairly impressive record of scholarship, allegedly killed three colleagues and wounded three others during a departmental faculty meeting. Bishop reportedly was quite bitter over her tenure review process, and was understandably concerned about her job prospects in a tight economy. Whether or not there were any procedural flaws, this episode is a grim reminder of the importance of transparency and due process.

TERMINATION AND LAYOFF

Even with careful employee screening, training, and supervision, there will be occasions that call for cutting ties with school employees. These occasions may involve staff downsizing or the elimination of certain departments or activities, but have no connection to job performance. Or, certain employees, because of poor job performance or improper conduct, may no longer be considered suitable for their job. Intermediate steps—such as medical leaves or referral to an Employee Assistance Program (EAP), may have been unsuccessful or considered inappropriate given the nature of the case. Regardless of the situation, employee layoff or terminations, as with tenure denials, must be handled with extreme care and sensitivity.

A common but fallacious assumption is that the problem of dishonest or even belligerent employees is the result of having failed to weed out undesirable job applicants due to inadequate pre-employment screening. While in many cases poor behavior stems from pre-existing character flaws, employee problems also can implicate inadequate training processes as well as ill-tempered or unfair supervision. Regardless, the decision to terminate an underperforming or badly performing worker requires careful planning and execution. Similarly, layoffs due to budget cuts or department closings must be handled with care and skill.

In either situation—termination or layoff—employees suffer in several respects: They lose not only their source of income, but often their sense of worth and their social network. It is critical, however, that they leave the job with their dignity intact, and that greatly depends on the nature of the termination and outplacement processes. A badly handled separation from the job can embitter the employee-suddenly-turned-ex-employee, thereby creating or intensifying the risk for violence, theft, or sabotage. It may also sour the remaining workforce. School administrators should, therefore, strive to invest as much time and effort in terminations as they do in recruitment.

One particularly important issue surrounds the timing of dismissal, where the conventional approach often fails to appreciate the human element. Martin Herman, for example, endorses the widely popular Friday firing strategy: "[Terminations are] best handled on a Friday, giving the employee a weekend away from the workplace to cool down and gain some perspective on his or her situation."[3] Not only are Friday afternoon (or worse, holiday eve) layoffs unnecessarily cruel, but they tend to be orchestrated for the benefit of the employer, not the employee. If an employee is terminated on Monday, then for him or her, Tuesday essentially becomes the start of a rather extended "weekend." More important, the early-in-the-week alternative would give the ill-fated employee the opportunity to call with follow-up questions or constructively start looking for another job, rather than to spend Saturday and Sunday passively reflecting on the injustice of it all.

The conventional wisdom among some within the security field maintains that a terminated employee must never be allowed back on the work site.

Kenneth Freimuth, for example, recommends that terminated employees should routinely be transported away from the workplace to a separate outplacement center so that they do not "loiter around outside of the plant and stew over what has happened to them."[4]

Although there may be instances in which the risk of violence, theft, or vandalism is so pronounced that barring access is necessary, most of the time such an approach will only make an angry, frustrated former employee even more angry and frustrated. Terminated employees need and, in most cases, deserve the opportunity to achieve closure on all their relationships with fellow co-workers. Similarly, the practice of having security personnel oversee employees as they clean out their desks of personal belongings can humiliate and inflame an already irate worker. If it is necessary to monitor a terminated employee as he or she cleans out the desk, a wise administrator may consider having a nonthreatening co-worker assist, rather than the director of security who may be perceived as an agent of "the enemy."

Finally, human resources can play a critical role in managing the termination process—responsible for far more than just handling the recovery of school property, including keys, and closing off access to the school's data systems. Human resources personnel are absolutely critical for resolving post-employment grievances, and even for confronting a vengeful ex-employee who may have the potential to become violent. With the assistance of human resources specialists—communicating of course with the security department—terminated employees should be treated with respect and compassion, and aided in making the transition to another job through aggressive and humane outplacement efforts. Not only may this help prevent an unfortunate episode, but it is also the ethical thing to do.

AFTERWORD

In 2001, in response to a request from the U.S. Congress, the National Research Council of the National Academies assembled a team of preeminent scholars, chaired by Professor Mark H. Moore of Harvard University, to study the recent spate of school massacres and to offer recommendations for prevention. After completing its broad-based research agenda, including detailed case studies and quantitative analyses of available data, the team had very few answers to give a concerned nation, but many questions to offer for future research.

Based on the review here of many aspects of school violence and security across the range of educational levels, we are left with a similarly less-than-complete understanding of how appropriately to respond. At best, we have concluded that:

- Despite several common elements, there is no useful profile of school avengers.
- Despite certain common precipitants and preconditions, it is not possible to predict school violence in a reliable way.
- Various security measures—physical or tactical—can help to reduce the risks of violence and property loss, but none is foolproof.
- Excess security can impair the learning environment and reinforce a sense of vulnerability.
- Even though certain forms of violent entertainment have strong negative effects, efforts to limit access to violent content can increase its appeal.
- Although consistent parental supervision is important, many parents are unable to increase their involvement.
- Although early prevention strategies are the most effective, it is not possible to identify at such an early stage of development those children who are the most likely to become future offenders.

- By the time an adolescent has reached the point of exhibiting truly worrisome behaviors, the prospects for intervention are considerably reduced.
- The more we obsess about school violence, the more we fuel the contagion effect.
- Punishing serious acts of violence with extreme measures like school exclusion (suspension or expulsion) may precipitate increased problems.

Nothing about this frustrating list of good intentions with disappointing outcomes should suggest that communities are powerless to make a significant difference in the well-being of children through the context of their schools. To the contrary, the school setting remains one of the better points of prevention and intervention. Significant benefits can come from such strategies as:

- smaller schools with close supervision
- increased mentoring by dedicated teachers, counselors, and coaches
- expanded extracurricular options
- more emphasis on social development and less on test scores
- greater focus on developing a school climate of respect and trust
- reliance on threat assessment and management rather than on profiling
- investment in effective yet unobtrusive security technology
- enhanced processes for recruitment, training, and supervision of school personnel

In short, we need a greater investment in schools, which is abundantly clear in view of the atrocious conditions that exist in many American schools—conditions that breed a malaise of hopelessness and despair and ultimately promote failure and disorder. Even if the risks of violence and disciplinary problems are not eliminated or even substantially reduced, we might still promote a wide array of positive outcomes for children in the process of trying.

Notes

CHAPTER 1

1. Dan Rather, *CBS Evening News*, March 5, 2001.

2. Kenneth S. Trump, Prepared statement for "Strengthening School Safety through the Prevention of Bullying," Joint hearing of the Subcommittee on Early Childhood, Elementary, Secondary Education and the Subcommittee on Healthy Families and Communities, U.S. House of Representatives Committee on Education and Labor, July 8, 2009.

3. For a similar analysis based on an earlier and shorter time frame, see M.A. Anderson, J. Kaufman, and T.R. Simon, et al., "School-Associated Violent Deaths in the United States, 1994–1999," *Journal of the American Medical Association* 286 (2001): 2695–702.

4. Survey of state regulations for use of bicycle helmets compiled by the Insurance Institute for Highway Safety. Available at: http://www.iihs.org/laws/mapbicyclehelmets. aspx.

5. Gail Russell Chaddock and Mark Clayton, "A Pattern in Rural School Shootings: Girls as Targets," *The Christian Science Monitor*, October 4, 2006.

6. Jessie Klein, "Teaching Her a Lesson: Media Misses Boys' Rage Relating to Girls in School Shootings," *Crime, Media, Culture* 1 (2005): 90.

7. Michael S. Kimmel and Matthew Mahler, "Adolescent Masculinity, Homophobia, and Violence," *American Behavioral Scientist* 46 (2003): 1439–58.

8. http://www.columbine-angels.com/School_Violence.htm.

9. James Alan Fox, "Violence, Victimization and Discipline in Four Boston High Schools. Report to the Safe Schools Commission," College of Criminal Justice and Center for Urban and Regional Economic Studies, November 1983.

10. Survey data involving sensitive questions, such as weapons possession, are subject to respondent underreporting (concealment) as well as overreporting (fabrication/boasting). See James Alan Fox and Paul E. Tracy, *Randomized Response: A Method for Sensitive Surveys* (Thousand Oaks, CA: Sage, 1986).

11. This Web site is no longer active.

12. *Mohat et al. v. Mentor Public School District Board of Education et al.*, Ohio Northern District Court, Case no. 1:2009cv00688.

13. Personal communication, February 13, 2009.

14. T.R. Nansel, M. Overpeck, R.S. Pilla, W.J., Ruan, B. Simons-Morton, and P. Scheidt, P., "Bullying Behaviors among U.S. Youth: Prevalence and Association with Psychosocial Adjustment," *Journal of the American Medical Association* 285 (2001), 2094–2100.

15. Dan Olweus, *Bullying at School* (Oxford: Blackwell, 1993).

16. Nansel, et al., "Bullying Behaviors."

17. E. Galinsky and K. Salmond, *Youth and Violence: Students Speak Out for a More Civil Society* (New York: Families and Work Institute, 2002).

18. Rana Sampson, "Bullying in Schools," Problem-Oriented Guides for Police Problem-Specific Guides Series, No. 12, Center for Problem-Oriented Policing, 2009, 4.

19. Rachel Dinkes, Emily Forrest Cataldi, Wendy Lin-Kelly, and Thomas D. Snyder, *Indicators of School Crime and Safety: 2007*. National Center for Education Statistics, Institute of Education Sciences, U.S. Department of Education, and Bureau of Justice Statistics, Office of Justice Programs, U.S. Department of Justice. Washington, DC, 34nn.

20. U.S. Department of Health and Human Services. Health Behavior in School-Aged Children, 2001–2002. Interuniversity Consortium for Political and Social Research, Data file #4372.

21. Meda Chesney-Lind and Katherine Irwin, *Beyond Bad Girls: Gender, Violence and Hype* (New York: Routledge, 2008): 106.

22. S. Hinduja and J.W. Patchin, "Cyberbullying: An Exploratory Analysis of Factors Related to Offending and Victimization," *Deviant Behavior* 29 (2008): 129–156.

23. R. Kaltiala-Heino, M. Rimpela, M. Marttunen, A. Rimpela, and P. Rantanen, "Bullying, Depression, and Suicidal Ideation in Finnish Adolescents: School Survey," *British Medical Journal* 319 (1999): 348–51.

24. K. Rigby and P. Slee, "Australia," in *The Nature of School Bullying: A Cross-National Perspective*, eds. P. Smith, Y. Morita, J. Junger-Tas, D. Olweus, R. Catalano, and P. Slee (London: Routledge, 1999).

25. D.S.J. Hawker and M.J. Boulton, "Twenty Years' Research on Peer Victimization and Psychological Maladjustment: A Meta-Analysis Review of Cross-Sectional Studies," *Journal of Child Psychology and Psychiatry* 41 (2000): 441–45.

26. Katrina Williams, Mike Chambers, Stuart Logan, and Derek Robinson, "Association of Common Health Symptoms with Bullying in Primary School Children," *British Medical Journal* 313 (1996): 17–19.

27. J.L. Haddow, "Residual Effects of Repeated Bully Victimization before the Age of 12 on Adolescent Functioning," *Journal of School Violence* 5 (2006): 37–52.

28. http://www.olweus.org.

29. http://www.cfchildren.org.

30. Michelle Kilpatrick Demaray and Christine Kerres Malecki, "A Review of the Use of Social Support in Anti-Bullying Programs," *Journal of School Violence* 5 (2003): 51–70.

31. Laura M. Crothers and Jered B. Kolbert, "Comparing Middle School Teachers' and Students' Views on Bullying and Anti-Bullying Interventions," *Journal of School Violence* 3 (2004): 17–32.

32. James D. Unnever and Dewey G. Cornell, "The Culture of Bullying in Middle School," *Journal of School Violence* 2 (2003): 5–27.

33. Peter Thunfors and Dewey Cornell, "The Popularity of Middle School Bullies," *Journal of School Violence* 7 (2008): 65–82.

34. Jean Decety, Kalina J. Michalska, Yuko Akitsuki, and Benjamin B. Lahey, "Atypical Empathic Responses in Adolescents with Aggressive Conduct Disorder: A Functional MRI Investigation," *Biological Psychology* 80 (2009): 203–11.

CHAPTER 2

1. Cook Counseling Center records for Seung-Hui Cho, December 14, 2005. Available at: http://static.mgnetwork.com/rtd/pdfs/2009-08-rmrecords.pdf.

2. Bryan Vossekuil, Marissa Reddy, Robert Fein, Randy Borum, and William Modzeleski, *The Final Report and Findings of the Safe School Initiative: Implications for the Prevention of School Attacks in the United States* (Washington, DC: U.S. Secret Service and U.S. Department of Education, 2002).

3. University of California Student Mental Health Committee, *Report of the University of California Student Mental Health Committee* (Berkeley: University of California Press, 2006).

4. James Alan Fox, "The Troubled Student and Campus Violence: Creating Better Safety Catches," *The Chronicle of Higher Education* 55 (November 14, 2008): A42.

5. James Alan Fox and Daryl A. Hellman, "Location and Other Correlates of Campus Crime," *Journal of Criminal Justice* 13 (1985): 429–44.

6. Lee R. McPheters, "Econometric Analysis of Factors Influencing Crime on Campus," *Journal of Criminal Justice* 6 (1978): 47–52.

7. 20 U.S.C. 1092(f)(1).

8. Sara Lipka, "In Campus-Crime Reports, There's Little Safety in the Numbers," *The Chronicle of Higher Education*, 55 (January 30, 2009): A1.

9. Ibid.

10. Sara Lipka, "A University Is Accused of Hushing Up a Murder," *The Chronicle of Higher Education*, 53 (March 23, 2007): A1.

11. C.P Krebs, C.H. Lindquist, T.D. Warner, B.S. Fisher, and S.L. Martin, "College Women's Experiences with Physically Forced, Alcohol- or Other Drug-Enabled, and Drug-Facilitated Sexual Assault before and since Entering College," *Journal of American College Health* 57 (2009): 639:47.

12. Bonnie S. Fisher, Francis T. Cullen, and Michael G. Turner, *The Sexual Victimization of College Women* (Washington, DC: U. S. Department of Justice, 2000).

CHAPTER 3

1. See Glenn W. Muschert, "Research in School Shooting," *Sociology Compass* 1 (2007):60–80.

2. Pew Research Center for the People and the Press, "A Year after Columbine: Public Looks to Parents More Than Schools to Prevent Violence," Washington, DC, April 19, 2000. Available at: http://people-press.org/reports/pdf/40.pdf.

3. Peter Langman, *Why Kids Kill: Inside the Minds of School Shooters* (New York: Palgrave Macmillan, 2009).

4. Citizen's Commission on Human Rights, "12 Recent School/Teen Shooters under the Influence of Psychiatric Drugs." Available at: http://www.cchr.org/media/pdfs/List_of_school_and_teen_shooters.pdf.

5. Lydia Saad, "Public Views Littleton Tragedy as Sign of Deeper Problems in Country," *Gallup News Service*, April 23, 1999.

6. *TIME*, May 31, 1999.

7. Marilyn Manson, "Marilyn Manson on Columbine," *Rolling Stone*, May 29, 1999, http://www.rollingstone.com/news/story/5927302/marilyn_manson_on_columbine.

8. Joseph A. Lieberman, *School Shootings: What Every Parent and Educator Needs to Know to Protect Our Children* (New York: Kensington Publishing Corp., 2008), 209. Note that Lieberman does not quote Harris's diary accurately, but the substance is not affected by the transcription error.

9. *James v. Meow Media, Inc.*, 300 F.3d 683, 687 (6th Cir. 2002).

10. Mary Ellen O'Toole, *The School Shooter: A Threat Assessment Perspective* (Washington, DC: Federal Bureau of Investigation, 2000), 20.

11. A. Bandura, D. Ross, and S.A. Ross, "Transmission of Aggression through Imitation of Aggressive Models," *Journal of Abnormal and Social Psychology* 63 (1961): 575−82; A. Bandura, D. Ross, and S.A. Ross, "Imitation of Film-Mediated Aggressive Models," *Journal of Abnormal and Social Psychology* 66 (1963): 3−11.

12. J. McIntyre and J.J. Teevan, "Television Violence and Deviant Behavior," in *Television and Social Behavior: Television and Adolescent Aggressiveness*, Vol. 3, eds. G.A. Comstock and E.A. Rubinstein (Washington, DC: U.S. Government Printing Office, 1972), 383−435.

13. E. Kuntsche, W. Pickett, M. Overpeck, W. Craig, W. Boyce, and M.G. deMatos, "Television Viewing and the Forms of Bullying among Adolescents from Eight Countries," *Journal of Adolescent Health* 39 (2006): 908−915.

14. L.D. Eron, L.R. Huesmann, M.M. Lefkowitz, and L.O. Walder, "Does Television Violence Cause Aggression?," *American Psychologist* 27 (1972): 253−63.

15. Aletha Huston, Edward Donnerstein, Halford Fairchild, Norma D. Feshbach, Phyllis A. Katz, John P. Murray, Eli A. Rubinstein, Brian L. Wilcox, and Diana Zuckerman, *Big World, Small Screen: The Role of Television in American Society* (Lincoln: University of Nebraska Press, 1992), 54.

16. D. Linz, E. Donnerstein, and S. Penrod, "The Effects of Multiple Exposures to Filmed Violence Against Women," *Journal of Communication* 34 (1984): 130−47; and D. Linz, E. Donnerstein, and S. Penrod, "Effects of Long-Term Exposure to Violent and Sexually Degrading Depictions of Women," *Journal of Personality and Social Psychology* 55 (1988): 758−68.

17. C.R. Mullin and D.G. Linz, "Desensitization and Resensitization to Sexualized Violence: Effects of Exposure to Sexually Violent Films on Judgments of Domestic Violence Victims," *Journal of Personality and Social Psychology* 69 (1995): 449−59.

18. Y. Wang, V.P. Mathews, A.J. Kalnin, K.M. Mosier, D.W. Dunn, and W.G. Kronenberger, "Short-Term Effects of Violent Video Game Playing: An fMRI Study," Indiana University School of Medicine, Indianapolis, IN, 2006.

19. C.A. Anderson, "An Update on the Effects of Playing Violent Video Games," *Journal of Adolescence* 27 (2004): 113−22.

20. Frank Newport, "Media Portrayals of Violence Seen by Many as Causes of Real-Life Violence, *Gallup News Service*, May 10, 1999.

21. Joanne Cantor and Kristen S. Harrison, "Ratings and Advisories for Television Programming," in *National Television Violence Study*, Vol. 1. (Thousand Oaks, CA: Sage Publications, 1996), 361−410.

22. Gary Kleck, "Mass Shootings in Schools: The Worst Possible Case for Gun Control," *American Behavioral Scientist* 52 (2009): 1447−64.

23. Mark Gillespie, "One in Three Say It Is Very Likely That Columbine-Type Shootings Could Happen in Their Community," *Gallup News Service*, April 20, 2000.

24. Regina G. Lawrence, and Thomas A. Birkland, "Guns, Hollywood, and School Safety: Defining the School-Shooting Problem across Public Arenas." *Social Science Quarterly* 85 (2004): 1193−1207.

25. Lydia Saad, "Before Recent Shootings, Gun-Control Support Was Fading: Americans Evenly Divided at 49% on Need for Stricter Gun Laws," *Gallup News Service*, April 8, 2009.

26. Thomas A. Birkland and Regina G. Lawrence, "Media Framing and Policy Change after Columbine," *American Behavioral Scientist* 52 (2009): 1405−25.

27. Brady Handgun Violence Prevention Act, Public Law 103−159, H.R. 1025, 103rd Congress; Violent Crime Control and Law Enforcement Act of 1994, H.R. 3355.

28. Frank Newport, "Before Recent Shootings, Most Parents Not Worried about School Safety," *Gallup News Service*, October 4, 2006.

29. ABC *20/20*, "If I Only Had a Gun," Episode 116, aired April 10, 2009.

30. Staff Council Office, Indiana University−Purdue University Indianapolis, "National Empty Holster Protest," *IUPUI Staff Council News*, April 18, 2008, 4. Available at: http://www.iupui.edu/~scouncil/documents/newsletters/volume1/issue05.pdf.

31. *Dist. of Columbia v. Heller*, 544 U.S. ___, 128 S. Ct. 2783, 2787 (2008).

32. Cutting Edge Ministries, "School Shootings Have a Pattern That Implicates the President and his Government—Gun Control Is the Objective! Black Magic Witchcraft Is the Power! " http://www.cuttingedge.org/news/n1344.cfm.

CHAPTER 4

1. U.S. Department of Health and Human Services, *What You Need To Know about Youth Violence Prevention* (Rockville, MD: U.S. Department of Health and Human Services, Substance Abuse and Mental Health Services Administration, Center for Mental Health Services, 2002), 60.

2. See J. David Hawkins, Todd I. Herrenkohl, David P. Farrington, Devon Brewer, Richard F. Catalano, Tracy W. Harachi, and Lynn Cothern, *Predictors of Youth Violence* (Washington, DC: Office of Juvenile Justice and Delinquency Prevention, 2000).

3. Rachel Dinkes, Jana Kemp, Katrina Baum, and Thomas D. Snyder, *Indicators of School Crime and Safety: 2008*, NCES 2009−022/NCJ 226343 (Washington, DC: National Center for Education Statistics, Institute of Education Sciences, U.S. Department of Education, and Bureau of Justice Statistics, Office of Justice Programs, U.S. Department of Justice, 2009).

4. K. Dwyer, D. Osher, and C. Warger, *Early Warning, Timely Response: A Guide to Safe Schools* (Washington, DC: U.S. Department of Education, 1998), 6.

5. Ibid., 6.

6. American Psychological Association, "Warning Signs." Available at: http://www.gripe4rkids.org/warning_signs.pdf.

7. http://www.schoolsafety.us/Checklist-of-Characteristics-of-Youth-Who-Have-Caused-School-Associated-Violent-Deaths-p-7.html.

8. Stephanie Verlinden, Michel Hersen, and Jay Thomas, "Risk Factors in School Shootings," *Clinical Psychology Review* 20 (2000): 3–56.

9. Stephen R. Band and Joseph A. Harpold, "School Violence: Lessons Learned," *FBI Law Enforcement Bulletin* 68 (September 1999), 9–16.

10. Mark H. Moore, Carol V. Petrie, Anthony A. Braga, and Brenda L. McLaughlin (Eds.), *Deadly Lessons: Understanding Lethal School Violence* (Washington, DC: National Academies Press, 2003): 4.

11. Katherine S. Newman, *Rampage: The Social Roots of School Shootings* (New York: Basic Books, 2004).

12. Marisa Reddy, Randy Borum, John Berglund, Bryan Vossekuil, Robert Fein, and William Modzeleski, "Evaluating Risk for Targeted Violence in Schools: Comparing Risk Assessment, Threat Assessment, and Other Approaches," *Psychology in the Schools* 38 (2001), 157–72.

13. Mary Ellen O'Toole, *The School Shooter: A Threat Assessment Perspective* (Quantico, VA: Federal Bureau of Investigation, 2000).

14. Ibid., 8–9.

15. Ibid., 10.

16. Bryan Vossekuil, Robert A. Fein, Marisa Reddy, Randy Borum, and William Modzeleski, *The Final Report and Findings of the Safe School Initiative: Implications for the Prevention of School Attacks in the United States* (Washington, DC: U.S. Secret Service and U.S. Department of Education, 2002).

17. Ibid., 31.

18. Ibid., 41.

19. Robert A. Fein and Bryan Vossekuil, *Protective Intelligence and Threat Assessment Investigations: A Guide for State and Local Law Enforcement Officials*, Publication No. NCJ 170612 (Washington, DC: National Institute of Justice, 1998).

20. Randy Borum, Robert Fein, Bryan Vossekuil, and John Berglund, "Threat Assessment: Defining an Approach for Evaluating Risk of Targeted Violence, *Behavioral Sciences and the Law* 17 (1999): 323–37.

21. Dewey G. Cornell, "Student Threat Assessment," in *Handbook of School Violence*, ed. Edwin R. Gerler (New York: Haworth Reference Press, 2004): 124.

22. D. Cornell, P. Sheras, A. Gregory, and X. Fan, "A Retrospective Study of School Safety Conditions in High Schools Using the Virginia Threat Assessment Guidelines versus Alternative Approaches," *School Psychology Quarterly* 24 (2009): 119–29.

23. Missouri Campus Security Task Force, *Securing Our Future: Making Colleges and Universities Safe Places to Learn and Grow*, State of Missouri Department of Public Safety, August 21, 2007.

24. M.A. Anderson, J. Kaufman, and D.R. Simon, et al., "School-Associated Violent Deaths in the United States, 1994–1999," *Journal of the American Medical Association* 286 (2001): 2695–702.

25. Denise C. Gottfredson, "School Size and School Disorder," Center for Social Organization of Schools, Johns Hopkins University, 1985.

26. http://www.schoolcounselor.org/content.asp?contentid=460.

27. Jack Levin and Heather Beth Johnson, "Youth Violence and the Urban Public School Response," *Journal of Research in Education* 7 (1997): 3–7.

28. Nichole Christian, "Is Smaller Perhaps Better?" *TIME Magazine*, May 31, 1999. http://www.time.com/time/magazine/article/0,9171,991127-1,00.html.

29. Emil J. Haller, "High School Size and Student Indiscipline: Another Aspect of the School Consolidation Issue?" *Educational Evaluation and Policy Analysis* 14 (1992): 145–56.

30. Ibid., 145.

CHAPTER 5

1. See http://www.utexas.edu/tower.

2. John J. DiIulio, "The Coming of the Super-Predators," *The Weekly Standard*, November 27, 1995.

3. S. Kostinsky, E.O. Bixler, and P. Kettl, P. "Threats of School Violence in Pennsylvania after Media Coverage of the Columbine High School Massacre," *Archives of Pediatric Adolescent Medicine* 155 (2001): 994–1001.

4. Associated Press, "School Threats Hit at Least 10 States Since Virginia Tech Shooting Massacre," April 18, 2007.

5. Katherine S. Newman, *Rampage: The Social Roots of School Shootings* (New York: Basic Books, 2004).

6. Kostinsky, et al., "Threats of School Violence in Pennsylvania."

7. Charles E. Menifield, Winfield H. Rose, John Homa, and Anita Brewer Cunningham, "The Media's Portrayal of Urban and Rural School Violence: A Preliminary Analysis," *Deviant Behavior* 22 (2001): 447–64.

8. Joseph A. Lieberman, *School Shootings: What Every Parent and Educator Needs to Know to Protect Our Children* (New York: Citadel Press, 2006).

9. Lauren Coleman, *The Copycat Effect: How the Media and Popular Culture Trigger the Mayhem in Tomorrow's Headlines* (New York: Pocket Books, 2004).

CHAPTER 6

1. George H. Gallup, "The 9th Annual Phi Delta Kappa/Gallup Poll of the Public's Attitude Toward the Public Schools," *Phi Delta Kappan*, 59 (September 1977): 33–48.

2. Linda Lyons, "Parents Concerned about School Safety," *Gallup News Service*, September 17, 2002.

3. Joseph Carroll, "The Divide between Public School Parents and Private School Parents," *Gallup News Service*, September 2007; "Children and Violence," http://www.gallup.com/poll/1588/Children-Violence.aspx.

4. Lynn A. Addington, "Students' Fear after Columbine: Findings from a Randomized Experiment," *Journal of Quantitative Criminology* 19 (2003): 367–87.

5. Mark Gillespie, "One in Three Say It Is Very Likely That Columbine-Type Shootings Could Happen in Their Community," *Gallup News Service*, April 20, 2000.

6. Heather Mason Kiefer, "Public: Society Powerless to Stop School Shootings," *Gallup News Service*, April 5, 2005.

7. http://www.psu.edu/ur/about/myths.html.

8. http://vids.myspace.com/index.cfm?fuseaction=vids.individual&VideoID=15484383.

9. http://www.safetybackpack.com.

10. Personal communication, March 24, 2009.

11. Guy J. Antinozzi and Alan Axelrod, *The Complete Idiot's Guide to Campus Safety* (New York: Penguin Books, 2008).

12. Alan Scher Zagier, "Colleges Confront Shootings with Survival Training," Associated Press, August 26, 2008.

13. Kyle Whitney, "Active Shooter Policy Required for Faculty," *North Wind Online*, March 12, 2009. Available at: http://media.www.thenorthwindonline.com/media/storage/paper1202/news/2009/03/12/News/Active.Shooter.Policy.Required.For.Faculty-3670189.shtml.

14. Guy Williams, "Next Up on U.S. Timetable: How to Survive Shootings," *The Independent* (London), August 28, 2008, 28.

15. http://www.odos.uiuc.edu/safety/safety.html.

16. http://www.kjrh.com/mediacenter/local.aspx?videoId=2589@kjrh.dayport.com.

17. Tina Kelley, "In an Era of School Shootings, Lockdowns Are the New Drill," *New York Times*, March 25, 2008, C14.

18. Diane Weaver Dunne, "FEMA Program Helps Schools Develop Emergency Response," *Education World*, May 30, 2000. Available at: http://www.education-world.com/a_issues/issues084.shtml.

19. Russell Skiba, Cecil R. Reynolds, Sandra Graham, Peter Sheras, Jane Close Conoley, and Enedina Garcia-Vazquez, "Are Zero Tolerance Policies Effective in the Schools?: An Evidentiary Review and Recommendations." A Report by the American Psychological Association Zero Tolerance Task Force, August 2006.

20. Russell J. Skiba and Reece L. Peterson, "School Discipline at a Crossroads: From Zero Tolerance to Early Response," *Exceptional Children* 66 (2000): 335–46.

21. R. Verdugo, "Race-Ethnicity, Social Class, and Zero-Tolerance Policies: The Cultural and Structural Wars," *Education and Urban Society* 35 (2002): 50–76.

22. R.J. Skiba, R.S. Michael, A.C. Nardo, and R. Peterson, *The Color of Discipline: Source of Racial and Gender Disproportionality in School Punishment* (Bloomington, IN: Indiana Education Policy Center, 2000).

23. Aaron Kupchik and Nicholas Ellis, "School Discipline and Security: Fair for All Students?" *Youth and Society* 39 (2008): 549–74.

CHAPTER 7

1. Paul Zielbauer, "Inquiry Uncovers School Bus Drivers' Pasts," *New York Times*, December 2, 2000, B6.

2. Stephanie Ebbert, "Student's Death Spurs New Effort on Bus Safety," *Boston Globe*, February 2, 2008, B3.

3. National Center for Statistics and Analysis, "School Transportation-Related Crashes," *Traffic Safety Facts—2006 Data* (Washington, DC: National Highway Traffic Safety). Available at: http://www-nrd.nhtsa.dot.gov/Pubs/810813.pdf.

4. C. Ray Jeffery, *Crime Prevention through Environmental Design* (Beverly Hills, CA: Sage Publications, 1971); Oscar Newman, *Defensible Space: Crime Prevention through Urban Design* (New York: Macmillan, 1972).

5. D. Finkelhor, H. Hammer, and A.J. Sedlak, *Nonfamily Abducted Children: National Estimates and Characteristics* (Washington, DC: U.S. Department of Justice, Office of Juvenile Justice and Delinquency Prevention, 2002).

6. H. Hammer, D. Finkelhor, and A.J. Sedlak, *Children Abducted by Family Members: National Estimates and Characteristics* (Washington, DC: U.S. Department of Justice, Office of Juvenile Justice and Delinquency Prevention, 2002).

7. Michael J. Karcher, "Connectedness and School Violence: A Framework for Developmental Interventions," in *Handbook of School Violence*, ed. Edwin R. Gerler (New York: Haworth Reference Press, 2004): 41–74.

8. Gregory D. Kutz, "Seclusions and Restraints: Selected Cases of Death and Abuse at Public and Private Schools and Treatment Centers" (Washington, DC: United States Government Accountability Office, May 19, 2009).

9. Sanford A. Newman, James Alan Fox, Edward A. Flynn, and William Christianson, *America's After-School Choice: The Prime Time for Juvenile Crime, or Youth Enrichment and Achievement*, Fight Crime: Invest in Kids, Washington, DC, October 6, 2000.

10. Public Agenda, "Teaching Interrupted: Do Discipline Policies in Today's Public Schools Foster the Common Good?" May 2004.

11. Rachel Dinkes, Jana Kemp, Katrina Baum, and Thomas D. Snyder, *Indicators of School Crime and Safety: 2008*, NCES 2009–022/NCJ 226343 (Washington, DC: National Center for Education Statistics, Institute of Education Sciences, U.S. Department of Education, and Bureau of Justice Statistics, Office of Justice Programs, U.S. Department of Justice, 2009), p. 112.

12. http://www.rtinetwork.org/Learn/Behavior/ar/SchoolwideBehavior.

13. Karen Gray-Adams, *Report on the Implementation of the Gun-Free Schools Act in the States and Outlying Areas, School Year 2003–04* (Washington, DC: U.S. Department of Education, 2007): 4. Available at: http://www.ed.gov/about/reports/annual/gfsa/gfsa03-04rpt.pdf.

14. Walter S. Gilliam, "Prekindergartners Left Behind: Expulsion Rates in State Prekindergarten Systems," Yale University Child Study Center, 2005.

15. Jon Oliver and Michael Ryan, *Lesson One: The ABCs for Life* (New York: Fireside, 2004).

16. Gilbert J. Botvin, *Life Skills Training: Promoting Health and Personnel Development* (Princeton, NJ: Princeton Health Press, 1998).

CHAPTER 8

1. The Associated Press, "Student Shot at a School in Memphis," *New York Times*, February 12, 2008, A18.

2. The Associated Press, "California: Boy Shot at School Dies," *New York Times*, February 16, 2008, A14.

3. The Associated Press, "Tennessee: Student Slain at School," *New York Times*, August 22, 2008, A14.

4. Peter Schworm, "Blacks Threatened at N.H. School," *Boston Globe*, February 25, 2008, B1.

5. Associated Press, "Hundreds of Students Brawl at a Los Angeles High School," *New York Times*, May 11, 2008.

6. Emily Ramshaw and Tawnell D. Hobbs, "Dallas ISD Records Show School Held 'Cage Fights,'" *Dallas Morning News*, March 20, 2009.

7. Dan Olweus, "Bully/Victim Problems among Schoolchildren: Basic Facts and Effects of a School-Based Intervention Program," in *The Development and Treatment of Childhood Aggression*, eds., D.J. Pepler and K.H. Rubin (Hillsdale, NJ: Erlbaum, 1991): 441–48.

8. S.P. Limber, "Implementation of the Olweus Bullying Prevention Program: Lessons Learned from the Field," in *Bullying in American Schools: A Social-Ecological Perspective on Prevention and Intervention*, eds., D. Espelage and S. Swearer (Mahwah, NJ:

Lawrence Erlbaum, 2004): 351–63; S. Black, "An Ongoing Evaluation of the Bullying Prevention Program In Philadelphia Schools: Student Survey and Student Observation Data." Paper presented at Centers for Disease Control and Prevention Safety in Numbers Conference, Atlanta, GA, 2003.

9. N. Bauer, P. Lozano, and F. Rivara, "The Effectiveness of the Olweus Bullying Prevention Program in Public Middle Schools: A Controlled Trial," *Journal of Adolescent Health* 40 (2007): 266–74.

10. Kenneth W. Merrell, Barbara A. Gueldner, Scott W. Ross, and Duane M. Isava, "How Effective Are School Bullying Intervention Programs? A Meta-Analysis of Intervention Research," *School Psychology Quarterly* 23 (2008): 26–42.

11. Maria M. Ttofi and David P. Farrington, "What Works in Preventing Bullying: Effective Elements of Anti-Bullying Programmes," *Journal of Aggression, Conflict and Peace Research* 1 (2009): 13–24.

12. David W. Johnson and Roger T. Johnson, "Conflict Resolution and Peer Mediation Programs in Elementary and Secondary Schools: A Review of the Research," *Review of Educational Research* 66 (1996): 459–506.

13. Rana Sampson, "Bullying in Schools," Problem-Oriented Guides for Police Problem-Specific Guides Series, No. 12, Center for Problem-Oriented Policing, 2009, p. 23.

14. Patrick Tolan, David Henry, Michael Schoeny, and Arin Bass, "Mentoring Interventions to Affect Juvenile Delinquency and Associated Problems," The Campbell Collaboration, 2008.

15. Ralph Frammolino, "Failing Grade for Safe Schools Plan," *Los Angeles Times*, September 6, 1998, A1.

16. See James Alan Fox, "Ganging Up," *Boston Globe*, December 1, 2003, A15; James Alan Fox and Marc L. Swatt, *The Recent Surge in Homicides Involving Young Black Males and Guns: Time to Reinvest in Prevention and Crime Control* (Boston: Northeastern University, December 2008).

17. Richard J. Caster, "2009 School Resource Office Survey," online presentation, http://nasro.org/presentations/2009_SRO_Survey.swf.

18. James C. Howell and James P. Lynch, *Youth Gangs in Schools* (Washington, DC: Office of Juvenile Justice and Delinquency Prevention, 2000, 4).

19. Michael J. Karcher, "Connectedness and School Violence: A Framework for Developmental Interventions," in *Handbook of School Violence*, ed., Edwin R. Gerler (New York: Haworth Reference Press, 2004): 41–74.

20. Finn-Aage Esbensen and D. Wayne Osgood, "National Evaluation of G.R.E.A.T.," National Institute of Justice, 1997, http://www.ncjrs.gov/txtfiles/167264.txt.

21. Finn-Aage Esbensen, Adrienne Freng, Terrance J. Taylor, Dana Peterson, and D. Wayne Osgood, "National Evaluation of the Gang Resistance Education and Training (G.R.E.A.T.) Program," in *Responding to Gangs: Evaluation and Research*, eds., Winifred L. Reed and Scott H. Decker (Washington, DC: National Institute of Justice, 2002): 162.

22. Office of Juvenile Justice and Delinquency Prevention, Best Practices to Address Community Gang Problems. U.S. Department of Justice, Office of Justice Programs: Washington, DC, 2008, http://www.ncjrs.gov/pdffiles1/ojjdp/222799.pdf.

23. S.R. Lal, D. Lal, and C.R. Achilles, *Handbook on Gangs in Schools: Strategies to Reduce Gang-Related Activities* (Newbury Park, CA: Corwin Press, 1993).

24. J. Hurdle, "Philadelphia Can't Set Gun Laws, Court Rules," *New York Times*, September 27, 2008, A18.

25. *Dist. of Columbia v. Heller*, 544 U.S. ___, 128 S. Ct. 2783, 2787 (2008).

26. See http://www.mayorsagainstillegalguns.org/html/federal/history_tiahrt.shtml.

27. P. L. 101-647, 18 USC Section 922(q) November 29, 1990.

28. *U.S. v. Lopez*, 514 U.S. 549 (1995).

29. *U.S. v. Morrison*, 529 U.S. 598 (2000).

30. Mary Ellen O'Toole, *The School Shooter: A Threat Assessment Perspective* (Quantico, VA: Federal Bureau of Investigation, 2000).

31. J. Daniels, I. Buck, S. Croxall, J. Gruber, P. Kime, and H. Govert, "A Content Analysis of News Reports of Averted School Rampages." *Journal of School Violence* 6 (2007): 83–99.

32. C. Brinkley and D.A. Saarnio, "Involving Students in School Violence Prevention: Are They Willing to Help?" *Journal of School Violence* 5 (2006): 93–106.

33. *New Jersey v. T.L.O.*, 469 U.S. 325, 334 (1985).

34. *Safford Unified Sch. Dist. No. 1 v. Redding*, 557 U.S. ___, 129 S. Ct. 2633, 2639 (2009).

35. Russell Skiba, Shana Ritter, Ada Simmons, Reece Peterson, and Courtney Miller, "The Safe and Responsive Schools Project: A School Reform Model for Implementing Best Practices in Violence Prevention," in *Handbook of School Violence and School Safety*, eds., Shane R. Jimerson and Michael J. Furlong (New York: Routledge, 2006): 631–50.

36. 7 Milton J. Valencia, "Parents Required to Join Students at Game," *Boston Globe*, September 18, 2008, B3.

37. R. Skiba and M. Rausch, "Zero Tolerance, Suspension, and Expulsion: Questions of Equity and Effectiveness," in *Handbook of Classroom Management: Research, Practice, and Contemporary Issues*, eds., C. Evertson and C. Weinstein (Mahwah, NJ: Erlbaum, 2006).

38. R. Dunham, and G. Alpert, "Keeping Marginal Youth in School: A Prevention Model," *Youth and Society* 17 (1986): 346–61; G. Morrison and R. Skiba, "Predicting Violence from School Misbehavior: Promises and Perils." *Psychology in the Schools* 38 (2001): 173–84.

39. Aviva M. Rich-Shea, "Action Research Project Examines the Impact of Race and Gender on Disciplinary Exclusions in Massachusetts Schools," *Women, Girls & Criminal Justice* 10 (December/January 2009): 3–4, 8–10.

40. Laura Mirsky and Ted Wachtel, eds., *Safer Saner Schools: Restorative Justice in Education* (Bethlehem, PA: IIRP, 2008); Dieter Burssens and Nicole Vettenburg, "Restorative Group Conferencing at School: A Constructive Response to Serious Incidents," *Journal of School Violence* 5 (2006): 5–17.

41. Office of Community Oriented Policing Service, "COPS in Schools," U.S. Department of Justice, Washington, DC, 2008. Available at: http://www.cops.usdoj.gov/Default.asp?Item=54.

42. Peter Finn and Jack McDevitt, *National Assessment of School Resource Office Programs Project Final Report*, National Institute of Justice, NCJRS Document No. 209273, March 2005.

43. Aaron Kupchik and Torin Monahan, "The New American School: Preparation for Post-Industrial Discipline," *British Journal of Sociology of Education* 27 (2006): 623.

44. Jack McDevitt and Jenn Panniello, "National Assessment of School Resource Officer Programs: Survey of Students in Three Large New SRO Programs," National Institute of Justice, NCJRS Document No. 209270, March 2005.

45. Matthew J. Mayer, "School Resource Officers (SROs)," Fact Sheet #5, Rutgers University, November 2008.

CHAPTER 9

1. Lydia Saad, "Americans Skeptical about Preventing Virginia Tech-Like Incidents," *Gallup News Service*, May 2, 2007.

2. *Mullins v. Pine Manor College*, 449 N.E.2d 331, 338 (Mass. 1983).

3. V.J. Nelson, "Howard Clery, Jr., 77; Lobbied for Increased Campus Security," *Boston Globe*, January 13, 2008, D17.

4. 20 U.S.C. 1092(f).

5. Associated Press, "Duquesne Players Sue Over Shooting," *New York Times*, June 24, 2008, C16.

6. Associated Press, "Officials Meet with Families about Virginia Tech Shootings," *New York Times*, October 20, 2008, A18.

7. Peter Schworm, "Attacks, Rowdiness Rattling Many at UMass-Amherst," *Boston Globe*, February 21, 2008, A1.

8. Shaila Dewan, "2 Withdraw from Petition to Rethink Drinking Age," *New York Times*, August 22, 2008, A16.

9. Geoff Edgers, "A Masterwork Goes Missing," *Boston Globe*, August 27, 2008, A1.

10. Geoff Edgers, "Davis Museum Director Resigns," *Boston Globe*, September 11, 2008, B1.

11. Brian A. Reaves, "Campus Law Enforcement, 2004–05," Bureau of Justice Statistics, Washington, DC, 2008 (Revised 2009). Available at: http://www.ojp.usdoj.gov/bjs/pub/pdf/cle0405.pdf.

12. Ibid., 3.

13. See http://www.criminaljustice.state.ny.us/ops/sgtraining.

14. Reaves, "Campus Law Enforcement, 2004–05," 9.

15. Tracy Jan, "Harvard Scrutinizing Its Police on Race," *Boston Globe*, August 27, 2008, A1.

16. Ralph C. Martin II (Chair) et al., "Committee Report on Improved University Policing Efforts in Response to the September 2008 Charge from Harvard University President Drew Gilpin Faust," April 2009, http://www.news.harvard.edu/press/pressdoc/090424_hupd_report.pdf.

17. Raymond H. Thrower, Steven J. Healy, Gary J. Margolis, Michael Lynch, Dolores Stafford, and William Taylor, *Overview of the Virginia Tech Tragedy and Implications for Campus Safety: The IACLEA Blueprint for Safer Campuses* (Hartford, CT: The International Association of Campus Law Enforcement Administrators, 2008).

18. Matthew Harwood, "Teaming Up to Reduce Risk," *Security Management* (April 2008): 66–78.

19. Gene Deisinger, Marisa Randazzo, Daniel O'Neil, and Jenna Savage, *The Handbook for Campus Threat Assessment and Management Teams* (Stoneham, MA: Applied Risk Management, LLC, 2008).

20. Harwood, "Teaming Up to Reduce Risk."

21. Martin Van Der Werf, "Florida Panel Says Privacy Laws Do Not Protect Dangerous Students," *Chronicle of Higher Education* 53 (June 8, 2007): A25.

22. NASPA—Student Affairs Administrators in Higher Education, "Balancing Student Privacy and School Safety: A Guide to The Family Educational Rights and Privacy Act for Colleges and Universities." Available at: http://www.naspa.org/divctr/pp/ferpa.cfm.

23. R. Hingson, T. Heeren, M. Winter, and H. Wechsler, "Magnitude of Alcohol-Related Mortality and Morbidity among U.S. College Students Ages 18–24: Changes from 1988 to 2001," *Annual Review of Public Health* 26 (2005): 259–79.

24. Elizabeth F. Farrell, "Counseling Centers Lack Resources to Help Troubled Students," *Chronicle of Higher Education* 54 (February 29, 2008): A1.

25. Ibid.

26. Reaves, "Campus Law Enforcement, 2004–05," 7.

27. S.F. Greenberg, "Active Shooters on College Campuses: Conflicting Advice, Roles of the Individual and First Responder, and the Need to Maintain Perspective," *Disaster Medicine and Public Health Preparedness* 1 (2007): 57–61.

28. Reaves, "Campus Law Enforcement, 2004–05," 19.

29. http://www.fas.org/irp/offdocs/nspd/hspd-5.html.

30. Daniel O'Neill, James Alan Fox, Roger Depue, and Elizabeth Englander, *Campus Violence Prevention and Response: Best Practices for Massachusetts Higher Education*, Report for the Campus Safety and Violence Prevention Work Group, Massachusetts Department of Higher Education, June 2008.

31. Alan Scher Zagier, "College Students Slow to Embrace Text Alerts," Associated Press, February 28, 2008.

32. Eric Hoover and Sara Lipka, "Colleges Weigh When to Alert Students to Danger," *Chronicle of Higher Education* 54 (December 7, 2007): A1.

33. Doug Lederman, "Emergency Overload," *Inside Higher Ed*, (September 24, 2008). Available at: http://www.insidehighered.com/news/2008/09/24/emergency.

CHAPTER 10

1. Kenneth S. Trump, "Lessons Learned," *District Administration* (April 2009): 28.

2. H.W. Arthurs, Roger A. Blais, and Jon Thompson, "Integrity in Scholarship: A Report to Concordia University," (Montreal, Quebec, Canada: April 1994). Available at: http://archives3.concordia.ca/timeline/histories/Arthurs_report.pdf; and John Scott Cowan, "Lessons from the Fabrikant File: A Report to the Board of Governors of Concordia University," May 1994. Available at: http://archives3.concordia.ca/timeline/histories/Cowan_report.pdf.

3. Martin B. Herman,"Planning for the Unpredictable," *Security Management*, November 1992, 37.

4. Kenneth C. Freimuth, "Recognizing the Risks of Employee Reductions," *Security Management*, October 1992, 78.

Appendix A

MAJOR EPISODES OF SCHOOL/CAMPUS HOMICIDE

The table below provides basic demographic and incident characteristics for school-related homicides that occurred over the past half-century (specifically, 1966 to 2008) and involved at least two fatalities (including an assailant's suicide). Of course, these few dozen episodes hardly reflect or represent the complete set of hundreds of school-related homicides that took place over that time frame. However, by virtue of extent—and, for some, the enormity—of the victim counts, these select cases attracted considerable public and media attention and have had an impact on public opinion and political action.

Multiple-Victim School Homicides in the United States, 1966 to Present

Date	Shooter(s)	Age	Gender	Student Status	State	School Level	No. of Victims	Description of Slain Victims
August 1, 1966	Charles Whitman	25	M	Y	Texas	College	14 killed; 31 wounded	Various people near campus tower; also killed wife and mother earlier
May 4, 1970	National Guardsmen	—	—	N	Ohio	College	4 killed; 9 wounded	Students
December 30, 1974	Anthony Barbaro	18	M	Y	New York	High school	3 killed; 11 wounded	Janitors and responding firemen
July 12, 1976	Edward Charles Allaway	37	M	N	California	College	7 killed; 2 wounded	Fellow employees
January 29, 1979	Brenda Spencer	16	F	N	California	Elementary	2 killed; 9 wounded	Principal and custodian killed; children and police officer wounded
January 20, 1983	David Lawler	14	M	Y	Missouri	Junior high	2 killed; 1 wounded	Student and suicide
February 24, 1984	Tyrone Mitchell	28	M	N	California	Elementary	2 killed; 11 wounded	Student and suicide
May 16, 1986	David and Doris Young	40s	M and F	N	Wyoming	Elementary	2 killed; 79 injured	Perpetrators killed; students and teachers injured from bomb blast
March 2, 1987	Nathan Faris	12	M	Y	Missouri	Middle school	2 killed	Student and suicide
September 26, 1988	James William Wilson Jr.	19	M	N	South Carolina	Elementary	2 killed; 7 wounded	Students

Date	Name	Age	Sex		State	School level	Casualties	Victims
January 17, 1989	Patrick Purdy	26	M	N	California	Elementary	6 killed; 30 wounded	Children and suicide
November 1, 1991	Gang Lu	28	M	Y	Iowa	College	6 killed; 1 wounded	College employees and suicide
May 1, 1992	Eric Houston	20	M	N	California	High school	4 killed; 10 wounded	Teacher and students
December 14, 1992	Wayne Lo	18	M	Y	Massachusetts	College	2 killed; 4 wounded	Student and professor
January 18, 1993	Gary Scott Pennington	17	M	Y	Kentucky	High school	2 killed	Teacher and custodian
November 7, 1994	Keith Ledeger	37	M	N	Ohio	Middle school	3 killed	Custodian, teacher, and assistant principal
October 12, 1995	Tony Sincino	16	M	Y	South Carolina	High school	2 killed; 1 wounded	Teacher and suicide
November 15, 1995	Jamie Rouse	17	M	Y	Tennessee	High school	2 killed; 1 wounded	Teacher and student
February 2, 1996	Barry Loukaitis	14	M	Y	Washington	Junior high	3 killed; 1 wounded	Teacher and students
August 15, 1996	Frederick Martin Davidson	36	M	Y	California	College	3 killed	Professors
February 19, 1997	Evan Ramsey	16	M	Y	Alaska	High school	2 killed; 2 wounded	School principal and a student
October 1, 1997	Luke Woodham	16	M	Y	Mississippi	High school	2 killed; 7 wounded	Two female students (including ex-girlfriend)

(Continued)

Multiple-Victim School Homicides in the United States, 1966 to Present (Continued)

Date	Shooter(s)	Age	Gender	Student Status	State	School Level	No. of Victims	Description of Slain Victims
December 1, 1997	Michael Carneal	14	M	Y	Kentucky	High school	3 killed; 5 wounded	Students
March 24, 1998	Mitchell Johnson & Andrew Golden	13 & 11	M	Y	Arkansas	Middle school	5 killed; 10 wounded	4 students and a teacher
May 21, 1998	Kip Kinkel	15	M	Y	Oregon	High school	2 killed; 25 wounded	Students
April 20, 1999	Eric Harris & Dylan Klebold	18 & 17	M	Y	Colorado	High school	15 killed; 23 wounded	Students, teacher, and 2 suicides
May 3, 1999	Steven Allen Abrams	39	M	N	California	Elementary	2 killed; many wounded	Students
March 10, 2000	Darrell Ingram	19	M	N	Georgia	High school	2 killed; 1 wounded	Students
August 28, 2000	James Easton Kelly	36	M	Y	Arkansas	College	2 killed	Professor and suicide
February 24, 2001	David Edward Attias	18	M	Y	California	College	4 killed; 1 wounded	Students
March 5, 2001	Charles Andrew Williams	15	M	Y	California	High school	2 killed; 13 wounded	Students
May 15, 2001	Jay Douglas Goodwin	16	M	Y	Texas	High school	2 killed	Female student and suicide
January 16, 2002	Peter Odighizuwa	42	M	N	Virginia	Law School	3 killed; 3 wounded	Dean, professor, and student
October 28, 2002	Robert Flores	41	M	Y	Arizona	College	4 killed	3 instructors and suicide

Date	Name	Age			State	School	Casualties	Notes
April 24, 2003	James Robert Sheets	14	M	Y	Pennsylvania	Junior high	2 killed	School principal and suicide
September 24, 2003	John Jason McLaughlin	15	M	Y	Minnesota	High school	2 killed	Students
March 21, 2005	Jeffrey James Weise	16	M	Y	Minnesota	High school	8 killed; 7 wounded	Security guard, teacher, 5 students, and suicide
September 2, 2006	Douglas Pennington	49	M	N	West Virginia	College	3 killed	Suicide and two sons
September 27, 2006	Duane R. Morrison	53	M	N	Colorado	High school	2 killed	One captive (16-year-old girl) and suicide
October 2, 2006	Charles Carl Roberts IV	32	M	N	Pennsylvania	Elementary	6 killed; 5 wounded	5 girls and suicide
April 2, 2007	Jonathan Rowan	41	M	N	Washington	College	2 killed	Ex-girlfriend and suicide
April 16, 2007	Seung-Hui Cho	23	M	Y	Virginia	College	33 killed; 25 wounded	32 killed and suicide
February 8, 2008	Latina Williams	23	F	Y	Louisiana	College	3 killed	2 female students and suicide
February 14, 2008	Steven Kazmierczak	27	M	N	Illinois	College	6 killed; 16 wounded	Students and suicide

Appendix B

GUN-FREE SCHOOL ZONES ACT OF 1990 AND THE GUN-FREE SCHOOLS ACT OF 1994

The Gun-Free School Zones Act, originally enacted in 1990 as part of the federal government's constitutionally authorized right to regulate interstate commerce, made it a federal offense, punishable by up to five years of imprisonment and up to a $5,000 fine, to possess a gun within 1,000 feet of any public, private, or parochial school. Subsequently, the U.S. Supreme Court ruled by a 5 to 4 decision in *U.S. v. Lopez* (514 U.S. 549, 551; 1995) that the 1990 law was unconstitutional because the issue of gun possession was not sufficiently linked to matters of commerce. However, Congress then passed the Gun-Free School Zone Amendment to Title 18 of the U.S. Code (Crimes and Criminal Procedure), which restored the prohibition against gun possession in the vicinity of a school.

In addition, in 1994, the U.S. Congress passed the Gun-Free School Act, as an amendment to the Elementary and Secondary Education Act (ESEA) of 1965, which specifically addressed student conduct associated with gun possession on school property. This legislation stipulated that any state receiving federal assistance under ESEA was to require all schools to expel for a minimum of one year any student bringing a firearm to school. The law did, however, provide school officials with the authority to modify the sanction on a case-by-case basis.

SECTION 922(Q) OF TITLE 18, UNITED STATES CODE

(q)

(1) The Congress finds and declares that—

(A) crime, particularly crime involving drugs and guns, is a pervasive, nationwide problem;

(B) crime at the local level is exacerbated by the interstate movement of drugs, guns, and criminal gangs;

(C) firearms and ammunition move easily in interstate commerce and have been found in increasing numbers in and around schools, as documented in numerous hearings in both the Committee on the Judiciary of the House of Representatives and the Committee on the Judiciary of the Senate;

(D) in fact, even before the sale of a firearm, the gun, its component parts, ammunition, and the raw materials from which they are made have considerably moved in interstate commerce;

(E) while criminals freely move from State to State, ordinary citizens and foreign visitors may fear to travel to or through certain parts of the country due to concern about violent crime and gun violence, and parents may decline to send their children to school for the same reason;

(F) the occurrence of violent crime in school zones has resulted in a decline in the quality of education in our country;

(G) this decline in the quality of education has an adverse impact on interstate commerce and the foreign commerce of the United States;

(H) States, localities, and school systems find it almost impossible to handle gun-related crime by themselves—even States, localities, and school systems that have made strong efforts to prevent, detect, and punish gun-related crime find their efforts unavailing due in part to the failure or inability of other States or localities to take strong measures; and

(I) the Congress has the power, under the interstate commerce clause and other provisions of the Constitution, to enact measures to ensure the integrity and safety of the Nation's schools by enactment of this subsection.

(2)

(A) It shall be unlawful for any individual knowingly to possess a firearm that has moved in or that otherwise affects interstate or foreign commerce at a place that the individual knows, or has reasonable cause to believe, is a school zone.

(B) Subparagraph (A) does not apply to the possession of a firearm—
   (i)   on private property not part of school grounds;
   (ii) if the individual possessing the firearm is licensed to do so by the State in which the school zone is located or a political subdivision of the State, and the law of the State or political subdivision requires that, before an individual obtains such a license, the law enforcement authorities of the State or political subdivision verify that the individual is qualified under law to receive the license;

    (iii) that is—
        (I) not loaded; and
        (II) in a locked container, or a locked firearms rack that is on a motor vehicle;
    (iv) by an individual for use in a program approved by a school in the school zone;
    (v) by an individual in accordance with a contract entered into between a school in the school zone and the individual or an employer of the individual;
    (vi) by a law enforcement officer acting in his or her official capacity; or
    (vii) that is unloaded and is possessed by an individual while traversing school premises for the purpose of gaining access to public or private lands open to hunting, if the entry on school premises is authorized by school authorities.

(3)

  (A) Except as provided in subparagraph (B), it shall be unlawful for any person, knowingly or with reckless disregard for the safety of another, to discharge or attempt to discharge a firearm that has moved in or that otherwise affects interstate or foreign commerce at a place that the person knows is a school zone.

  (B) Subparagraph (A) does not apply to the discharge of a firearm—
    (i) on private property not part of school grounds;
    (ii) as part of a program approved by a school in the school zone, by an individual who is participating in the program;
    (iii) by an individual in accordance with a contract entered into between a school in a school zone and the individual or an employer of the individual; or
    (iv) by a law enforcement officer acting in his or her official capacity.

(4) Nothing in this subsection shall be construed as preempting or preventing a State or local government from enacting a statute establishing gun free school zones as provided in this subsection.

GUN-FREE SCHOOLS ACT OF 1994

Requirements—

(1) In General—Except as provided in paragraph (3), each state receiving Federal funds under this act shall have in effect a state law requiring local educational agencies to expel from school for a period of not less than one year a student who is determined to have brought a weapon to a school under the jurisdiction of local educational agencies in that

state, except that such state law allow the chief administrative officer of such local educational agency to modify such expulsion requirement for a student on a case-by-case basis.

(2) Construction—Nothing in this title shall be construed to prevent a State from allowing a local educational agency that has expelled a student from such a student's regular school setting from providing educational services in an alternative setting.

(3) Special Rule—

(A) Any State that has a law in effect prior to the date of enactment of the Improving America's Schools Act of 1994 which is in conflict with the not less than one year expulsion requirement described in paragraph (1) shall have the period of time described in subparagraph (B) to comply with such requirement.

(B) The period of time shall be the period beginning on the date of enactment of the Improving America's Schools Act and ending one year after such date.

(4) Definition—For the purpose of this section, the term "weapon" means a firearm as such term is defined in Section 921 of Title 18, United States Code.

(c) Special Rule—The provisions of this section shall be construed in a manner consistent with the Individuals with Disabilities Education Act.

(d) Report to State—Each local educational agency requesting assistance from the State educational agency that is to be provided from funds made available to the State under the Act shall provide to the State, in the application requesting such assistance—

(1) an assurance that such local educational agency is in compliance with the State law required by subsection (b); and

(2) a description of the circumstances surrounding any expulsions imposed under the State law required by subsection (b), including—

(A) the name of the school concerned;

(B) the number of students expelled from such school; and

(C) the type of weapons concerned.

(e) Reporting—Each State shall report the information described in subsection (c) to the Secretary on an annual basis.

(f) Report to Congress—Two years after the date of enactment of the Improving America's Schools Act of 1994, the Secretary shall report to Congress if any State is not in compliance with the requirements of this title.

SEC. 14602. POLICY REGARDING CRIMINAL JUSTICE SYSTEM REFERRAL

(a) In General—No funds shall be made available under this Act to any local educational agency unless such agency has a policy requiring referral to the criminal justice or juvenile delinquency system of any student who brings a firearm or weapon to a school served by such agency.

(b) Definitions—For the purpose of this section, the terms "firearm" and "school" have the same meaning given to such terms by section 921(a) of Title 18, United States Code.

Appendix C

BULLYING PREVENTION PROGRAMS

Ever since Dan Olweus first developed his now widely used bullying prevention program some 25 years ago, the number and range of alternative strategies implemented in schools around the country and the world have grown dramatically. The following table highlights many of the more prominent initiatives, including their intended age populations, programmatic features, and Web addresses. Their relative effectiveness is, however, a topic for scientific inquiry, and is not considered in this list.

Major Bullying Prevention Programs

Program	Organizational Sponsor or Developer	Intended Grades	Web site	Approach
The Bully Free Classroom	Bully Free Systems	Pre-K–12	www.bullyfree.com	Uses an "it's the small things that matter most" approach to teach children acceptance and belonging
The R Time Program	Bully Safe Schools	Pre-K–5	www.stopbullyingnow.net	Teaches students manners and positive speaking through interactive classroom assignments
Promoting Alternative Thinking Strategies (PATHS)	Channing Bete	K–6	www.channing-bete.com/prevention-programs/paths	Uses classroom activities to teach children nonviolent problem solving skills, as well as character development skills
Club Ophelia	Cheryl Dellasega	6–8	www.clubophelia.com/clubophelia/home.php	Teaches girls to understand the effects their actions and words have on other people, how to make positive and empowering choices, and how to identify and address bullying

Second Step Program	Committee for Children	Pre-K–8	www.cfchildren.org	Focuses on teaching vital social skills, such as empathy, emotion management, problem solving, and cooperation
Steps to Respect	Committee for Children	3–6	www.cfchildren.org	Provides training and lesson plans for teachers and administrators on how to recognize and respond to bullying, and how to teach respect
Safe School Ambassadors	Community Matters	4–12	http://www.safeschoolambassadors.org	Engages influential students from cliques and groups within the school in anti-bullying training and discussions
Bully-Proofing Your School	Creating Caring Communities	Pre-K–12	www.bullyproofing.org	Instructs school teachers and administrators, through literature and consultations, how to counteract bullying in their schools

(Continued)

Major Bullying Prevention Programs (Continued)

Program	Organizational Sponsor or Developer	Intended Grades	Web site	Approach
Aggressors, Victims, and Bystanders: Thinking and Acting to Prevent Violence	Education Development Center	6–9	www.thtm.org	Helps children to understand the roles of aggressors, victims, and bystanders; to develop conflict-resolution skills through practice; and to change beliefs that support violence
MetLife Foundation Read for Health Program	Education Development Center: Health and Human Development	6–12	http://www.hhd.org/resources/curriculum/metlife-foundation-read-health-program-taking-action-stop-bullying-literacy-bas	Uses video and lesson plans to assist teachers in using the power of literature to build reading and writing skills while teaching anti-bullying strategies
Educators for Social Responsibility	Educators for Social Responsibility	K–12	www.esrnational.org/	Provides workshops and consultations for teachers on how to educate students in social and emotional learning, diversity issues, and conflict resolution

Program	Organization	Grade	Website	Description
Olweus Bullying Prevention Program	Institute on Family & Neighborhood Life, Clemson University	K–12	www.clemson.edu/olweus	Uses the cooperation of students, administrators, parents, and teachers in a series of meetings, training, activities, and surveys to implement an ongoing climate of intolerance for bullies
The ABCs for Life	Lesson One Company	K–6	www.lessonone.org	Promotes life skills as a means of anti-bullying, with materials for parents and teachers to assist the child in integrating the lessons into daily life
Don't Laugh at Me	Operation Respect	2–8	www.operationrespect.org	Teaches social and emotional principles, and how to connect with peers, through music, video, and classroom activities
Linking the Interests of Families and Teachers (LIFT)	Oregon Social Learning Center	1 and 5	http://www.oslc.org/projects/popups-projects/link-family-teacher.html	Encourage pro-social and positive peer interactions, and coordinates school and home life for students

(Continued)

Major Bullying Prevention Programs (Continued)

Program	Organizational Sponsor or Developer	Intended Grades	Web site	Approach
BullySafe USA	SuEllen Fried	K–12	www.bullysafeusa.com	Focuses on the idea that words are important and students must use them to communicate mutual respect
Get Connected	Synergy Services	6–8	www.synergyservices.org	Educates on how to promote positive peer relationships for students, teachers, administrators, parents, and the community
Power Through Choices	Synergy Services	Pre-K–12	www.synergyservices.org	Teaches students life skills for dealing with age-specific issues such as relationships, abuse, effective decision-making, and self-esteem
STEP Up	Synergy Services	6–8	www.synergyservices.org	Addresses issues associated with bullying among girls
The Incredible Years	The Incredible Years	Pre-K–2	www.incredibleyears.com	Teaches self-control and coping skills, awareness and confidence, and positive thinking and problem-solving skills

Appendix D
THE CLERY ACT

The Jeanne Clery Disclosure of Campus Security Policy and Campus Crime Statistics Act (originally the Crime Awareness and Campus Security Act of 1990) requires all public and private colleges and universities that participate in federal student aid programs to collect, report, and disseminate statistics on a range of offense categories (homicide, rape and sexual assault, robbery, aggravated assault, burglary, auto theft, and arson), on arrests and student disciplinary actions, and on hate crimes. Campus police or public safety departments must provide an annual report of these crime statistics to all enrolled students and employees of the school, as well as to prospective students who request the information.

Although very well-intentioned, the implementation of the Clery requirements has not been uniform across the spectrum of over 8,000 schools participating in the initiative. Moreover, the available data do not nearly provide a complete, reliable, and accurate representation of the state of campus safety in America.

DISCLOSURE OF CAMPUS SECURITY POLICY AND CAMPUS CRIME STATISTICS § 20 U.S.C. § 1092(F)

(1) Each eligible institution participating in any program under this title, other than a foreign institution of higher education, shall on August 1, 1991, begin to collect the following information with respect to campus crime statistics and campus security policies of that institution, and beginning September 1, 1992, and each year thereafter, prepare, publish, and distribute, through appropriate publications or mailings, to all current students and employees, and to any applicant for enrollment or

employment upon request, an annual security report containing at least the following information with respect to the campus security policies and campus crime statistics of that institution:

(A) A statement of current campus policies regarding procedures and facilities for students and others to report criminal actions or other emergencies occurring on campus and policies concerning the institution's response to such reports.

(B) A statement of current policies concerning security and access to campus facilities, including campus residences, and security considerations used in the maintenance of campus facilities.

(C) A statement of current policies concerning campus law enforcement, including—

   (i) the law enforcement authority of campus security personnel;

   (ii) the working relationship of campus security personnel with State and local law enforcement agencies, including whether the institution has agreements with such agencies, such as written memoranda of understanding, for the investigation of alleged criminal offenses; and

   (iii) policies which encourage accurate and prompt reporting of all crimes to the campus police and the appropriate law enforcement agencies.

(D) A description of the type and frequency of programs designed to inform students and employees about campus security procedures and practices and to encourage students and employees to be responsible for their own security and the security of others.

(E) A description of programs designed to inform students and employees about the prevention of crimes.

(F) Statistics concerning the occurrence on campus, in or on noncampus buildings or property, and on public property during the most recent calendar year, and during the 2 preceding calendar years for which data are available—

   (i) of the following criminal offenses reported to campus security authorities or local police agencies:

      (I) murder;

      (II) sex offenses, forcible or nonforcible;

      (III) robbery;

      (IV) aggravated assault;

      (V) burglary;

      (VI) motor vehicle theft;

      (VII) manslaughter;

      (VIII) arson; and

      (IX) arrests or persons referred for campus disciplinary action for liquor law violations, drug-related violations, and weapons possession; and

(ii) of the crimes described in subclauses (I) through (VIII) of clause (i), of larceny-theft, simple assault, intimidation, and destruction, damage, or vandalism of property, and of other crimes involving bodily injury to any person, in which the victim is intentionally selected because of the actual or perceived race, gender, religion, sexual orientation, ethnicity, or disability of the victim that are reported to campus security authorities or local police agencies, which data shall be collected and reported according to category of prejudice.

(G) A statement of policy concerning the monitoring and recording through local police agencies of criminal activity at off-campus student organizations which are recognized by the institution and that are engaged in by students attending the institution, including those student organizations with off-campus housing facilities.

(H) A statement of policy regarding the possession, use, and sale of alcoholic beverages and enforcement of State underage drinking laws and a statement of policy regarding the possession, use, and sale of illegal drugs and enforcement of Federal and State drug laws and a description of any drug or alcohol abuse education programs as required under section 120 of this Act [20 USCS § 1011i].

(I) A statement advising the campus community where law enforcement agency information provided by a State under section 170101(j) of the Violent Crime Control and Law Enforcement Act of 1994 (42 U.S.C. 14071(j)), concerning registered sex offenders may be obtained, such as the law enforcement office of the institution, a local law enforcement agency with jurisdiction for the campus, or a computer network address.

(J) A statement of current campus policies regarding immediate emergency response and evacuation procedures, including the use of electronic and cellular communication (if appropriate), which policies shall include procedures to-

(i) immediately notify the campus community upon the confirmation of a significant emergency or dangerous situation involving an immediate threat to the health or safety of students or staff occurring on the campus, as defined in paragraph (6), unless issuing a notification will compromise efforts to contain the emergency;

(ii) publicize emergency response and evacuation procedures on an annual basis in a manner designed to reach students and staff; and

(iii) test emergency response and evacuation procedures on an annual basis.

(2) Nothing in this subsection shall be construed to authorize the Secretary to require particular policies, procedures, or practices by institutions of higher education with respect to campus crimes or campus security.

(3) Each institution participating in any program under this title shall make timely reports to the campus community on crimes considered to be a threat to other students and employees described in paragraph (1)(F) that are reported to campus security or local law police agencies. Such reports shall be provided to students and employees in a manner that is timely and that will aid in the prevention of similar occurrences.

(4)

   (A) Each institution participating in any program under this title that maintains a police or security department of any kind shall make, keep, and maintain a daily log, written in a form that can be easily understood, recording all crimes reported to such police or security department, including—

      (i) the nature, date, time, and general location of each crime; and

      (ii) the disposition of the complaint, if known.

   (B)

      (i) All entries that are required pursuant to this paragraph shall, except where disclosure of such information is prohibited by law or such disclosure would jeopardize the confidentiality of the victim, be open to public inspection within two business days of the initial report being made to the department or a campus security authority.

      (ii) If new information about an entry into a log becomes available to a police or security department, then the new information shall be recorded in the log not later than two business days after the information becomes available to the police or security department.

      (iii) If there is clear and convincing evidence that the release of such information would jeopardize an ongoing criminal investigation or the safety of an individual, cause a suspect to flee or evade detection, or result in the destruction of evidence, such information may be withheld until that damage is no longer likely to occur from the release of such information.

(5) On an annual basis, each institution participating in any program under this title shall submit to the Secretary a copy of the statistics required to be made available under paragraph (1)(F). The Secretary shall—

   (A) review such statistics and report to the authorizing committees on campus crime statistics by September 1, 2000;

   (B) make copies of the statistics submitted to the Secretary available to the public; and

   (C) in coordination with representatives of institutions of higher education, identify exemplary campus security policies, procedures, and practices and disseminate information concerning those policies, procedures, and practices that have proven effective in the reduction of campus crime.

(6)

   (A) In this subsection:

      (i) The term "campus" means—

         (I) any building or property owned or controlled by an institution of higher education within the same reasonably contiguous geographic area of the institution and used by the institution in direct support of, or in a manner related to, the institution's educational purposes, including residence halls; and

         (II) property within the same reasonably contiguous geographic area of the institution that is owned by the institution but controlled by another person, is used by students, and supports institutional purposes (such as a food or other retail vendor).

      (ii) The term "noncampus building or property" means—

         (I) any building or property owned or controlled by a student organization recognized by the institution; and

         (II) any building or property (other than a branch campus) owned or controlled by an institution of higher education that is used in direct support of, or in relation to, the institution's educational purposes, is used by students, and is not within the same reasonably contiguous geographic area of the institution.

      (iii) The term "public property" means all public property that is within the same reasonably contiguous geographic area of the institution, such as a sidewalk, a street, other thoroughfare, or parking facility, and is adjacent to a facility owned or controlled by the institution if the facility is used by the institution in direct support of, or in a manner related to the institution's educational purposes.

   (B) In cases where branch campuses of an institution of higher education, schools within an institution of higher education, or administrative divisions within an institution are not within a reasonably contiguous geographic area, such entities shall be considered separate campuses for purposes of the reporting requirements of this section.

(7) The statistics described in paragraph (1)(F) shall be compiled in accordance with the definitions used in the uniform crime reporting system of the Department of Justice, Federal Bureau of Investigation, and the modifications in such definitions as implemented pursuant to the Hate Crime Statistics Act [28 USCS § 534 note]. Such statistics shall not identify victims of crimes or persons accused of crimes.

(8)

   (A) Each institution of higher education participating in any program under this title shall develop and distribute as part of the report described in paragraph (1) a statement of policy regarding—

   (i) such institution's campus sexual assault programs, which shall be aimed at prevention of sex offenses; and

   (ii) the procedures followed once a sex offense has occurred.

  (B) The policy described in subparagraph (A) shall address the following areas:

   (i) Education programs to promote the awareness of rape, acquaintance rape, and other sex offenses.

   (ii) Possible sanctions to be imposed following the final determination of an on-campus disciplinary procedure regarding rape, acquaintance rape, or other sex offenses, forcible or nonforcible.

   (iii) Procedures students should follow if a sex offense occurs, including who should be contacted, the importance of preserving evidence as may be necessary to the proof of criminal sexual assault, and to whom the alleged offense should be reported.

   (iv) Procedures for on-campus disciplinary action in cases of alleged sexual assault, which shall include a clear statement that—

    (I) the accuser and the accused are entitled to the same opportunities to have others present during a campus disciplinary proceeding; and

    (II) both the accuser and the accused shall be informed of the outcome of any campus disciplinary proceeding brought alleging a sexual assault.

   (v) Informing students of their options to notify proper law enforcement authorities, including on-campus and local police, and the option to be assisted by campus authorities in notifying such authorities, if the student so chooses.

   (vi) Notification of students of existing counseling, mental health or student services for victims of sexual assault, both on campus and in the community.

   (vii) Notification of students of options for, and available assistance in, changing academic and living situations after an alleged sexual assault incident, if so requested by the victim and if such changes are reasonably available.

  (C) Nothing in this paragraph shall be construed to confer a private right of action upon any person to enforce the provisions of this paragraph.

 (9) The Secretary shall provide technical assistance in complying with the provisions of this section to an institution of higher education who requests such assistance.

 (10) Nothing in this section shall be construed to require the reporting or disclosure of privileged information.

(11) The Secretary shall report to the appropriate committees of Congress each institution of higher education that the Secretary determines is not in compliance with the reporting requirements of this subsection.

(12) For purposes of reporting the statistics with respect to crimes described in paragraph (1)(F), an institution of higher education shall distinguish, by means of separate categories, any criminal offenses that occur—

(A) on campus;

(B) in or on a noncampus building or property;

(C) on public property; and

(D) in dormitories or other residential facilities for students on campus.

(13) Upon a determination pursuant to section 487(c)(3)(B) [20 USCS § 1094(c)(3)(B)] that an institution of higher education has substantially misrepresented the number, location, or nature of the crimes required to be reported under this subsection, the Secretary shall impose a civil penalty upon the institution in the same amount and pursuant to the same procedures as a civil penalty is imposed under section 487(c)(3)(B) [20 USCS § 1094(c)(3)(B)].

(14)

(A) Nothing in this subsection may be construed to—

(i) create a cause of action against any institution of higher education or any employee of such an institution for any civil liability; or

(ii) establish any standard of care.

(B) Notwithstanding any other provision of law, evidence regarding compliance or noncompliance with this subsection shall not be admissible as evidence in any proceeding of any court, agency, board, or other entity, except with respect to an action to enforce this subsection.

(15) The Secretary shall annually report to the authorizing committees regarding compliance with this subsection by institutions of higher education, including an up-to-date report on the Secretary's monitoring of such compliance.

(16) The Secretary may seek the advice and counsel of the Attorney General concerning the development, and dissemination to institutions of higher education, of best practices information about campus safety and emergencies.

(17) Nothing in this subsection shall be construed to permit an institution, or an officer, employee, or agent of an institution, participating in any program under this title to retaliate, intimidate, threaten, coerce, or otherwise discriminate against any individual with respect to the implementation of any provision of this subsection.

(18) This subsection may be cited as the "Jeanne Clery Disclosure of Campus Security Policy and Campus Crime Statistics Act."

Appendix E
SCHOOL SECURITY DESIGN, TECHNOLOGY, AND OPERATION

Implementing physical security for schools and colleges incorporates a range of methods and strategies, each of which involves decisions concerning type, complexity, and cost. The following list identifies many of the issues surrounding school security planning:

School design
- Number of buildings
- Number of entry points
- Door and locking devices
- Types and size of windows
- Internal sight lines
- Open areas and hallways
- Exterior lighting and landscaping
- Pedestrian and vehicle paths/flow
- Campus perimeter

Video surveillance
- Monitored versus nonmonitored
- Black and white versus color
- Digital versus analog recording
- Fixed versus pan-tilt-zoom cameras
- Conventional versus "smart" video-analytic detection
- Hardwired versus wireless systems
- Video formats and resolution/pixels
- Camera placement, housing, and field of view
- Lighting requirements and nighttime applications
- Hidden cameras and posted warnings
- Centralized versus distributed systems
- Image storage—VCR, DVR, or NVR (network video recorder)

Metal detection
- Walk-through metal detectors
- Hand-held scanners
- X-ray property scanners
- Restrictions on property/containers (e.g., backpacks)

Access control
- Limiting entry/exit points
- Hours of operation and access
- Sign-in and sign-out procedures
- Security guard posts
- ID card/badge with automatic reader
- PIN number with keypad
- Biometric feature recognition devices
- Piggy-backing
- Doors versus turnstiles
- Alarms and alarm monitoring
- Sensing devices—occupancy, motion detection, glass breakage, and proximity

Physical barriers
- Fences and walls
- Trees, bodies of water, earth berms, and other natural barriers
- Bollard posts

Communications
- Hard-wired telephones and intercom networks
- Blue-light emergency phone installations
- Radio versus cell phone networks
- Repeaters and routers for radio and cell service enhancement
- GPS tracking devices
- Interoperability with local police/emergency communication systems

Alarm and notification systems
- Panic buttons and manual alarms
- Automatic sirens
- Mass notification over e-mail, phone, and text-messaging

A significant number and array of resources are available for background on each aspect of school security operations and technology. The following are particularly recommended:

1. The National Clearinghouse for Educational Facilities, established in 1997 by the U.S. Department of Education and managed by the National Institute of Building Sciences, publishes an array of up-to-date advisory documents concerning physical security for schools and colleges. Primary among their recent reports are:
   (a) National Clearinghouse for Educational Facilities, *Door Locking Options in School.* Washington, DC, 2009.
      - URL: http://www.edfacilities.org/pubs/door_locks.pdf

(b) National Clearinghouse for Educational Facilities, *Emergency Response Information for School Facilities*. Washington, DC, 2008.
  • URL: http://www.ncef.org/pubs/emergency_response.pdf
(c) National Clearinghouse for Educational Facilities, *Improving School Access Control*. Washington, DC, 2008.
  • URL: http://www.ncef.org/pubs/accesscontrol.pdf
(d) National Clearinghouse for Educational Facilities, *Low-Cost Security Measures for School Facilities*. Washington, DC, 2008.
  • URL: http://www.ncef.org/pubs/low_cost_measures.pdf
(e) National Clearinghouse for Educational Facilities, *Mass Notification for Higher Education*. Washington, DC, 2009.
  • URL: http://www.ncef.org/pubs/notification.pdf
(f) National Clearinghouse for Educational Facilities, *Mitigating Hazards in School*. Washington, DC, 2008.
  • URL: http://www.ncef.org/pubs/mitigating_hazards.pdf
(g) National Clearinghouse for Educational Facilities, *School Security Technologies*. Washington, DC, 2009.
  • URL: http://www.ncef.org/pubs/security_technologies.pdf
(h) National Clearinghouse for Educational Facilities, *Selecting Security Technology Providers*. Washington, DC, 2009.
  • URL: http://www.ncef.org/pubs/providers.pdf

2. Applied Risk Management (ARM) of Stoneham, Massachusetts has published a multifaceted guide to assist campuses in blending critical security needs with overarching goals for energy sustainability:
(a) Dan O'Neill, Roger Rueda, and Jenna Savage, *Security Design for Sustainable Buildings and Campuses*, Applied Risk Management, Stoneham, MA, 2009.
  • URL: http://www.arm-security.com/pdf/ARM_Security_Design_for_Sustainable_Buildings_Campuses.pdf

3. Although published a decade ago, Sandia National Laboratories in Albuquerque, New Mexico, with support from the National Institute of Justice, produced a still salient guidebook for school administrators and law enforcement personnel regarding physical security concerns and strategies for schools:
(a) Mary W. Green, *The Appropriate and Effective Use of Security Technologies in U.S. Schools: A Guide for Schools and Law Enforcement Agencies*. National Institute of Justice, Washington, DC, September 1999.
  • URL: http://www.ncjrs.org/school/home.html

4. ASIS International, the main professional organization in the security field, sponsors the publication of *The Protection of Assets (POA) Manual*, a comprehensive and regularly updated reference (both print and online editions) on various aspects of security:
(a) ASIS International, *The Protection of Assets (POA) Manual*. Alexandria, VA.
  • URL: http://www.protectionofassets.com

Appendix F

STUDENT PRIVACY RIGHTS

The Fourth Amendment to the United States Constitution guarantees "the right of the people to be secure in their persons, houses, papers, and effects, against unreasonable searches and seizures." "School" has not been identified explicitly as a place of privacy, and the U.S. Supreme Court has not determined that the usual rights of privacy extend automatically to students while at school.

Although there is no governing legislation concerning student searches, the accumulation of court holdings to date indicates the following set of standards:

- Any contraband in plain view can be seized without probable cause.
- Locker searches are generally permissible, either as part of a random sweep or a targeted search.
- School officials must have "reasonable suspicion" to search personal items, such as book bags and purses.
- Pat-down searches that are minimally intrusive are permissible regardless of level of suspicion. However, strip searches require clear-cut and reasonable suspicion of contraband, including weapons, illicit drugs, and prohibited prescription medications.

The landmark Supreme Court decision in *New Jersey v. T.L.O.* (469 U.S. at 325; 1985) case, involving a search of a student's purse related to suspicion of her having violated the school's no-smoking policy, has been considered a model for legitimate school action. Complicating matters, and literally turning the episode into a federal case, was that much more than tobacco was discovered in the course of the search. The court concluded that school officials acted properly and, given that they had reasonable grounds for their suspicion, did not require a warrant to conduct the search.

Over two decades later, in 2009, the U.S. Supreme Court heard a challenge to the limits of the student search guidelines set forth in the *New Jersey v. T.L.O.* decision. The case involved an Arizona civil suit over the partial strip search of a 13-year-old female student for suspicion of possessing over-the-counter pain medication for the purpose of distributing to classmates. The Court held that, while a search of the student's personal property (backpack and outer clothing) was appropriate, the nature of the contraband and the likelihood that she was hiding it on her body were not sufficient to justify such invasion of her privacy.

Thus, even though the Court did not indicate that strip searches of students by school personnel were necessarily a violation of the Fourth Amendment rights, their reasonableness must be assessed based on the nature of the contraband and the likelihood of finding it. As the majority stated, "The indignity of the search does not, of course, outlaw it, but it does implicate the rule of reasonableness as stated in *T. L. O.*"

NEW JERSEY V. T. L. O.

SUPREME COURT OF THE UNITED STATES
469 U.S. 325
January 15, 1985, Decided

JUSTICE WHITE delivered the opinion of the Court.

We granted certiorari in this case to examine the appropriateness of the exclusionary rule as a remedy for searches carried out in violation of the Fourth Amendment by public school authorities. Our consideration of the proper application of the Fourth Amendment to the public schools, however, has led us to conclude that the search that gave rise to the case now before us did not violate the Fourth Amendment. Accordingly, we here address only the questions of the proper standard for assessing the legality of searches conducted by public school officials and the application of that standard to the facts of this case.

On March 7, 1980, a teacher at Piscataway High school in Middlesex County, N.J., discovered two girls smoking in a lavatory. One of the two girls was the respondent T. L. O., who at that time was a 14-year-old High school freshman. Because smoking in the lavatory was a violation of a school rule, the teacher took the two girls to the Principal's office, where they met with Assistant Vice Principal Theodore Choplick. In response to questioning by Mr. Choplick, T. L. O.'s companion admitted that she had violated the rule. T. L. O., however, denied that she had been smoking in the lavatory and claimed that she did not smoke at all.

Mr. Choplick asked T. L. O. to come into his private office and demanded to see her purse. Opening the purse, he found a pack of cigarettes, which he removed from the purse and held before T. L. O. as he accused her of having lied to him. As he reached into the purse for the cigarettes, Mr. Choplick also noticed a package of cigarette rolling papers. In his experience, possession of rolling papers by High school students was closely associated with the use of marihuana. Suspecting that a closer examination of the purse might yield further evidence of drug use, Mr. Choplick proceeded to search the purse thoroughly. The search revealed a small amount of marihuana, a pipe, a number of empty plastic bags, a substantial quantity of money in one-dollar bills, an index card that appeared to be a list of students who owed T. L. O. money, and two letters that implicated T. L. O. in marihuana dealing.

Mr. Choplick notified T. L. O.'s mother and the police, and turned the evidence of drug dealing over to the police. At the request of the police, T. L. O.'s mother took her daughter to police headquarters, where T. L. O. confessed that she had been selling marihuana at the High school. On the basis of the confession and the evidence seized by Mr. Choplick, the State brought delinquency charges against T. L. O. in the Juvenile and Domestic Relations Court of Middlesex County. Contending that Mr. Choplick's search of her purse violated the Fourth Amendment, T. L. O. moved to suppress the evidence found in her purse as well as her confession, which, she argued, was tainted by the allegedly unlawful search.

The New Jersey Supreme Court agreed with the lower courts that the Fourth Amendment applies to searches conducted by school officials. The court also rejected the State of New Jersey's argument that the exclusionary rule should not be employed to prevent the use in juvenile proceedings of evidence unlawfully seized by school officials.

With respect to the question of the legality of the search before it, the court agreed with the Juvenile Court that a warrantless search by a school official does not violate the Fourth Amendment so long as the official "has reasonable grounds to believe that a student possesses evidence of illegal activity or activity that would interfere with school discipline and order." According to the majority, the contents of T. L. O.'s purse had no bearing on the accusation against T. L. O., for possession of cigarettes (as opposed to smoking them in the lavatory) did not violate school rules, and a mere desire for evidence that would impeach T. L. O.'s claim that she did not smoke cigarettes could not justify the search. Moreover, even if a reasonable suspicion that T. L. O. had cigarettes in her purse would justify a search, Mr. Choplick had no such suspicion, as no one had furnished him with any specific information that there were cigarettes in the purse. Finally, leaving aside the question whether Mr. Choplick was justified in opening the purse, the court held that the evidence of drug use that he saw inside did not justify the extensive "rummaging" through T. L. O.'s papers and effects that followed.

We granted the State of New Jersey's petition for certiorari.

In determining whether the search at issue in this case violated the Fourth Amendment, we are faced initially with the question whether that Amendment's prohibition on unreasonable searches and seizures applies to searches conducted by public school officials. We hold that it does.

It is now beyond dispute that "the Federal Constitution, by virtue of the Fourteenth Amendment, prohibits unreasonable searches and seizures by state officers." Equally indisputable is the proposition that the Fourteenth Amendment protects the rights of students against encroachment by public school officials. These two propositions—that the Fourth Amendment applies to the States through the Fourteenth Amendment, and that the actions of public school officials are subject to the limits placed on state action by the Fourteenth Amendment—might appear sufficient to answer the suggestion that the Fourth Amendment does not proscribe unreasonable searches by school officials. On reargument, however, the State of New Jersey has argued that the history of the Fourth Amendment indicates that the Amendment was intended to regulate only searches and seizures carried out by law enforcement officers; accordingly, although public school officials are concededly state agents for purposes of the Fourteenth Amendment, the Fourth Amendment creates no rights enforceable against them.

It may well be true that the evil toward which the Fourth Amendment was primarily directed was the resurrection of the pre-Revolutionary practice of using general warrants or "writs of assistance" to authorize searches for contraband by officers of the Crown. But this Court has never limited the Amendment's prohibition on unreasonable searches and seizures to operations conducted by the police. Rather, the Court has long spoken of the Fourth Amendment's strictures as restraints imposed upon "governmental action"—that is, "upon the activities of sovereign authority." Accordingly, we have held the Fourth Amendment applicable to the activities of civil as well as criminal authorities: building inspectors, Occupational Safety and Health Act inspectors, and even firemen entering privately owned premises to battle a fire are all subject to the restraints imposed by the Fourth Amendment. "[The] basic purpose of this Amendment, as recognized in countless decisions of this Court, is to safeguard the privacy and security of individuals against arbitrary invasions by governmental officials."

Notwithstanding the general applicability of the Fourth Amendment to the activities of civil authorities, a few courts have concluded that school officials are exempt from the dictates of the Fourth Amendment by virtue of the special nature of their authority over schoolchildren. Such reasoning is in tension with contemporary reality and the teachings of this Court. We have held school officials subject to the commands of the First Amendment, and the Due Process Clause of the Fourteenth Amendment. If school authorities are state actors for purposes of the constitutional guarantees of freedom of expression and due process, it is difficult to understand why they should be deemed to be exercising parental rather than public authority when conducting searches of their students.

To hold that the Fourth Amendment applies to searches conducted by school authorities is only to begin the inquiry into the standards governing such searches. Although the underlying command of the Fourth Amendment is always that searches and seizures be reasonable, what is reasonable depends on the context within which a search takes place. The determination of the standard of reasonableness governing any specific class of searches requires "balancing the need to search against the invasion which the search entails." On one side of the balance are arrayed the individual's legitimate expectations of privacy and personal security; on the other, the government's need for effective methods to deal with breaches of public order.

We have recognized that even a limited search of the person is a substantial invasion of privacy. We have also recognized that searches of closed items of personal luggage are intrusions on protected privacy interests, for "the Fourth Amendment provides protection to the owner of every container that conceals its contents from plain view." A search of a child's person or of a closed purse or other bag carried on her person, no less than a similar search carried out on an adult, is undoubtedly a severe violation of subjective expectations of privacy. (We do not address the question, not presented by this case, whether a schoolchild has a legitimate expectation of privacy in lockers, desks, or other school property provided for the storage of school supplies.)

Of course, the Fourth Amendment does not protect subjective expectations of privacy that are unreasonable or otherwise "illegitimate." The State of New Jersey has argued that because of the pervasive supervision to which children in the schools are necessarily subject, a child has virtually no legitimate expectation of privacy in articles of personal property "unnecessarily" carried into a school. This argument has two factual premises: (1) the fundamental incompatibility of expectations of privacy with the maintenance of a sound educational environment; and (2) the minimal interest of the child in bringing any items of personal property into the school. Both premises are severely flawed. . . .

Against the child's interest in privacy must be set the substantial interest of teachers and administrators in maintaining discipline in the classroom and on school grounds. Maintaining order in the classroom has never been easy, but in recent years, school disorder has often taken particularly ugly forms: drug use and violent crime in the schools have become major social problems. How, then, should we strike the balance between the schoolchild's legitimate expectations of privacy and the school's equally legitimate need to maintain an environment in which learning can take place? It is evident that the school setting requires some easing of the restrictions to which searches by public authorities are ordinarily subject. The warrant requirement, in particular, is unsuited to the school environment: requiring a teacher to obtain a warrant before searching a child suspected of an infraction of school rules (or of the criminal law) would unduly interfere with the maintenance of the swift and informal disciplinary procedures needed in the schools. Just as we have in other cases dispensed with the warrant requirement when "the burden of obtaining a warrant is likely to frustrate the governmental purpose behind the search," we hold today that school officials need not obtain a warrant before searching a student who is under their authority.

The school setting also requires some modification of the level of suspicion of illicit activity needed to justify a search. Ordinarily, a search—even one that may permissibly be carried out without a warrant—must be based upon "probable cause" to believe that a violation of the law has occurred. However, "probable cause" is not an irreducible requirement of a valid search. The fundamental command of the Fourth Amendment is that searches and seizures be reasonable, and although "both the concept of probable cause and the requirement of a warrant bear on the reasonableness of a search, . . . in certain limited circumstances neither is required." Where a careful balancing of governmental and private interests suggests that the public interest is best served by a Fourth Amendment standard of reasonableness that stops short of probable cause, we have not hesitated to adopt such a standard.

We join the majority of courts that have examined this issue in concluding that the accommodation of the privacy interests of schoolchildren with the substantial need of teachers and administrators for freedom to maintain order in the schools does not require strict adherence to the requirement that searches be based on probable cause to believe that the subject of the search has violated or is violating the law. Rather, the legality of a search of a student should depend simply on the reasonableness, under all the circumstances, of the search. Determining the reasonableness of any search involves a twofold inquiry: first, one must consider "whether the . . . action was justified at its inception;" second, one must determine whether the search as actually conducted "was reasonably related in scope to the circumstances which justified the interference in the first place." Under ordinary circumstances, a search of a student by a teacher or other school official will be "justified at its inception" when there are reasonable grounds for suspecting that the search will turn up evidence that the student has violated or is violating either the law or the rules of the school. Such a search will be permissible in its scope when the measures adopted are reasonably related to the objectives of the search and not excessively intrusive in light of the age and sex of the student and the nature of the infraction.

This standard will, we trust, neither unduly burden the efforts of school authorities to maintain order in their schools nor authorize unrestrained intrusions upon the privacy of schoolchildren. By focusing attention on the question of reasonableness, the standard will spare teachers and school administrators the necessity of schooling themselves in the niceties of probable cause and permit them to regulate their conduct according to the dictates of reason and common sense. At the same time, the reasonableness standard should ensure that the interests of students will be invaded no more than is necessary to achieve the legitimate end of preserving order in the schools.

SUPREME COURT OF THE UNITED STATES
Syllabus

SAFFORD UNIFIED SCHOOL DISTRICT #1 ET AL. v. REDDING CERTIORARI TO THE UNITED STATES COURT OF APPEALS FOR THE NINTH CIRCUIT

No. 08–479. Argued April 21, 2009—Decided June 25, 2009
After escorting 13-year-old Savana Redding from her middle school classroom to his office, Assistant Principal Wilson showed her a day planner

containing knives and other contraband. She admitted owning the planner, but said that she had lent it to her friend Marissa and that the contraband was not hers. He then produced four prescription-strength, and one over-the-counter, pain relief pills, all of which are banned under school rules without advance permission. She denied knowledge of them, but Wilson said that he had a report that she was giving pills to fellow students. She denied it and agreed to let him search her belongings. He and Helen Romero, an administrative assistant, searched Savana's backpack, finding nothing. Wilson then had Romero take Savana to the school nurse's office to search her clothes for pills. After Romero and the nurse, Peggy Schwallier, had Savana remove her outer clothing, they told her to pull her bra out and shake it, and to pull out the elastic on her underpants, thus exposing her breasts and pelvic area to some degree. No pills were found. Savana's mother filed suit against petitioner school district (Safford), Wilson, Romero, and Schwallier, alleging that the strip search violated Savana's Fourth Amendment rights. Claiming qualified immunity, the individuals (hereinafter petitioners) moved for summary judgment. The District Court granted the motion, finding that there was no Fourth Amendment violation, and the en banc Ninth Circuit reversed. Following the protocol for evaluating qualified immunity claims, see *Saucier v. Katz*, 533 U.S. 194, 200, the court held that the strip search was unjustified under the Fourth Amendment test for searches of children by school officials set out in *New Jersey v. T. L. O.*, 469 U.S. 325. It then applied the test for qualified immunity. Finding that Savana's right was clearly established at the time of the search, it reversed the summary judgment as to Wilson, but affirmed as to Schwallier and Romero because they were not independent decision makers.

Held:

1. The search of Savana's underwear violated the Fourth Amendment.

   (a) For school searches, "the public interest is best served by a Fourth Amendment standard of reasonableness that stops short of probable cause." *T. L. O.*, 469 U.S., at 341. Under the resulting reasonable suspicion standard, a school search "will be permissible . . . when the measures adopted are reasonably related to the objectives of the search and not excessively intrusive in light of the age and sex of the student and the nature of the infraction." Id., at 342. The required knowledge component of reasonable suspicion for a school administrator's evidence search is that it raise a moderate chance of finding evidence of wrongdoing.

   (b) Wilson had sufficient suspicion to justify searching Savana's backpack and outer clothing. A week earlier, a student, Jordan, had told the principal and Wilson that students were bringing drugs and weapons to school and that he had gotten sick from some pills. On the day of the search, Jordan gave Wilson a pill that he said came from Marissa. Learning that the pill was prescription strength, Wilson called Marissa out of class and was handed the day planner.

Once in his office, Wilson, with Romero present, had Marissa turn
out her pockets and open her wallet, producing, inter alia, an over-
the-counter pill that Marissa claimed was Savana's. She also denied
knowing about the day planner's contents. Wilson did not ask her
when she received the pills from Savana or where Savana might be
hiding them. After a search of Marissa's underwear by Romero and
Schwallier revealed no additional pills, Wilson called Savana into his
office. He showed her the day planner and confirmed her relationship with Marissa. He knew that the girls had been identified as part
of an unusually rowdy group at a school dance, during which alcohol and cigarettes were found in the girls' bathroom. He had other
reasons to connect them with this contraband, for Jordan had told
the principal that before the dance, he had attended a party at Savana's house where alcohol was served. Thus, Marissa's statement that
the pills came from Savana was sufficiently plausible to warrant suspicion that Savana was involved in pill distribution. A student who
is reasonably suspected of giving out contraband pills is reasonably
suspected of carrying them on her person and in her backpack.
Looking into Savana's bag, in her presence and in the relative privacy of Wilson's office, was not excessively intrusive, any more than
Romero's subsequent search of her outer clothing.

(c) Because the suspected facts pointing to Savana did not indicate that
the drugs presented a danger to students or were concealed in her
underwear, Wilson did not have sufficient suspicion to warrant
extending the search to the point of making Savana pull out her
underwear. Romero and Schwallier said that they did not see anything
when Savana pulled out her underwear, but a strip search and its
Fourth Amendment consequences are not defined by who was looking
and how much was seen. Savana's actions in their presence necessarily
exposed her breasts and pelvic area to some degree, and both subjective and reasonable societal expectations of personal privacy support
the treatment of such a search as categorically distinct, requiring distinct elements of justification on the part of school authorities for
going beyond a search of outer clothing and belongings. Savana's subjective expectation of privacy is inherent in her account of it as embarrassing, frightening, and humiliating. The reasonableness of her
expectation is indicated by the common reaction of other young people similarly searched, whose adolescent vulnerability intensifies the
exposure's patent intrusiveness. Its indignity does not outlaw the
search, but it does implicate the rule that "the search [be] 'reasonably
related in scope to the circumstances which justified the interference
in the first place.'" T. L. O., supra, at 341. Here, the content of the suspicion failed to match the degree of intrusion. Because Wilson knew
that the pills were common pain relievers, he must have known of

their nature and limited threat and had no reason to suspect that large amounts were being passed around or that individual students had great quantities. Nor could he have suspected that Savana was hiding common painkillers in her underwear. When suspected facts must support the categorically extreme intrusiveness of a search down to an adolescent's body, petitioners' general belief that students hide contraband in their clothing falls short; a reasonable search that extensive calls for suspicion that it will succeed. Non-dangerous school contraband does not conjure up the specter of stashes in intimate places, and there is no evidence of such behavior at the school; neither Jordan nor Marissa suggested that Savana was doing that, and the search of Marissa yielded nothing. Wilson also never determined when Marissa had received the pills from Savana; had it been a few days before, that would weigh heavily against any reasonable conclusion that Savana presently had the pills on her person, much less in her underwear.

2. Although the strip search violated Savana's Fourth Amendment rights, petitioners Wilson, Romero, and Schwallier are protected from liability by qualified immunity because "clearly established law [did]not show that the search violated the Fourth Amendment," *Pearson v. Callahan*, 555 U.S. The intrusiveness of the strip search here cannot, under *T. L. O.*, be seen as justifiably related to the circumstances, but lower court cases viewing school strip searches differently are numerous enough, with well-reasoned majority and dissenting opinions, to counsel doubt about the clarity with which the right was previously stated.

3. The issue of petitioner Safford's liability under *Monell v. New York City Dept. of Social Servs.*, 436 U.S. 658, 694, should be addressed on remand.

531 F. 3d 1071, affirmed in part, reversed in part, and remanded.

SOUTER, J., delivered the opinion of the Court, in which ROBERTS, C. J., and SCALIA, KENNEDY, BREYER, and ALITO, JJ., joined, and in which STEVENS and GINSBURG, JJ., joined as to Parts I–III. STEVENS, J., filed an opinion concurring in part and dissenting in part, in which GINSBURG, J., joined. GINSBURG, J., filed an opinion concurring in part and dissenting in part. THOMAS, J., filed an opinion concurring in the judgment in part and dissenting in part.

Appendix G

Family Educational Rights and Privacy Act

The Family Educational Rights and Privacy Act (FERPA) was enacted in 1974 to protect the confidentiality of student education records, and pertains to all schools, regardless of type or level, that receive funds from the U.S. Department of Education. For minor children, the rights afforded by FERPA are granted to their parents. However, once a student reaches the age of 18 or attends a school above the high school level, the rights of privacy under FERPA are then shifted to his or her control as a so-called "eligible student." Only if an eligible student signs a waiver may the parents or guardians have access to school records.

As provided by FERPA, a parent or eligible student has the right to examine the education records maintained by the school and to request that the school correct any inaccuracies. If the school declines to amend the record as requested, the inquiring party has the right to a formal hearing and, if still unsuccessful in having the record changed, the right to include a written statement in the school file.

In addition, a school must secure the written permission of a parent or eligible student before releasing any information to a third party. However, schools are permitted to release information contained in school records without consent in a limited set of legitimate circumstances, most notably in sharing school records with appropriate officials in the case of health or safety emergencies. Moreover, law enforcement records as well as school records pertaining to medical or psychological treatment for students who are over age 18 or attending a post-secondary school are exempt from the privacy provisions of FERPA.

Finally, the usual privacy rights under the Health Insurance Portability and Accountability Act (HIPAA) do not extend to health information contained in education records of post-secondary schools. Instead, FERPA regulations and exclusions govern the privacy and appropriate release of school-based health and counseling records of college students.

FAMILY EDUCATIONAL RIGHTS AND PRIVACY ACT (20 USC S. 1232G)

S. 1232g. Family educational and privacy rights

(a) Conditions for availability of funds to educational agencies or institutions; inspection and review of education records; specific information to be made available; procedure for access to education records; reasonableness of time for such access; hearings; written explanations by parents; definitions.

(1)

(A) No funds shall be made available under any applicable program to any educational agency or institution which has a policy of denying, or which effectively prevents, the parents of students who are or have been in attendance at a school of such agency or at such institution, as the case may be, the right to inspect and review the education records of their children. If any material or document in the education record of a student includes information on more than one student, the parents of one of such students shall have the right to inspect and review only such part of such material or document as relates to such student or to be informed of the specific information contained in such part of such material. Each educational agency or institution shall establish appropriate procedures for the granting of a request by parents for access to the education records of their children within a reasonable period of time, but in no case more than forty-five days after the request has been made.

(B) The first sentence of subparagraph (A) shall not operate to make available to students in institutions of postsecondary education the following materials:

(i) financial records of the parents of the student or any information contained therein;

(ii) confidential letters and statements of recommendation, which were placed in the education records prior to January 1, 1975, if such letters or statements are not used for purposes other than those for which they were specifically intended;

(iii) if the student has signed a waiver of the student's right of access under this subsection in accordance with subparagraph (C), confidential recommendations—

(I) respecting admission to any educational agency or institution,

(II) respecting an application for employment, and

(III) respecting the receipt of an honor or honorary recognition.

(C) A student or a person applying for admission may waive his right of access to confidential statements described in clause (iii) of subparagraph (B), except that such waiver shall apply to recommendations only if (i) the student is, upon request, notified of the names of all persons making confidential recommendations and (ii) such recommendations are used solely for the purpose for which they were specifically intended. Such waivers may not be required as a condition for admission to, receipt of financial aid from, or receipt of any other services or benefits from such agency or institution.

(2) No funds shall be made available under any applicable program to any educational agency or institution unless the parents of students who are or have been in attendance at a school of such agency or at such institution are provided an opportunity for a hearing by such agency or institution, in accordance with regulations of the Secretary, to challenge the content of such student's education records, in order to insure that the records are not inaccurate, misleading, or otherwise in violation of the privacy or other rights of students, and to provide an opportunity for the correction or deletion of any such inaccurate, misleading, or otherwise inappropriate data contained therein and to insert into such records a written explanation of the parents respecting the content of such records.

(3) For the purposes of this section the term "educational agency or institution" means any public or private agency or institution which is the recipient of funds under any applicable program.

(4)

(A) For the purposes of this section, the term "education records" means, except as may be provided otherwise in subparagraph (B), those records, files, documents, and other materials which—
    (i) contain information directly related to a student; and
    (ii) are maintained by an educational agency or institution or by a person acting for such agency or institution.

(B) The term "education records" does not include—
    (i) records of instructional, supervisory, and administrative personnel and educational personnel ancillary thereto which are in the sole possession of the maker thereof and which are not accessible or revealed to any other person except a substitute;
    (ii) records maintained by a law enforcement unit of the educational agency or institution that were created by that law enforcement unit for the purpose of law enforcement.
    (iii) in the case of persons who are employed by an educational agency or institution but who are not in attendance at such agency or institution, records made and maintained in the normal course of business which relate exclusively

to such person in that person's capacity as an employee and are not available for use for any other purpose; or

(iv) records on a student who is eighteen years of age or older, or is attending an institution of postsecondary education, which are made or maintained by a physician, psychiatrist, psychologist, or other recognized professional or paraprofessional acting in his professional or paraprofessional capacity, or assisting in that capacity, and which are made, maintained, or used only in connection with the provision of treatment to the student, and are not available to anyone other than persons providing such treatment, except that such records can be personally reviewed by a physician or other appropriate professional of the student's choice.

(5)

(A) For the purposes of this section the term "directory information" relating to a student includes the following: the student's name, address, telephone listing, date and place of birth, major field of study, participation in officially recognized activities and sports, weight and height of members of athletic teams, dates of attendance, degrees and awards received, and the most recent previous educational agency or institution attended by the student.

(B) Any educational agency or institution making public directory information shall give public notice of the categories of information which it has designated as such information with respect to each student attending the institution or agency and shall allow a reasonable period of time after such notice has been given for a parent to inform the institution or agency that any or all of the information designated should not be released without the parent's prior consent.

(6) For the purposes of this section, the term "student" includes any person with respect to whom an educational agency or institution maintains education records or personally identifiable information, but does not include a person who has not been in attendance at such agency or institution.

(b) Release of education records; parental consent requirement; exceptions; compliance with judicial orders and subpoenas; audit and evaluation of Federally-supported education programs; recordkeeping.

(1) No funds shall be made available under any applicable program to any educational agency or institution which has a policy or practice of permitting the release of educational records (or personally identifiable information contained therein other than directory information, as defined in paragraph (5) of subsection (a)) of students without the written consent of their parents to any individual, agency, or organization, other than to the following—

      (A)   other school officials, including teachers within the educational institution or local educational agency, who have been determined by such agency or institution to have legitimate educational interests;

      (B)   officials of other schools or school systems in which the student seeks or intends to enroll, upon condition that the student's parents be notified of the transfer, receive a copy of the record if desired, and have an opportunity for a hearing to challenge the content of the record;

      (C)   authorized representatives of (i) the Comptroller General of the United States, (ii) the Secretary, (iii) an administrative head of an educational agency (as defined in section 408(c), or (iv) State educational authorities, under the conditions set forth in paragraph (3) of this subsection;

      (D)   in connection with a student's application for, or receipt of, financial aid;

      (E)   State and local officials or authorities to whom such information is specifically required to be reported or disclosed pursuant to State statute adopted prior to November 19, 1974;

      (F)   organizations conducting studies for, or on behalf of, educational agencies or institutions for the purpose of developing, validating, or administering predictive tests, administering student aid programs, and improving instruction, if such studies are conducted in such a manner as will not permit the personal identification of students and their parents by persons other than representatives of such organizations and such information will be destroyed when no longer needed for the purpose for which it is conducted;

      (G)   accrediting organizations in order to carry out their accrediting functions;

      (H)   parents of a dependent student of such parents, as defined in section 152 of the Internal Revenue Code of 1954; and

      (I)   subject to regulations of the Secretary, in connection with an emergency, appropriate persons if the knowledge of such information is necessary to protect the health or safety of the student or other persons.

Nothing in clause (E) of this paragraph shall prevent a State from further limiting the number or type of State or local officials who will continue to have access thereunder.

    (2) No funds shall be made available under any applicable program to any educational agency or institution which has a policy or practice of releasing, or providing access to, any personally identifiable information in education records other than directory information, or as is permitted under paragraph (1) of this subsection unless—

(A) there is written consent from the student's parents specifying records to be released, the reasons for such release, and to whom, and with a copy of the records to be released to the student's parents and the student if desired by the parents, or

(B) such information is furnished in compliance with judicial order, or pursuant to any lawfully issued subpoena, upon condition that parents and the students are notified of all such orders or subpoenas in advance of the compliance therewith by the educational institution or agency.

(3) Nothing contained in this section shall preclude authorized representatives of (A) the Comptroller General of the United States, (B) the Secretary, (C) an administrative head of an education agency or (D) State educational authorities from having access to student or other records which may be necessary in connection with the audit and evaluation of Federally-supported education program, or in connection with the enforcement of the Federal legal requirements which relate to such programs: Provided, That except when collection of personally identifiable information is specifically authorized by Federal law, any data collected by such officials shall be protected in a manner which will not permit the personal identification of students and their parents by other than those officials, and such personally identifiable data shall be destroyed when no longer needed for such audit, evaluation, and enforcement of Federal legal requirements.

(4)

(A) Each educational agency or institution shall maintain a record, kept with the education records of each student, which will indicate all individuals (other than those specified in paragraph (1)(A) of this subsection), agencies, or organizations which have requested or obtained access to a student's education records maintained by such educational agency or institution, and which will indicate specifically the legitimate interest that each such person, agency, or organization has in obtaining this information. Such record of access shall be available only to parents, to the school official and his assistants who are responsible for the custody of such records, and to persons or organizations authorized in, and under the conditions of, clauses (A) and (C) of paragraph (1) as a means of auditing the operation of the system.

(B) With respect to this subsection, personal information shall only be transferred to a third party on the condition that such party will not permit any other party to have access to such information without the written consent of the parents of the student.

(5) Nothing in this section shall be construed to prohibit State and local educational officials from having access to student or other records which may be necessary in connection with the audit and evaluation of any federally or State supported education program or in connection with the enforcement of the Federal legal requirements which relate to any such program, subject to the conditions specified in the proviso in paragraph (3).

(6) Nothing in this section shall be construed to prohibit an institution of postsecondary education from disclosing, to an alleged victim of any crime of violence (as that term is defined in section 16 of title 18, United States Code), the results of any disciplinary proceeding conducted by such institution against the alleged perpetrator of such crime with respect to such crime.

(c) Surveys or data-gathering activities; regulations. The Secretary shall adopt appropriate regulations to protect the rights of privacy of students and their families in connection with any surveys or data-gathering activities conducted, assisted, or authorized by the Secretary or an administrative head of an education agency. Regulations established under this subsection shall include provisions controlling the use, dissemination, and protection of such data. No survey or data-gathering activities shall be conducted by the Secretary, or an administrative head of an education agency under an applicable program, unless such activities are authorized by law.

(d) Students' rather than parents' permission or consent. For the purposes of this section, whenever a student has attained eighteen years of age, or is attending an institution of postsecondary education, the permission or consent required of and the rights accorded to the parents of the student shall thereafter only be required of and accorded to the student.

(e) Informing parents or students of rights under this section. No funds shall be made available under any applicable program to any educational agency or institution unless such agency or institution informs the parents of students, or the students, if they are eighteen years of age or older, or are attending an institution of postsecondary education, of the rights accorded them by this section.

(f) Enforcement; termination of assistance. The Secretary, or an administrative head of an education agency, shall take appropriate actions to enforce provisions of this section and to deal with violations of this section, according to the provisions of this Act, except that action to terminate assistance may be taken only if the Secretary finds there has been a failure to comply with the provisions of this section, and he has determined that compliance cannot be secured by voluntary means.

(g) Office and review board; creation; functions. The Secretary shall establish or designate an office and review board within the Department of Health, Education, and Welfare for the purpose of investigating, processing, reviewing, and adjudicating violations of the provisions of this section and complaints which may be filed concerning alleged violations of this section. Except for the conduct of hearings, none of the functions of the Secretary under this section shall be carried out in any of the regional offices of such Department.

Appendix H

HIGHER EDUCATION ACT OF 2008

The mass shootings at Virginia Tech and Northern Illinois University prompted the U.S. Congress to include in the Higher Education Opportunity Act of 2008 sections related to the preparedness of colleges and universities for a variety of emergency situations, including threats of violence. While other pieces of the legislation concerned natural disasters, Sections 821 and 822 of Part L established a federal grant program to assist schools in developing and implementing emergency communications systems, emergency response plans, and protocols for their use. The legislation encourages schools to provide timely information to the campus community when confronted with emergency situations, but resisted a broader requirement contained in a House of Representatives version of the bill for launching a campus alert. The legislation also called for a federal initiative to develop and disseminate a set of model emergency response policies, procedures, and practices.

Finally, in the context of Sections 825 and 826, the Congress recognized the existing level of confusion among many college officials about the limits of Family Educational Rights and Privacy Act (FERPA) restrictions in cases involving mental health matters and the potential for violent behavior. It called on the U.S. Department of Education to clarify the rules applicable to these situations.

HIGHER EDUCATION OPPORTUNITY ACT OF 2008

PART L—STUDENT SAFETY AND CAMPUS EMERGENCY MANAGEMENT
SEC. 821. STUDENT SAFETY AND CAMPUS EMERGENCY MANAGEMENT.
    (a) GRANTS AUTHORIZED.—
        (1) IN GENERAL.—From the amounts appropriated under subsection
          (g), the Secretary is authorized to award grants, on a competitive

basis, to institutions of higher education or consortia of institutions of higher education to enable institutions of higher education or consortia to pay the Federal share of the cost of carrying out the authorized activities described in subsection (c).

(2) CONSULTATION WITH THE ATTORNEY GENERAL AND THE SECRETARY OF HOMELAND SECURITY.—Where appropriate, the Secretary shall award grants under this section in consultation with the Attorney General and the Secretary of Homeland Security.

(3) DURATION.—The Secretary shall award each grant under this section for a period of two years.

(4) LIMITATION ON INSTITUTIONS AND CONSORTIA.—An institution of higher education or consortium shall be eligible for only one grant under this section.

(b) FEDERAL SHARE; NON-FEDERAL SHARE.—

(1) IN GENERAL.—The Federal share of the activities described in subsection (c) shall be 50 percent.

(2) NON-FEDERAL SHARE.—An institution of higher education or consortium that receives a grant under this section shall provide the non-Federal share, which may be provided from State and local resources dedicated to emergency preparedness and response.

(c) AUTHORIZED ACTIVITIES.—Each institution of higher education or consortium receiving a grant under this section may use the grant funds to carry out one or more of the following:

(1) Developing and implementing a state-of-the-art emergency communications system for each campus of an institution of higher education or consortium, in order to contact students via cellular, text message, or other state-of-the-art communications methods when a significant emergency or dangerous situation occurs. An institution or consortium using grant funds to carry out this paragraph shall also, in coordination with the appropriate State and local emergency management authorities—

(A) develop procedures that students, employees, and others on a campus of an institution of higher education or consortium will be directed to follow in the event of a significant emergency or dangerous situation; and (B) develop procedures the institution of higher education or consortium shall follow to inform, within a reasonable and timely manner, students, employees, and others on a campus in the event of a significant emergency or dangerous situation, which procedures shall include the emergency communications system described in this paragraph.

(2) Supporting measures to improve safety at the institution of higher education or consortium, such as—

(A) security assessments;

(B) security training of personnel and students at the institution of higher education or consortium;

(C) where appropriate, coordination of campus preparedness and response efforts with local law enforcement, local emergency management authorities, and other agencies, to improve coordinated responses in emergencies among such entities;

(D) establishing a hotline that allows a student or staff member at an institution or consortium to report another student or staff member at the institution or consortium who the reporting student or staff member believes may be a danger to the reported student or staff member or to others; and

(E) acquisition and installation of access control, video surveillance, intrusion detection, and perimeter security technologies and systems. H. R. 4137–333

(3) Coordinating with appropriate local entities for the provision of mental health services for students and staff of the institution of higher education or consortium, including mental health crisis response and intervention services for students and staff affected by a campus or community emergency.

(d) APPLICATION.—Each institution of higher education or consortium desiring a grant under this section shall submit an application to the Secretary at such time, in such manner, and containing such information as the Secretary may require.

(e) TECHNICAL ASSISTANCE.—The Secretary shall coordinate technical assistance provided by State and local emergency management agencies, the Department of Homeland Security, and other agencies as appropriate, to institutions of higher education or consortia that request assistance in developing and implementing the activities assisted under this section.

(f) AUTHORIZATION OF APPROPRIATIONS.—There are authorized to be appropriated to carry out this part such sums as may be necessary for fiscal year 2009 and each of the five succeeding fiscal years.

SEC. 822. MODEL EMERGENCY RESPONSE POLICIES, PROCEDURES, AND PRACTICES.
The Secretary, in consultation with the Attorney General and the Secretary of Homeland Security, shall continue to—

(1) advise institutions of higher education on model emergency response policies, procedures, and practices; and

(2) disseminate information concerning those policies, procedures, and practices.

SEC. 825. GUIDANCE ON MENTAL HEALTH DISCLOSURES FOR STUDENT SAFETY.

(a) GUIDANCE.—The Secretary shall continue to provide guidance that clarifies the role of institutions of higher education with respect to the disclosure of education records, including to a parent or legal guardian of a dependent student, in the event that such student demonstrates that the student poses a significant risk of harm to himself or herself or to others, including a significant risk of suicide, homicide, or assault. Such guidance shall further clarify that an institution of higher education that, in good faith, discloses education records or other information in accordance with the requirements of this Act and section 444 of the General Education Provisions Act (the Family Educational Rights and Privacy Act of 1974) shall not be liable to any person for that disclosure.

(b) INFORMATION TO CONGRESS.—The Secretary shall provide an update to the authorizing committees on the Secretary's activities under subsection (a) not later than 180 days after the date of enactment of the Higher Education Opportunity Act.

SEC. 826. RULE OF CONSTRUCTION.
Nothing in this part shall be construed—

(1) to provide a private right of action to any person to enforce any provision of this section;

(2) to create a cause of action against any institution of higher education or any employee of the institution for any civil liability; or

(3) to affect section 444 of the General Education Provisions Act (the Family Educational Rights and Privacy Act of 1974) or the regulations issued under section 264 of the Health Insurance Portability and Accountability Act of 1996 (42 U.S.C. 1320d–2 note).

INDEX

About the Authors

JAMES ALAN FOX, Ph.D., is The Lipman Family Professor of Criminology, Law and Public Policy at Northeastern University in Boston. He has published 17 books, including several on homicide and youth violence. He served on a White House advisory group on school violence and recently collaborated on a major report on campus violence and security for the Massachusetts Board of Higher Education.

HARVEY BURSTEIN, J.D., David B. Schulman Professor of Security Emeritus at the College of Criminal Justice, Northeastern University, Boston, MA, has more than 50 years of hands-on security management and consulting experience and is the author of 11 books in the field.